Annual Review of Addictions and Offender Counseling, Volume III

Best Practices

Annual Review of Addictions and Offender Counseling, Volume III

Best Practices

EDITED BY

PAMELA S. LASSITER

and TREVOR J. BUSER

RESOURCE *Publications* • Eugene, Oregon

ANNUAL REVIEW OF ADDICTIONS AND OFFENDER COUNSELING VOLUME III
Best Practices

Copyright © 2017 Wipf and Stock Publishers. All rights reserved. Except for brief quotations in critical publications or reviews, no part of this book may be reproduced in any manner without prior written permission from the publisher. Write: Permissions, Wipf and Stock Publishers, 199 W. 8th Ave., Suite 3, Eugene, OR 97401.

Resource Publications
An Imprint of Wipf and Stock Publishers
199 W. 8th Ave., Suite 3
Eugene, OR 97401

www.wipfandstock.com

PAPERBACK ISBN: 978-1-5326-1348-7
HARDCOVER ISBN: 978-1-5326-1350-0
EBOOK ISBN: 978-1-5326-1349-4

Manufactured in the U.S.A.   FEBRUARY 2, 2017

Contents

1   Editorial   1

2   Synthetic Drugs: What School and Mental Health Counselors Need to Know   7
    LaShauna M. Dean

3   Beyond the Prescription: The Other Side of Opioid Painkillers   22
    Shainna Ali, Gulnora Hundley, and M. Kristina DePue

4   Social Skills Training for Youth in Treatment for Substance Use Disorder   40
    Oksana Kravets and Jenepher Lennox Terrion

5   Promoting Resilience in Children of Alcoholics: A Family Perspective   64
    Shaywanna Harris and S. Kent Butler

6   The Professionals and Procedures Involved in Drug Courts   79
    John T. Petko

7   Avatar Assisted Therapy: A Novel Technology Based Intervention to Treat Substance Use Disorders   97
    Michael S. Gordon, Steven B. Carswell, Erica N. Peters, Susan Tangires, Timothy W. Kinlock, Frank J. Vocci, and Lauren Restivo

8   Best Practices in Counseling Gay Male Youth With Substance
    Use Disorders   116
       Michael D. Brubaker and Michael P. Chaney

9   The Importance of Storytelling for older Women in Alcoholics
    Anonymous   140
       Lauren S. Ermann, Gerard Lawson, and Penny L. Burge

10 The Impact of Addictions Education on Attitudes
    of Students   163
       *Amanuel Haile Asfaw, Kevin Vance, Kyoungho Lee, David
       Meggitt, Jane Warren, Jennifer Weatherford, and Grant Sasse*

11 Wearing their Shoes: Creating Counselors' Understanding of
    Addiction through Empathy   186
       Christina Rosen and Geoffrey Yager

12 The New Leaf Experience: College Student Substance Use
    Treatment and Addiction Counselor Training Clinic   204
       *Amy E. Williams, Eleni M. Honderich, and
       Charles F. Gressard*

Editorial

The *Annual Review of Addictions and Offender Counseling, Volume III: Best Practices* is the third volume in a series of peer-reviewed edited books sponsored by the International Association of Addiction and Offender Counselors (IAAOC), a division of the American Counseling Association (ACA). All of the articles included in this volume have been peer reviewed by the Editorial Board of the *Journal of Addictions and Offender Counseling (JAOC)*. As a product of IAAOC, the mission of the *Annual Review* is to produce high quality publications representing practice-focused scholarship and innovations in the field. Continuing the mission of the first two volumes, this volume provides a forum for publications addressing a broad array of topics in the field of addictions and offender counseling, including drug education, intervention strategies, multicultural considerations, and counselor education.

The following section provides a description of each chapter included in this volume.

Synthetic Drugs: What School and Mental Health Counselors Need to Know

LaShauna M. Dean

This chapter provides information on synthetic drugs, specifically Spice, Bath Salts, and Flakka. Dosage, legal, and historical information are discussed and common effects and trends of each drug are addressed. Implications for counselors are also provided.

Beyond the Prescription: The Other Side of Opioid Painkillers

SHAINNA ALI, GULNORA HUNDLEY, AND M. KRISTINA DEPUE

Counselors should be aware of the national prescription opioid pandemic, knowledgeable about implications for users and society, and familiar with and skilled in the necessary methods of assisting clients with dependence on painkillers. This chapter provides essential information for counselors concerning use, misuse, and abuse of opioids in order to effectively assist clients.

Social Skills Training for Youth in Treatment for Substance Use Disorder

OKSANA KRAVETS AND JENEPHER LENNOX TERRION

Social competence is both a protective factor and a risk factor for substance use disorder in adolescent males so providing training in social skills development should be part of addiction counseling efforts. This paper recommends training approaches and techniques to be used in addiction and offender counselling.

Promoting Resilience in Children of Alcoholics: A Family Perspective

SHAYWANNA HARRIS AND S. KENT BUTLER

Children of Alcoholics (COAs) research has provided pertinent data on risk and protective factors as well as best practices and interventions that may promote resilience within this population. Familial relationships have been identified as a major protective factor for COAs, however, research promoting family therapy as an enhancement to resilience is scarce. The purpose of this chapter is to provide counselors with a current resilience-based and alcoholism-focused family therapy model and interventions that may improve resilience in COAs.

The Professionals and Procedures Involved in Drug Courts

JOHN T. PETKO

Counseling students who graduate from programs have coursework on addiction counseling but are often unfamiliar with the processes that are involved in drug courts. This chapter provides a brief history of drugs courts, defines what a drug court is, and identifies the processes that are involved in drug courts as well as the professionals who comprise the drug court team. Resources for counselors working in drug courts are provided.

Avatar Assisted Therapy: A Novel Technology Based Intervention to Treat Substance Use Disorders

MICHAEL S. GORDON, STEVEN B. CARSWELL, ERICA N. PETERS, SUSAN TANGIRES, TIMOTHY W. KINLOCK, FRANK J. VOCCI, AND LAUREN RESTIVO

Avatar assisted therapy (AAT) allows treatment providers and clients to interact from separate and remote locations in real time via a web based platform using avatars, which are digital self-representations within virtual environments. This chapter discusses this novel technology based intervention, including its strengths and limitations. Initial results of a pilot study ($N = 54$) suggest that AAT is a feasible means of providing substance abuse counseling via the Internet and there was significant patient interest in participation based on scheduling convenience and the ability to be anonymous.

Best Practices in Counseling Gay Male Youth With Substance Use Disorders

MICHAEL D. BRUBAKER AND MICHAEL P. CHANEY

Substance use rates are higher among gay male youth than their heterosexual counterparts, often corresponding with high-risk behaviors that compromise their health and well-being. This chapter explores the etiology of substance abuse among this population and recommends best practices to effectively treat gay male youth. A case study demonstrates the application of gay-affirming treatment principles. Clinical implications and future directions are discussed.

The Importance of Storytelling for older Women in Alcoholics Anonymous
Lauren S. Ermann, Gerard Lawson, and Penny L. Burge

This phenomenological study explores storytelling and older women in Alcoholics Anonymous (AA). Results suggest a number of significant benefits associated with both recounting and listening to stories in AA. Implications for counselors are discussed.

The Impact of Addictions Education on Attitudes of Students:
Amanuel Haile Asfaw, Kevin Vance, Kyoungho Lee, David Meggitt, Jane Warren, Jennifer Weatherford, and Grant Sasse

Negative attitudes and beliefs towards addictions can impair effective interventions; education enhances empathy and intervention skills. This study measured changes in addictions attitudes in Master's students for two years following completion of a 15-week addictions counseling course. Treatment optimism scores increased significantly.

Wearing their Shoes: Creating Counselors' Understanding of Addiction through Empathy
Christina Rosen and Geoffrey G. Yager

Empathy is an essential building block to an effective therapeutic alliance. Empathy is particularly crucial for substance abuse counselors. This chapter describes a self-instructional approach assisting counselors to develop awareness of themselves and of their clients' internal world.

The New Leaf Experience: College Student Substance Use Treatment and Addiction Counselor Training Clinic
Amy E. Williams, Eleni M. Honderich, and Charles F. Gressard

The history of a college-based substance abuse clinic (New Leaf) is described. Along with servicing college students, the clinic provides training in motivational interviewing (MI) and supervision for counseling students alongside opportunities for conducting research. Considerations for developing similar programs are included.

Acknowledgements

As editors, we would like to acknowledge the excellent work of the *JAOC* Editorial Board. Their careful reviews and wise advice helped our authors refine their work in meaningful ways, raising the quality of each contribution. The *JAOC* Editorial Board includes the following dedicated professionals:

    Lyndon Abrams, The University of North Carolina at Charlotte
    Shainna Ali, University of Central Florida
    Wanda P. Briggs, Winthrop University
    Kathleen Brown-Rice, University of South Dakota
    Michael Chaney, Oakland University
    Rochelle Cade, Mississippi College
    Christine Chasek, University of Nebraska at Kearney
    Philip Clarke, Wake Forest University
    Angela Colistra, Drexel University
    John Culbreth, The University of North Carolina at Charlotte
    M. Kristina Depue, University of Florida
    Kevin Doyle, Longwood University
    Susan R. Furr, The University of North Carolina at Charlotte
    Sandy Gibson, The College of New Jersey
    Amanda Giordano, The University of North Texas
    Kristopher M. Goodrich, University of New Mexico
    Shaywanna Harris, University of Central Florida
    Leigh Falls Holman, The University of Memphis
    Melanie Iarussi, Auburn University
    Nathaniel Ivers, Wake Forest University
    Dayle Jones, University of Central Florida
    Gerald A. Juhnke, The University of Texas at San Antonio
    John M. Laux, The University of Toledo
    Todd F. Lewis, North Dakota State University
    Gabriel I. Lomas, Western Connecticut State University
    Virginia Magnus, University of Tennessee at Chattanooga
    Keith Morgen, Centenary College
    Samir Patel, Murray State University
    Dilani Perera-Diltz, Lamar University
    Christina Hamme Peterson, Rider University
    Edward Wahesh, Villanova University
    Joshua Watson, Texas A&M University-Corpus Christi

Additionally, we would like to offer special thanks to Corrine C. Rutt, Daniella L. Muller and Mena S. Farag (Editorial Assistants) from Rider University and to Dr. Kathleen Brown-Rice (*JAOC*, Assistant Editor) for all of their hard work in the editorial and manuscript management process.

Pamela S. Lassiter
Department of Counseling
The University of North Carolina at Charlotte
Charlotte, North Carolina

Trevor J. Buser
Department of Graduate Education, Leadership, and Counseling
Rider University
Lawrenceville, New Jersey

2

Synthetic Drugs

What School and Mental Health Counselors Need to Know

LaShauna M. Dean[1]

Synthetic Drugs

Synthetic drugs include a variety of man-made, synthesized drugs. This article will focus on Spice, Bath Salts, and Flakka. This class of drugs has rapidly become a public health crisis, with over 400 overdoses being reported on the East Coast alone since April 2015 (New Jersey Regional Operations Intelligence Center Drug Monitoring Initiative, 2015). Additionally, synthetic drugs have been labeled the emergent drug of abuse among college students and young adults, making synthetics a necessary class of drugs to understand for counseling professionals (Hu, Primack, Barnett, & Cook, 2011; Saha, Wilson, & Adger, 2012; Van Pelt,

---

1. LaShauna M. Dean, Department of Special Education and Professional Counseling, William Paterson University. Correspondence concerning this article should be addressed to LaShauna M. Dean, Department of Special Education and Counseling, William Paterson University, 1600 Valley Road, Wayne, NJ 07470 (e-mail: deanL3@wpunj.edu).

2012). All of the synthetic drugs in this class share the commonalities of being highly addictive, unpredictable in their effects, and having an ever-changing list of chemical compounds in their ingredients. This article will provide background and dosage information, will review physical and mental health effects, and rates of occurrence for each drug. Educational and clinical implications for counselors will be addressed as well.

Spice

Spice is a synthetic cannabinoid originally created to study how marijuana affects brain function in the relief of chronic pain by scientist, John W. Huffman (Zucchino, 2011). Huffman and colleagues at Clemson University created a compound that chemically replicated the effects of the active ingredient in marijuana, Tetrahydrocannabinol. Hoffman reported that he never intended for the synthetic marijuana he created to be used as a new drug on the market, but somehow the formula got into the hands of illegal drug producers and became available on the market in the mid 2000's (Cohen, 2014; Zucchino, 2011). Since then, Spice has been widely used by people who were seeking to avoid detection on urine drug screens, primarily those in the criminal justice system, adolescents and young adults, and individuals in the military (Cohen, 2014; Substance Abuse and Mental Health Services Administration [SAMHSA], 2014). Spice is difficult to detect on urine and blood drug tests due to the changing chemical structure of the drug. As manufacturers of the drug alter the chemical compounds in Spice, drug-testing companies have a difficult time creating tests that will identify those compounds.

The psychoactive chemicals in Spice are sprayed onto shredded plant materials and sold in small packets (Saha et al., 2012; SAMSHA, 2014). Users can then either roll it in traditional wrapper-paper used in marijuana joints for smoking or they can add it an e-cigarette to be vaporized. Unfortunately, the actual chemical formula of Spice is unknown as producers are constantly changing the compounds used to avoid detection by government officials (SAMSHA, 2014; Van Pelt, 2012). This presents one of the greatest dangers to users, as there is no set list of chemicals in each Spice packet (Papanti et al., 2013). In 2011, the Drug Enforcement Administration (DEA) placed a temporary ban on the five most commonly found synthetic marijuana compounds: JWH-018, JWH-073,

JWH-200, CP-47,497, and cannabicyclohexanol (SAMSHA, 2014). In July 2012, a full federal ban was enacted on synthetic marijuana making it a Schedule I drug, meaning that it is highly addictive and has no medical value (SAMSHA, 2014).

Spice is easily obtainable on the Internet and in neighborhood stores. It is typically more expensive than marijuana, with 2.5 grams costing around $30, making it more popular among White and Hispanic males from more affluent families (Cohen, 2014; Stogner & Miller, 2014). It is being marketed as "not for human consumption" to avoid the application of the Analogue Act. According to Cohen (2014), the Analogue Act states that *analogues,* which are similar versions of other scheduled drugs, can be treated as a controlled substance if its effects are similar to or greater than the original drug its meant to mimic. By labeling Spice, and other synthetic drugs, as "not for human consumption," drug manufactures were able to largely avoid federal prosecution. It is commonly sold under names such as: K2, Spice, Spice Gold, Skunk, Yucatan Fire, Zen, Cloud Nine, Artic Synergy, Black Mamba, Mr. Nice Guy, Natures Organic, Genie, and Bombay Blue (Papanti et al., 2013; SAMSHA, 2014, p. 1).

Effects of Spice

Users of Spice have reported experiencing short-term symptoms such as dry mouth, dehydration, rapid heart rate, nausea and vomiting, agitation, seizures, confusion, and heart attacks (National Institute on Drug Abuse [NIDA], 2012a; Saha et al., 2012; SAMSHA, 2014). Spice often has severe psychoaffective effects such as euphoria, anxiety, aggression, sadness, paranoia, delusions, hallucinations, and psychosis (NIDA, 2012a; Saha et al., 2012; SAMSHA, 2014). In fact, Papanti et al. (2013) coined the term "spiceophrenia" which is a state of psychosis characterized by hallucinations and delusions in chronic and acute users of synthetic cannabinoid (p. 379). The long-term effects of spice are largely unknown as this is a relatively new drug on the market (SAMSHA, 2014). However, it is important to note that the chemist who created the chemical compounds commonly found in Spice has warned about the long-term consequences of use, saying that "serious and unpredictable psychological effects" are possible (Cohen, 2014; Zucchino, 2011, para. 14).

Deaths have been associated with Spice usage, with the Centers for Disease Control and Prevention reporting 15 deaths related to Spice usage in the first six months of 2015 (Kraft, 2015). These deaths are often caused by a reduced blood supply to the heart, which can lead to a heart attack (SAMSHA, 2014). Additionally, users have reported experiencing physical and psychiatric withdrawal symptoms as well as signs of addiction (SAMSHA, 2014; Wagner et al., 2014). These effects highlight the differences in marijuana use and the dangers of using synthetic cannabinoids, with the main differences being the increased potential for addiction, death, and severe and long lasting psychological effects seen in synthetic cannabinoids.

Occurrence

According to the 2012 *Monitoring the Future Survey*, Spice was the second most widely used substance among 10th and 12th graders after marijuana, and third among 8th graders after marijuana and inhalants (NIDA, 2012b). Part of its popularity among younger individuals could be due in part to marketing (Cohen, 2014; SAMSHA, 2014). Packets of Spice are widely available on the Internet and local stores (i.e. convenience stores, gas stations, and local smoke shops) and are sold with very misleading labels such as pictures of Buddha, serenity, and nature, leading users to believe that it is organic, safe and legal (Cohen, 2014). However, these marketing strategies are extremely misleading as it is highly addictive and causes a more intense and prolonged high than marijuana (SAMSHA, 2014).

Calls to US poison control centers regarding negative reactions to the drug increased by 330% from January 2015 to April 2015 according to the Centers for Disease Control (as cited by Law, Schier, Martin, Chang, & Wolkin, 2015). This is not surprising as SAMSHA (2014) reported that spice is four to 100 times more potent than the psychoactive ingredient found in marijuana, and often lacks the antipsychotic properties found in marijuana, a fact that many users may not know. In addition, the overall effects of the drug are largely unknown due to the changing combination of ingredients used in synthetic cannabinoids (Cohen, 2014; Wagner et al., 2014).

Bath Salts

Bath salts are synthetic cathinones that replicate the effects of amphetamines (NIDA, 2015a; SAMSHA, 2014). Cathinone occurs naturally in the Khat plant, which is a flowering evergreen shrub native to East Africa and the Arabian Peninsula, and acts as an amphetamine-like stimulant (SAMSHA, 2014). The active ingredient in bath salts is Methylenedioxypyrovalerone (MDPV), which was designated a Schedule I drug by the DEA (Office of National Drug Control Policy, 2015). MDPV is reported to be ten times stronger than cocaine (Marder, 2015; NIDA, 2015a). Methylone (Methylenedioxy-N-methylcathinone) is another common active ingredient found in bath salts (Wagner et al., 2014); MDVP is more expensive and potent whereas Methylone is less expensive and requires higher doses for the intended high (Wagner et al., 2014; Winder, Stern, & Hosanagar, 2013. However, while the main chemicals in bath salts have been banned, manufacturers are expected to create chemically similar ingredients, by making minor changes to the original chemical formula, with the aim of evading the legal restrictions, making this an extremely dangerous and unpredictable drug to use (NIDA, 2015a).

Bath salts have the appearance of crystallized rocks or as white or off-white powder and can be smoked, injected, or snorted (NIDA, 2015a; SAMSHA, 2014). Saha et al. (2012) additionally reported that some users are using bath salts rectally. Similar to Spice, it is commonly sold online and in local neighborhood stores under names such as: Ivory Wave, Blow, Red Dove, and Vanilla. Typically, packets of bath salts range in dosage/concentration of between 200-500 mgs and retail for between $20 and $75 (Cohen, 2014; Miotto, Striebel, Cho, & Wang, 2013). Again, the label "not for human consumption" is used to avoid federal regulation (Miotto et al., 2013, p. 2). Bath salts often look like commonly used bath products or aromatic potpourri, deceptively leading users to feel that can be used to relax the user in a safe way (Miotto et al., 2013).

Effects of Bath Salts

The most common effects of bath salt use are psychoaffective effects which include severe paranoia, delirium, delusions, anxiety which can trigger panic attacks, anger, stimulation resulting in a decreased need for sleep, self-injurious behavior, psychosis, and violent, aggressive behavior

(NIDA, 2015a; Saha et al., 2012; SAMSHA, 2014). These psychoactive symptoms have been described as "horrible" with users reporting seeing demons, monsters, and foreign soldiers or aliens (Allegany Health Department, 2015). However, the most notable effect of using bath salts is violent and self-injurious behavior. Marder (2015) reported on a 21-year old male named Dickie Sanders who reportedly had no prior history of mental illness. However after ingesting bath salts in November 2010, he experienced strange and psychotic behavior for five days which included having a frightening delusion that 25 police officers were outside of his house, leading him to slit his own throat. While he survived that suicide attempt and was reportedly feeling better, his psychotic symptoms reemerged and he fatally shot himself in the middle of the night, even after receiving treatment at a hospital for the hallucinations. That is one of many similar stories in which new psychosis or exacerbated psychosis has been reported following the use of bath salts, and while a causal link has not been established, further study is needed to understand the long-term psychiatric effects of bath salts.

Additionally, due to its similarity to amphetamines, bath salt usage also leads to several adverse physical health effects such as rapid heart rate, high blood pressure, muscle spasms, strokes, heart attacks, seizures, decreased appetite, severe perspiration, and a risk for organ failure due to the body temperature raising to dangerous levels (NIDA, 2015a; Miotto et al., 2013; Saha et al., 2012; SAMSHA, 2014). These effects are complicated by the problem of dosage variability, ranging from five to 90 mgs or more depending on the active ingredients in the product (Winder et al., 2013). Scientists tested one package of bath salts for the amount of MDPV and found only 17 milligrams while another package contained 2,000 milligrams accounting for the varied effects on users (Marder, 2015).

Occurrence

While reports indicate that synthetic cathinones were available in the 1920s, it reemerged on the Internet around 2008 and 2009 (Saha et al., 2012). Calls related to overdosing on bath salts have increased by 20 times between 2010-2011 according to the American Association of Poison Control Centers (Hu et al., 2011; Van Pelt, 2012). Additionally, this drug has been found to be prevalent in individuals in their twenties (Hu et al., 2011; SAMSHA, 2014; Van Pelt, 2012), with 63% of emergency room visits in Michigan, for example, being males between the ages of 20 and 29. Like the marketing for Spice, the packing for bath salts gives users the illusion that it is safe and can be used for stress-relieving properties. Common packaging includes words like euphoric and soothing are complimented by spa-like pictures of serene flowers and colors (Miotto et al., 2013). However, the adverse psychoaffective and physiological reactions are far from euphoric.

Flakka

Flakka is a relatively new synthetic that emerged on the market in 2010 (NIDA, 2015b). However, its history dates back to the 1960s when drug developers created it as a central nervous stimulant (Katselou et al., 2016). It is chemically similar to bath salts and is also a synthetic cathinone. The active ingredient in Flakka is Alpha-pyrrolidinopentiophenone (alpha-PDP), which was classified as a Schedule I drug and banned by the DEA in 2014 (NIDA, 2015b). Flakka derives its name from *flaca* meaning a thin, pretty woman in Spanish (Califano, 2015) and is sometimes called "gravel." Flakka has the appearance of a white or pink, foul smelling crystal and is often sold under the labels of plant food, bath salts, stain removers, or jewelry cleaners (Katselou et al., 2016). Like the other drugs in the group, it is also labeled not for human consumption Users can eat, snort, inject, or more commonly vaporize it in an e-cigarette. Vaporizing Flakka sends the drug very quickly into the blood stream making an overdose more likely (Califano, 2015; NIDA, 2015b). Average doses/concentration of the drug vary depending on route of administration: 10mg if the drug is smoked; 35mg if taken orally; and 400mg if vaporized; however an effective dose starts at 100mg requiring users to sometimes take larger amounts for the intended effect (Katselou et al., 2016).

Effects of Flakka

Flakka has similar physical and psychoactive effects as bath salts (NIDA, 2015a). It also causes the body to overheat leading to many users stripping their clothes off. The noticeable difference occurs in a psychoactive state known as "excited delirium" (Glatter, 2015, para. 2). Excited delirium is a state of hyperstimulation and paranoia in which users experience hallucinations and violent, aggressive behaviors, and potentially multiple organ failure and abnormally rapid heart rate (Katselou et al., 2016). During this state, "superhuman strength" is also reported making it difficult for bystanders and/or police officers to subdue the individual (Califano, 2015, p. 28). Additional physical signs of adverse reactions which could lead to an overdose often include cardiovascular problems such as: hypertension, difficulty breathing, heart rhythm abnormalities and palpitations, and heart attacks (Katselou et al., 2016).

According to Miotto et al. (2013), most deaths involving cathinones occur after individuals experience excited delirium and other cardiovascular abnormalities. The effects of the Flakka usually last between three and four hours, however the effects can linger on for several days (Glatter, 2015). The NIDA and other sources have reported several deaths related to using Flakka, including heart attacks, death by suicide, and a premature baby who died after his mother used Flakka during her pregnancy (Alanez, 2015; Arnold, 2015; Katselou et al., 2016; Laughlin, 2015; NIDA, 2015b), making this another extremely unpredictable and dangerous drug.

Occurrence

Flakka is available worldwide however it is most prevalent in Florida, with other reported use in Texas, Ohio, and Tennessee (Califano, 2015; Glatter, 2015). Flakka is typically manufactured in China, Pakistan, and India and is available online in larger quantities, then sold on the streets for as little as five dollars. This highlights two major concerns of using Flakka; the first being that its low cost makes it more easily available and therefore easier to abuse (Rizzio & Rice, 2015). The second issue is that the contents and dosage within the packets are largely unknown so users are not aware of how much they are taking. According to Califano (2015), Flakka may also often be cut with heroin, cocaine, or marijuana thereby exacerbating the already adverse and potentially deadly effects of the drug.

Implications for Counselors

So how should counselors respond to the emergence of synthetic drugs? The answer to that question is not simple and involves many layers starting with becoming more knowledgeable about not only synthetic drugs but also the youth that use them. There has been a cultural shift in how our society views using drugs as seen by calls for decriminalization of marijuana and more acceptability of using harm reduction techniques (Fisher & Harrison, 2013; Swift, 2013). Treatment of synthetic drugs should begin with prevention efforts (Wagner et al., 2014). Additionally, our role as counselors may have to shift from mostly advocating with the client through empowerment and counseling, to advocating for change within the personal, social, and political systems with which our clients exist (Lewis, Arnold, House, & Toporek, 2003).

A Cultural Shift

Views of acceptable drug use have changed within the last forty years. According to a recent Gallop poll, 58% of Americans want marijuana legalized, up from 12% in 1969 (Swift, 2013). These changing beliefs about illicit drugs are concerning, possibly leading one to question how other illicit drugs will be viewed in the future. The Drug Enforcement Administration (DEA) contributes to this changing attitude about decriminalization, and in part, to misleading information from entities that seek to legalize narcotics (DEA, 2010). The DEA takes an absolute stance against decriminalization of drugs, which is seen as outdated and over politicized by advocates for decriminalization of marijuana. While the DEA has put out drug facts supported by research, advocates for decriminalization have published misleading information that further complicates this issue.

Additionally, the way young adults obtain and research information about drugs has drastically changed. In the past, users passed information from person to person. However, in today's society, individuals can utilize drug information sharing websites, such as bluelight.org and partyvibe.org, to research various aspects of drugs. These drug sharing sites offer information on how to use various drugs, the effects of use, and how to mix two or more drugs to get more powerful effects (Chiauzzi, DasMahapatra, Lobo, & Barratt, 2013; Winder et al., 2013). These websites often feature colorful designs with a *club*/party feel, which are appealing to young adults. As mentioned previously, the marketing for these websites is very misleading as the *party-like* feel of these websites may lead the user to underestimate the dangers associated with the drugs discussed on the site. With this information being easily accessible, often the users of synthetics, and other drugs, are more knowledgeable about drugs than counselors treating the issue. Continuing education and training is needed if you are a school or mental health counselor as it is likely that synthetic drug use will grow (Van Pelt, 2012).

Continued Education

Helping professionals will play a key role in bringing awareness about synthetic drugs and prevention efforts to clients and their families (SAMSHA, 2014; Van Pelt, 2012). Users of synthetic drugs may not fully understand the dangers of using synthetic drugs, in part due to deceptive labeling (Winder et al., 2013). Wagner et al. (2014) found that almost half of their sample believed that bath salts were legal, showing that many users are uninformed. As mentioned previously, users also may not be aware of the varying doses available in packages or how intended effects may vary depending on route of administration. With so much misinformation available in online drug forums and the Internet as a whole, counselors can take a key role of providing preventative education about synthetic drugs such as common myths, information on overdoses, and long-term psychological and physiological effects.

Van Pelt (2012) posited that those in the helping field need to understand trends of synthetic use, common symptoms, effects of use, and how to use appropriate drug terminology with clients or students. For example, the author warned against using common street names of synthetic drugs with teens as the use of common terms may lead teens to become more comfortable with the drug and actually increase their likelihood of using the drug (Van Pelt, 2012). Winder et al. (2013) also called for addiction practitioners to stay current on new trends emerging in their communities. Counselors can stay current by taking advantage of continuing education opportunities and viewing government-sponsored drug information sites such as the NIDA and SAMSHA, which have factsheets, publications, webinars, and news briefs on emerging drugs. Additionally, most states have a local task force on drugs that can serve as a valuable resource. For example, New Jersey has the Governor's Council on Alcoholism and Drug Abuse, which launched a statewide awareness campaign, available at www.knowaddiction.nj.gov. This website has valuable information about a variety of drugs and available treatment options in the state. While counselor education around synthetic drug use is crucial, further advocacy steps must be taken to ensure that the public is informed as well.

Van Pelt (2012) highlighted the importance of educating parents and local schools about synthetic drugs. This touches on the importance of advocacy espoused by the Advocacy Competencies created to help counselors understand how they can advocate on behalf of or with clients while working within their personal, social, and political systems (Lewis et al., 2003). Counselors can act on behalf of students/clients at the client level by disseminating information to parents and within local communities that may be affected by synthetic drug use. The larger challenge is advocacy at the system level, which is complicated by the lack of treatment-related research available on synthetic drugs (Miotto et al., 2013; Winder et al., 2013). At the systems level, counselors can partner with allies in the criminal justice system to discover better ways of recognizing signs of synthetic drug use and abuse, identifying factors that increase a person's likelihood of using synthetic drugs, and more effective ways to test for synthetic drug use. Additionally, while many synthetic drug users are treated in a hospital setting, leading to some users going untreated. Counselors can help reduce the problem of under treatment, by being sure to report client use of synthetics to local poison control centers and state drug task forces.

What to Do If You Encounter Synthetics?

Due to the severity and range of symptoms experienced by users of synthetics drugs, counselors may need to assess the involvement of medical intervention. In some synthetic drugs, withdrawal can be severe and may need to be medically monitored (Miotto et al., 2013; SAMSHA, 2014; Winder et al., 2013). Further supporting the need for possible medical intervention is the fact that SAMSHA (2014) reported that Spice, more potent than marijuana, can lead to a variety of physical and psychoaffective changes for which a counselor may need to send a client to the hospital for medical monitoring and/or detox. Miotto et al. (2013) highlighted that many synthetic drug users required hospital admission, which was often followed up by inpatient or outpatient addiction treatment.

As mentioned previously, many of the synthetic drugs also trigger violent episodes, therefore Califano (2015) recommended that safety be assessed first, possibly necessitating involvement of law enforcement. In the case of Flakka intoxication, Califano (2015) suggested the acronym *PRIORITY* to assess for excited delirium syndrome which stands for: Psychological issues, Recent drug/alcohol use, Incoherent thought processes, Off (clothes) and sweating, Resistant to presence/dialogue, Inanimate objects/shiny/glass—violent or assessing whether the individual is using objects in violent ways, Tough, unstoppable, superhuman strength, and Yelling (p. 2). This acronym, PRIORITY, can be used as beginning steps for identifying and assessing possible synthetic drug use in clients as it touches on key differences in synthetics such as the state of excited delirium and other physical state differences. Califano (2015) advised that treatment providers look for each symptom in the acronym as a possible clue that the person is experiencing Flakka intoxication, which is very similar to bath salt intoxication as they are both cathinones.

Once safety of the client and the counselor has been established, counselors can further assess the client for synthetic drug use. SAMSHA (2014) recommended that behavioral health providers ask specific questions about synthetic drugs not only during the intake but also throughout the duration of treatment. SAMSHA (2014) also warns that the continued monitoring of abstinence may be difficult due to the chemical compounds of synthetic drugs constantly changing at a faster pace than urine drug screens can update the substances tested. A further consideration is that urine drug screens that have specific panels for synthetics usually have to be sent to specialized labs to measure concentration levels, which is more costly than traditional, immediate response tests. These complications stress the importance of constant screening on behalf of the counselor as urine drug screens may not reveal or confirm synthetic drug use.

There is a dearth in the literature about effective treatment interventions for synthetic drug users. Medical professionals have used antipsychotic and benzodiazepines to treat the withdrawal symptoms of cathinones (Winder et al., 2013), which was then followed up by an intensive outpatient treatment program. However, two treatment considerations are clear in the literature: (1) due to the state of excited delirium, counselors should continually monitor clients for self-harm and/or suicidal ideation; and (2) a full medical evaluation should occur when clients admit to using synthetics, as dose amounts vary so greatly that clients need to be monitored as the drug leaves the system (Miotto et al., 2013; Winder et al., 2013). Lastly, due to the lack of treatment-related research on synthetics, counselors have an opportunity to conduct research that furthers the knowledge of how to effectively address and treat synthetic drug use.

Conclusion

While the importance of synthetic drug use may seem distant for some counselors, its growth is likely to spread (Van Pelt, 2012). Counselors as a whole are encouraged to be proactive vs. reactive when dealing with how to prevent and treat synthetic drug abuse (Van Pelt, 2012; SAMSHA, 2014). Knowledge of the effects of each drug in this class is the first line of defense in prevention, as some urine drug screens will not detect synthetic drugs. Fortunately, there are many reliable resources available to help counselors stay up to date on emergent drugs and how to treat clients who use them. Although treatment recommendations with this group of drugs are sparse, counselors are in a key position to advance the research.

References

Alanez, T. (2015, October 8). Broward's first Flakka baby: Born premature, he only lived an hour. *Sun Sentinel*. Retrieved from http://www.sun-sentinel.com/local/broward/fl-flakka-baby-death-20151008-story.html

Allegany Health Department. (2015). *Synthetic drugs*. Retrieved from http://www.alleganyhealthdept.com/addictions/Synthetic%20Drugs%20-%20ACHD%20web.pdf

Arnold, R. (2015, September 4). Synthetic drug Flakka causing Houston-area deaths. *Click2Houston*. Retrieved from http://www.click2houston.com/news/synthetic-drug-flakka-causing-houston-area-deaths

Califano, F. (2015). Flakka: A new EMS challenge. *Fire Engineering, 168*(9), 28-30.

Chiauzzi, E., DasMahapatra, P., Lobo, K., & Barratt, M. J. (2013). Participatory research with an online drug forum: A survey of user characteristics, information sharing, and harm reduction views. *Substance Use & Misuse, 48*, 661-670. doi:10.3109/10826084.2013.800117

Cohen, J. A. (2014). The highs of tomorrow: Why new laws and policies are needed to meet the unique challenges of synthetic drugs. *Journal of Law & Health, 27*(2), 164-185.

Drug Enforcement Administration. (2010). *Speaking out against drug legalization*. Retrieved from http://www.dea.gov/pr/multimedia-library/publications/speaking_out.pdf

Fisher, G. L., & Harrison, T. C. (2013). *Substance abuse: Information for social workers, therapists, and counselors* (5th ed.). Upper Saddle River, NJ: Pearson.

Glatter, R. (2015. April 4). Flakka: The new designer drug you need to know about. *Forbes*. Retrieved from http://www.forbes.com/sites/robertglatter/2015/04/04/flakka-the-new-drug-you-need-to-know-about/#5efd850a20bf

Hu, X., Primack, B. A., Barnett, T. E., & Cook, R. L. (2011). College students and use of K2: An emerging drug of abuse in young persons. *Substance Abuse Treatment, Prevention, & Policy, 6*, 16-19.

Katselou, M., Papoutis, I., Nikolaou, Panagiota, Spiliopoulou, C., & Athanaselis, S. (2016). Alpha—PVP ("flakka"): A new synthetic cathinone invades the drug arena. *Forensic Toxicology, 34*, 41-50. doi:10.1007/s11419-015-0298-1

Kraft, A. (2015, June 11). Big increase in deaths, poisonings from synthetic marijuana. *CBS News*. Retrieved from http://www.cbsnews.com/news/deaths-poisonings-from-synthetic marijuana-spice-k2/

Laughlin, M. (2015, August 23). Broward grand jury to investigate Flakka after 33 deaths. *Orlando Sentinel*. Retrieved from http://www.orlandosentinel.com/news/breaking-news/os-ap-broward-grand-jury-flakka-20150823-story.html

Law, R., Schier, J., Martin, C., Chang, A., & Wolkin, A. (2015, June 12). Notes from the field: Increase in reported adverse health effects related to synthetic cannabinoid use—United States, January—May 2015. *Morbidity & Mortality Weekly Report, 64*(22), 618-619.

Lewis, J., Arnold, M., House, R., & Toporek, R. (2003). *Advocacy competencies*. Retrieved from http://www.counseling.org/docs/default-source/competencies/advocacy_competencies.pdf

Marder, J. (2015). *The drug that never lets go*. Retrieved from http://www.pbs.org/newshour/spc/multimedia/bath-salts/

Miotto, K., Striebel, J., Cho, A. K., & Wang, C. (2013). Clinical and pharmacological aspects of bath salt use: A review of the literature and case reports. *Drug and Alcohol Dependence, 132*, 1-12. doi:10.1016/j.drugalcdep.2013.06.016.

National Institute of Drug Abuse (NIDA). (2012a). *Drugfacts: Spice.* Retrieved from http://www.drugabuse.gov/publications/drugfacts/k2spice-synthetic-marijuana.

National Institute of Drug Abuse (NIDA). (2012b). *Monitoring the future 2012 survey results.* Retrieved from http://www.drugabuse.gov/related-topics/trends-statistics/infographics/monitoring-future-2012-survey-results

National Institute of Drug Abuse (NIDA). (2015a). *Drugfacts: Synthetic cathinones ("bath salts").* Retrieved from http://www.drugabuse.gov/publications/drugfacts/synthetic-cathinones-bath-salts.

National Institute of Drug Abuse (NIDA). (2015b). *Emerging trends.* Retrieved from http://www.drugabuse.gov/drugs-abuse/emerging-trends.

New Jersey Regional Operations Intelligence Center Drug Monitoring Initiative. (2015). *Public awareness: Synthetic drugs.* Retrieved from http://www.knowaddiction.nj.gov/.

Office of National Drug Control Policy, White House. (2015). *Synthetic drugs (a.k.a. K2, Spice, Bath Salts, etc.).* Retrieved from https://www.whitehouse.gov/ondcp/ondcp-fact-sheets/synthetic-drugs-k2-spice-bath-salts.

Papanti, D., Schifano, F., Botteon, G., Bertossi, F., Mannix, J., Vidoni, D., . . . Bonavigo, T. (2013). "Spiceophrenia": A systematic overview of "Spice"-related psychological issues and a case report. *Human Psychopharmacology: Clinical & Experimental, 28,* 379-389. doi:10.1002/hup

Rizzo, T., & Rice, G. E. (2015, August 14). Flakka, the new killer drug, is spreading across the country. *The Kansas City Star.* Retrieved from http://ht.ly/ShpvF

Saha, S., Wilson, J. D., Adger, H. (2012). K2, Spice, and bath salts: Drugs of abuse commercially available. *Contemporary Pediatrics, 29*(10), 22-28.

Stogner, J. M., & Miller, B. L. (2014). A spicy kind of high: A profile of synthetic cannabinoid users. *Journal of Substance Use, 19*(1-2), 199-205. doi:10.3109/146598 91.2013.770571

Substance Abuse and Mental Health Services Administration (SAMHSA). (2014). Spice, bath salts, and behavioral health. *Advisory, 13*(2).

Swift, A. (2013, October 22). For first time, Americans favor legalizing marijuana. *Gallup.* Retrieved from http://www.gallup.com/poll/165539/first-time-americans-favor legalizing-marijuana.aspx

Van Pelt, J. (2012). Synthetic drugs: Fake substances, real dangers. *Social Work Today, 12*(4), 12-21.

Wagner, K. D., Armenta, R. F., Roth, A. M., Maxwell, J. C., Cuevas-Mota, J., & Garfein, R. S. (2014). Use of synthetic cathinones and cannabinimetics among injection drug users in San Diego, California. *Drug and Alcohol Dependence, 141,* 99-106. doi:10.106/j.drugalcdep.2014.05.007.

Winder, G. S., Stern, N., & Hosanagar, A. (2013). Are "Bath Salts" the next generation of stimulant abuse? *Journal of Substance Abuse Treatment, 44,* 42-45. doi:10.1016/j.jsat.2012.02.003

Zucchino, D. (2011, September 28). Scientist's research produces a dangerous high. *Los Angeles Times.* Retrieved from http://articles.latimes.com/2011/sep/28/nation/la-na-killer-weed-20110928

3

Beyond the Prescription

The Other Side of Opioid Painkillers

Shainna Ali, Gulnora Hundley, and M. Kristina DePue[1]

From 1991 to 2009, prescriptions for opioids tripled to more than 200 million (National Institute on Drug Abuse [NIDA], 2011). Currently, an average of 50 Americans die every day from prescription painkiller overdoses (Centers for Disease Control and Prevention [CDC], 2011). Prescription opioids, including oxycodone (OxyContin), hydrocodone (Vicodin), and meperidine (Demerol), are the second most commonly abused substance (Hanson, 2010), following alcohol. Distinct from illicit drugs, prescribed opioids have unique implications that must be taken into consideration during substance abuse treatment. Ease of accessibility to painkillers, unlike that of illicit substances, contributes to widespread availability, fuels federal addiction statistics, and changes treatment implications for opioid addiction (Substance Abuse and Mental Health Services Administration [SAMHSA], 2011; Unick, Rosenblum, Mars, & Ciccarone, 2013).

1. Shainna Ali, Gulnora Hundley, Department of Department of Child, Family, & Community Sciences, University of Central Florida, M. Kristina DePue, School of Human Development and Organizational Studies in Education, University of Florida. Correspondence concerning this article should be addressed to Shainna Ali, ShainnaAli@ knights.ucf.edu.

It is important to address this changing face of opioid addiction in order to better understand and assist clients suffering from opioid addiction. Although recognition of the prescription opioid pandemic is growing, there is little attention paid to the potential ramifications of prescription opioid use, misuse, and abuse in the counseling literature. This paper is an attempt to address these limitations as we (a) explain the medical processes and risks associated with prescription opioids, (b) outline the spectrum of prescription use, misuse, and abuse, and (c) highlight key counseling implications associated with prescription opioids.

Opioids and Opioid Antagonists: Neurobiology

This section describes how opioids affect the brain's chemical processes that contribute to cravings and the subsequent development of tolerance, dependence, and addiction with regard to opioids. Additionally, attention is given to the neurobiology of opioid antagonists. While it is widely accepted that socioeconomic and psychological factors play a role in opioid addiction, recent evidence clearly suggests a neurobiological component as well, for both beginning and , especially, continuing drug use (Stahl, 2013).

Opioids

Acting in the central nervous system (CNS), opioids produce analgesia, a sense of tranquility, decreased sense of apprehension, and a suppression of the cough reflex. Some of these actions are the primary CNS actions for which opioids are prescribed. However, opioids can produce nausea, vomiting, decreased respiration, constriction of the pupils, alterations in temperature regulation and a variety of changes in the neuroendocrine system (Preston, O'Neal, & Talaga, 2013). Through brain imaging, quantitative autoradiography, and other techniques such as genetic cloning, many brain reward system sites of drug action have been well established. These reward systems also involve neurotransmitters, or neuropeptides and receptors that mediate various pharmacological effects of the opioid drugs (Greenwald, Stitzer, & Haberny, 1997).

Opioid receptors, which are highly specific sites on nerve cells, are found throughout the brain and spinal cord, in neural plexuses in the gastrointestinal tract and other parts of the autonomic nervous system, and on white blood cells (De Vries & Shippenberg, 2002). Therefore, it is not surprising that opioid drugs have various actions on and interact with many parts of the human body. The most prominent effects—and the effects for which opioids are most commonly prescribed— occur the central nervous system (CNS) and the gastrointestinal tract (King, Ho & Schluger, 1999).

Three major types of opioid receptors have been identified (mu, delta and kappa), which appear to produce different physiological functions (Stimmel, 2007). When heroin, oxycodone, or any other opioid circulates through the bloodstream and enters the CNS, the molecules of these drugs attach to specialized proteins, called mu and delta opioid receptors, on the surfaces of opioid-sensitive neurons. Some animal studies have shown that mu and delta receptors may be responsible for the euphoria (Bryant, Zaki, Carrol, & Evans, 2005). On the other hand, kappa receptors appear to be responsible for dysphoria and may play a role in opioid withdrawal (De Vries & Shippenberg, 2002).

One of the brain circuits activated by opioids is the mesolimbic (midbrain) reward system. This system produces signals in a part of the brain called the ventral tegmental area (VTA) that result in the release of the neurotransmitter dopamine (DA) in another part of the brain, the nucleus accumbens (NAc) (Kreek, Schluger, & Borg, 1999). The release of DA into the NAc causes feelings of pleasure. Opioid tolerance occurs because the brain cells with opioid receptors gradually become less responsive to the opioid stimulation (Volkow, Frieden, Hyde, & Cha, 2014). That is, after continual use, more opioids are needed to stimulate the VTA brain cells of the mesolimbic reward system to release the same amount of DA and, in turn, produce euphoria similar to that initially provided.

Opioid dependence and most of the opioid withdrawal symptoms stem from changes in another important brain system called the locus ceruleus (LC), an area at the base of the brain. Neurons in the LC release the neurotransmitter, noradrenaline (NA), and distribute it to other parts of the brain where it stimulates wakefulness, breathing, blood pressure, and general alertness, among other functions (Sadock, Sadock, & Ruiz, 2009). When opioid molecules link to mu receptors on brain cells in the LC, they suppress the neurons' release of NA, resulting in drowsiness, slowed respiration, low blood pressure—familiar effects of opioid intoxication. With constant exposure to opioids, however, LC neurons adjust by increasing their level of activity. When opioids are present, their suppressive impact is compensated by this heightened activity, resulting in roughly normal amounts of NA being released and, therefore, the lack of pain-relieving effects for the patient. When opioids are not present to suppress the LC brain cells' enhanced activity, however, the neurons release excessive amounts of NA, triggering "the jitters," anxiety, muscle cramps, and diarrhea. Indeed, the antianxiety actions of opioids are likely due in part to their capacity to hinder LC activity (Bryant, Zaki, Carrol, & Evans, 2005).

Opioid Antagonists

Opioid drugs are defined and categorized in terms of their capacity to bind to and then activate these various receptor types (Stahl, 2013). Drugs that bind to and activate a receptor are agonists at that receptor. Those that bind to but do not activate a receptor function as antagonists at that receptor (De Vries & Shippenberg, 2002). Antagonists help addicts to avoid relapse by occupying opioid receptor sites and blocking the effects of agonists at the cellular level. Naltrexone has emerged as the most extensively studied agent among the opioid antagonists (Stimmel, 2007). Despite its minimal side effects, naltrexone has not been widely accepted by those struggling with addiction. This may be due to absence of feelings of well-being and euphoria. Methadone and levo-alpha-acetylmethadol (LAAM), the derivative of methadone, are synthetic opioid agonists. The higher the dose of methadone and LAAM, the greater the "blocking" effect of euphoria from heroin and other short-acting opioids. It is also important to emphasize that maintenance therapy with methadone is effective only for opioid drugs and does not have any effect in preventing withdrawal from or craving for any other group of mood-altering substances (Stimmel, 2007).

Unlike methadone and LAAM, buprenorphine (Suboxone) may be described as a partial agonist. While buprenorphine has been used effectively to substitute for other opioids and suppresses the development of opioid withdrawal signs and symptoms, its partial agonist properties are also responsible for increasing the potential for rapid opioid withdrawal syndrome under certain conditions (Volkow et al., 2014). As is true for methadone and LAAM, buprenorphine should be considered as having a potential for abuse. Each of these medications can play a unique role in comprehensive treatment for opioid addiction, but since no single medication is appropriate for every individual, it is important that clinicians have a variety of therapeutic agents available to them (Bryant, Zaki, Carrol, & Evans, 2005).

The molecular mechanisms of opioid abuse are highly complex processes that involve not only the endogenous opioid system (e.g., endorphins and enkephalins) but also many other neurotransmitter and receptor systems. The neurobiology of opioid dependence and pharmacokinetics of these drugs must be appreciated if better approaches to the treatment of opioid addiction are to be achieved. However, a detailed discussion regarding neurobiological advances of opioid addictions lies beyond the scope of this paper. If the reader desires additional information on this topic, the authors recommend the work of De Vries and Shippenberg (2002).

Understanding Prescription Opioid Use, Misuse, and Abuse

Prescription Use

Prescription opioid use can be defined as the general utilization of an opioid prescribed by a qualified clinical professional for medical concerns. Prescription opioids are consumed annually by millions of Americans (NIDA, 2011), and the legitimate use of prescription painkillers cannot be denied (Center for Lawful Access and Abuse Deterrence [CLAAD], 2011; Garcia, 2013; McCabe & Boyd, 2012). Medications are utilized to ameliorate pain for a number of medical concerns from basic injury to cancer (Davis, Walsh, Lagman, & LeGrand, 2005; Mandalà, Moro, Labianca, Cremonesi, & Barni, 2006). Chronic pain affects more than 116 million adults in the United States, which is more than the total affected by heart disease, cancer, and diabetes combined (Institute of Medicine, 2011). The utilization of prescription painkillers is currently the primary method of combating pain (Holman, Stoddard, & Higgins, 2013). For millions of individuals suffering from chronic pain, prescription painkillers dramatically improve their quality of life; however, the pairing of pain and prescription opioids may facilitate addictive behavior (Garland, Froeliger, Passik, & Howard, 2013; Florida Department of Health [FLDH], 2011). The necessity and legitimate use of prescription opioids do not prevent the potential for opioid misuse or abuse.

Whereas substances like heroin must be obtained illicitly and their possession can result in legal consequences, painkillers are usually prescribed and obtained legally. A doctor's validation and authorization for the use of prescription painkillers can prompt individuals to overlook risks paralleling those of illegal drugs. The concept of a prescription suggests a best practice recommendation from a credentialed provider; therefore, the potential ramifications associated with prescription painkillers are often unknown, overlooked, and misunderstood by users. Such confusion regarding the danger of prescription opioids puts users' safety at risk.

Prescription Misuse

Prescription opioid misuse can be defined as the nonmedical utilization of a prescription opioid. Nonmedical use of prescription painkillers is widespread in America (CDC, 2011; NIDA 2011; Office of the National Drug Control Policy [ONDCP], 2011). The motivations underpinning prescription opioid misuse are varied. As with illicit drugs, individuals may utilize prescription pills as a method of sensation-seeking. Individuals, who would have otherwise used illegal substances such as heroin, may turn to prescription opioids in an effort to achieve a similar high (McCabe & Boyd, 2012).

More than 75% of people who misuse prescription painkillers obtain drugs prescribed to someone else (SAMSA, 2011). The scope of acquisition misuse encompasses family and friends, theft, signature-forged prescriptions, the internet, and the street market. More than half of nonmedical users obtain prescription painkillers from a friend or relative (CLAAD, 2011; Hanson, 2010). According to the 2010 National Survey on Drug Use and Health, 55% of individuals who misuse prescription painkillers get the pills for free, 11.4% of users purchase them, and 4.8 % of users steal them from a friend or family member (SAMHSA, 2011). Jones, Fullwood, and Hawthorn (2012) highlighted the fact that parents typically focus on the prevention of illicit drug use; parents are often uninformed about the potential concerns (e.g., dependence) that cause prescription opioids to be as dangerous as having an illicit drug in the home.

Prescription opioid misuse may also stem from legitimate use. Individuals who were originally prescribed painkillers for a legitimate concern may continue to use them recreationally or for self-treatments not intended by the medical provider. When faced with prescription dependence and the inability to obtain more prescription pills, individuals who began use with a legitimate prescription may turn to heroin, due to its lower cost and ease of accessibility, or prescription drug diversion (Mars, Bourgois, Karandinos, Montero, & Ciccarone, 2014; Peavy et al., 2012). Prescription drug diversion is the illegal redirection of drugs from legitimate to illegitimate sources. A main method of prescription diversion is doctor shopping, or seeking multiple prescriptions for the same drug from numerous doctors in an effort to acquire a substantial supply for personal consumption or illegal resale (Cepeda, Fife, Wing, Mastrogiovanni, & Henderson, 2012; CLAAD, 2011; Trust for America's Health, 2013). According to NIDA (2011), more than half of patients who received an opioid prescription in 2009 had already filled an opioid prescription within the previous 30 days.

Prescription monitoring programs (PMPs) have been increasing in number in response to the growing need to manage prescription drug diversion. Currently, 49 states have a PMP, the District of Columbia has a proposal pending and Missouri is the only state that does not have a monitoring program (Garcia, 2013; Hanson, 2010). Within the last decade, the practice of doctor shopping has been particularly popular in states that did not have PMPs, as doctor shoppers flocked to locations in which they were less likely to be tracked, monitored or suffer from legal ramifications (CDC, 2011; Hanson, 2010). For example, prior to the establishment of a PMP, Florida was a hot bed for prescription drug diversion. Individuals from states with a PMP (e.g., Ohio, Tennessee, and Kentucky) traveled to Florida to acquire medication from the state's infamous "pill mills" (Kuehn, 2014). Nonregulated pain clinics in Florida offered cash-only, on-site dispensing and hence fostered prescription diversion (Rigg, March, & Inciardi, 2010). A sudden increase in the movement of individuals to states without a PMP has been noted in several states; however, Missouri remains without a PMP and corresponding legislation. Thus, the issues of diversion continue to be a concern within this state and for the nation.

It may be too early to determine the efficacy of PMPs. Loopholes in state-based initiatives to monitor prescription painkillers may simply increase diversion rather than decrease prescription drug misuse. For example, since PMPs are state-based initiatives, the lack of interstate sharing makes it difficult to track diversion across state lines.

Moreover, studies have shown that supply-based interventions may simply lead individuals to shift the substance consumed (Unick et al., 2013). For example, increased monitoring may cause an individual to turn to illegal opioids, rather than prescribed opioids. Finally, in addition to prescription drug diversion, opioid misuse encapsulates unprescribed acquisition (e.g., obtaining medications from family members), making it difficult to measure the extent of prescription misuse at large.

"Prescription drug abuse is the intentional use of a medication without a prescription; in a way other than as prescribed; or for the experience or feeling it causes" (NIDA, 2011, p.1). Unlike use, which pertains to the general utilization of a prescription drug, or misuse, which is the inappropriate use stemming from legitimate use, the key difference with prescription drug abuse is the awareness paired with the conscientious illegitimate utilization of a medication for a purpose beyond medical. The consequences associated with prescription opioid abuse are reaching devastating statistics nationwide (NIDA, 2011). Misperceptions of danger foster the seamless development from prescription opioid use to misuse, and subsequently to abuse. The annual estimated societal cost of prescription opioid abuse is more than 55 billion dollars (Birnbaum, et al., 2011). In 2008, prescription painkiller overdoses killed nearly 15,000 individuals, triple the number of similar fatalities in 1999 (CDC, 2011). Opioid pill morbidity is the leading cause of accidental death in more than half of the United States (Holman et al., 2013).

The legal ramifications are dissimilar from illicit drugs, which prompt the perception that prescription pills are less dangerous; therefore, the seriousness is undernoted (CLAAD, 2011). Unlike illegal substances, since pills are legal and are often prescribed by a medical professional, it is difficult to prove abuse. Additionally, levels of pain may be difficult to test and prove, thus complicating the potential to track when appropriate use has evolved into abuse.

Counseling Implications

Prescription opioid dependence poses unique challenges that make the recovery process difficult and daunting for clients. Unlike those using illicit drugs, consumers of prescription opioids can spiral from legitimate use into dependence and diversion. Therefore, implications for prescription opioid abuse are distinct, and treatments should not be a duplicate of non pill opioid treatment. Unfortunately, as noted by various authors, inadequate treatment exists for individuals who suffer from prescription opioid use (Bell, 2010; Schmidt, Bischof, Harting, & Rumpf, 2009). This section will outline various methods and techniques that counselors may implement to effectively assist clients in the domains of (a) understanding the problem, (b) assessment, (c) detox, and (d) counseling techniques. Whereas administration of a comprehensive treatment program may be the ultimate goal, there are clear steps that counselors should take when working with this population.

Recognizing the Problem

In order for counselors to begin supporting clients who are facing prescription opioid abuse and dependence, their first step is education. It is essential for counselors to be informed and educated about the prescription pandemic (Frauger et al., 2012; Trust for America's Health, 2013). Knowledgeable counselors can help guide clients through their withdrawal from prescription opioid dependence in a safe environment that facilitates lasting recovery. Although this paper is an effort to educate counselors on the primary issues of prescription opioid abuse, counselors should also explore the magnitude of prescription drug use in their area and services that are already in place. Further, we encourage counselors to be informed about the dangers of prescription opioid abuse and the difficulties clients face as they stop using drugs, particularly when considering the potential complications of chemical dependence.

In order to stay informed, counselors can use helpful websites such as www.samhsa.gov, www.Mayo Clinic.org, and www.drugfreeworld.org. The SAMHSA (2014) website provides helpful information on common drugs, considerations with specific populations, and helpful statistics to understand the breadth of the opioid concern. The Mayo Clinic (2015) includes helpful lists such as signs and symptoms, causes, risk factors, complications, and prevention of opioid abuse. The Foundation for a Drug-Free World (2015) provides street names, mental and physiological effects, causes, a brief history, and warning signs of opioid abuse. Additionally, excerpts from individuals who were affected by prescription opioid abuse are included; these segments may assist counselors in understanding the client's perspective.

Assessment

Proper assessment for prescription opioid concerns begins at the intake and continues throughout counseling. It is essential that a counselor is competent to identify a client who may be misusing and/or abusing prescription painkillers. However, it is difficult to gauge divergence from prescribed use without a thorough assessment. Without understanding the signs, symptoms, and consequences of prescription opioid abuse, accurate assessment is difficult. Counselors should employ formal and informal methods in an effort to gain a better perspective and arrive at a thorough assessment (Hanson, 2010; Trust for America's Health, 2013). Examples of useful formal measures include the Drug Abuse Screening Test (DAST-20; Skinner, 1982), the Opioid Risk Tool (Webster & Webster, 2005), the Brief Pain Inventory (BPI, Cleeland et al., 1994), and the American Psychiatric Association adapted NIDA Modified ASSIST (NIDA, 2014). Accurate assessment is critical to match clients with appropriate treatment mechanisms.

The assessment process needs to go beyond the dichotomous categories of "user" and "nonuser." Instead, the counselor should explore active and historical use, purposes for use, and potential methods of maintenance (Rosenblatt & Mekhail, 2005). Clients may fail to identify prescription opioid use on substance abuse sections of the biopsychosocial assessment form. As such, we encourage counselors to ask detailed questions about clients' current and past usage of prescription opioids to assess whether there is prescription abuse or dependence present and then to aid in appropriate referrals for treatment. In conducting a broad assessment of prescription use, be sure to question the (a) generic name of the drug; (b) brand name of the drug; (c) prescribing doctor; (d) start date and changes since; (e) purpose; (f) dose; (g) schedule, interactions with other drugs; (h) potential complaints associated; and (i) client's perception of whether the drug is working. For informal assessment, the following are suggested questions that a counselor may use during the assessment process:

- Tell me the names of and use for any prescription drugs that you currently use or have used in the past, whether prescribed or not prescribed.
- Have you ever used prescription medication for the relief of pain?
- If you use a medication for pain relief, what condition is it prescribed for?
- If you have used prescription medication for pain relief, how long did you use the medication and did you use it as prescribed?
- If you have used prescription medication for pain relief, has your dosage increased to achieve same level of relief as when the pain management program was started?
- Have you ever been in a situation in which multiple doctors had to prescribe pain medication in a closely related time frame?
- Have you ever run out of pain medication before your next prescription was due?
- Do you feel that doctors have adequately treated your pain?
- Have you ever been to the emergency room to get pain medication?
- Some clients feel very strong cravings for these drugs over time. Have you ever felt such cravings that you considered forging a prescription to get the drug?

Responses to these questions can provide useful information about the use, misuse, and abuse of prescription opioids and alert the counselor about possible signs of a problem with prescription drug abuse. If there is enough information from the client to suggest there could be a problem, then we suggest a useful screening tool called the CAGE Questionnaire (Rosenblatt & Mekhail, 2005). CAGE is a four-item screening tool that assesses possible abuse along four dimensions: attempts to cut down use, other people's annoyance at use, guilty feelings about use, and early day usage to reduce negative feelings. Clients who answer affirmatively to two or more items may have a problem with the substance. Although CAGE screening was originally developed for alcoholism and does not give the full picture of drug use, it can be useful in providing feedback and eliciting conversations about current opioid use.

Medical Detoxification

Because of the unique effects of prescription opioid use on the CNS, clients experience withdrawal symptoms, such as flu-like symptoms, physical pain, and intense craving for the drug (Wesson & Ling, 2003). Opioids trick the body into thinking it is in pain. Therefore, the body functions as if it is in pain during opioid use and endorphin levels begin to rise after taking the drug. Consequently, when opioid use ceases, the individual's pain receptors are no longer able to differentiate real from phantom pain, and the body overacts to pain stimuli. In fact, running water on the skin may induce painful sensations for someone who recently stopped opioid use (Stahl, 2013). Continued drug use often occurs as a result of avoiding the aforementioned withdrawal symptoms.

These withdrawal symptoms are unique to opioid use, and medical detoxification is a central component of successful recovery from prescription opioid use. There are essentially two types of medical detoxification: (a) medication assisted therapies (MATs), and (b) symptom monitoring and treatment. Medical detoxification through the use of MATs, such as Suboxone and Methadone, can help prevent the client from a return to use when withdrawal symptoms (i.e., pain and aches) begin (Volkow et al.,2014). Maintenance drugs are used to treat opioid addiction and help curb cravings for opioids. There is much debate on the continued use of maintenance drugs because they can be habit forming (Stimmel, 2007); however, we suggest that short-term use for acute withdrawal symptoms may be beneficial to the client and help deter relapse (Volkow et al., 2014).

Treatment centers frequently use the aforementioned medications to help reduce the severity of withdrawal and help to ameliorate initial cravings for opioids. If counselors and clients are not interested in maintenance medications, then a medical detoxification program that focuses on withdrawal-symptom treatment is strongly suggested, because of the potential fatal aspects of withdrawal symptoms. An example of a lethal repercussion of withdrawal include excessive vomiting which may infiltrate the lungs (aspiration) and cause a deadly infection (Stahl, 2013).

Further, vomiting and diarrhea may lead to terminal hydrolyte depletion. Locating medical detoxification programs that specialize in opioid addiction in your area and gaining information about the methods of detoxification used by the center are important steps to consider.

Counseling Techniques

Many clients may not recognize the potential ramifications of prescription opioid use, given that physicians prescribe the medications. Clients generally lack knowledge regarding the dangers of opioid use. Thus, it is imperative that counselors utilize psychoeducation therapy (PET) to empower clients to deal with prescription opioid abuse. PET is useful to teach clients about the signs, symptoms, and dangers of long-term prescription opioid use and is a first step to helping clients understand what is happening in their minds and to their bodies. Careless use of prescription drugs can lead to dependence that is not only misunderstood but can also provoke shame and guilt. As such, working with clients to normalize their experience with prescription opiate dependence can facilitate self-compassion, understanding, and motivation to change unwanted dependence.

Psychoeducation about treatment options and the provision of coping strategies to recover from dependence can also empower clients to have autonomy over their recovery. Moreover, the recovery process can be full of unknowns for clients; thus, educating clients about detoxification and maintenance strategies may aid in reducing anxieties and fears. Education is one of the four major areas of the Obama Administration's National Drug Control Strategy (2011) to reduce prescription drug abuse. The NIDA (2014) and the Foundation for a Drug-Free World (2014) provide helpful reports than can be utilized for psychoeducation. Additionally, Taite Adam's (2013) *Opiate Addiction: The Painkiller Addiction Epidemic, Heroin Addiction and the Way Out* is a text that could be integrated into counseling for psychoeducation. This text is user-friendly and covers topics such as how opiates work, pain pill addiction, chronic pain, treatment, and detoxification.

Withdrawal symptoms of opioid prescription drugs are both psychologically and physically challenging, and client resistance to treatment is common (Pollack et al., 2002). Psychoeducation may help with client resistance, but additional counseling techniques, such as Motivational

Interviewing (MI), can help decrease client resistance to discontinuation of prescription opioid use (Miller & Rollnick, 1991). MI considers the client's motivation level and readiness to change by assessing the client's Stage of Change (SOC; Prochaska & DiClemente, 1982). SOC consists of five stages that move from the least aware and least motivated to sustain recovery: precontemplation, contemplation, preparation, action, and maintenance. Assessment of the presence of a prescription opioid abuse problem is paramount, but assessing the client's motivation and awareness levels is also important in helping formulate the counseling process. For example, in the stage of precontemplation a client is not considering change and needs information to link problems experienced with substance problems. At this stage, it is appropriate to elicit the client's perceptions of the problem, explore pros and cons of substance use, and examine discrepancies between the client's perceptions of behavior and others' perceptions. Awareness, motivation, and needs in the precontemplation stage differ from the preparation stage in which a client has decided to change and begin steps toward recovery. During this time, it is helpful to clarify goals and strategies for change, offer a menu of options for change, and have the client publicly assert plans to change. Adequate assessment of stage is essential to meet the different needs of the stage and appropriately guide the client towards recovery. More information on the SOC can be found by reading *Changing for Good* by Prochaska, Norcross, and DiClemente (1994). Additional information and training on Motivation Interviewing can be found at www.motivationalinterviewing.org.

Another counseling technique that may be useful when working with prescription opioid abuse is harm reduction. Harm reduction coincides with psychoeducation, as educating clients regarding the harmful aspects of the drugs is foundational to the technique. Harm reduction takes a pragmatic approach with clients, using the notion of acceptance that prescription opioid use is common place (Lushin & Anastas, 2011). The goals of the approach are then to reduce the levels of harm associated with the drug intake. Stemming from pragmatism, harm reduction evaluates social functioning, social context, risks, and support as individuals are seen as complex beings. From this perspective, insistence on permanent cessation is seen as non-pragmatic and may deter a client from treatment (Lushin & Anastas, 2011). An easy way to think of harm reduction is a balance of cost and benefit; therefore, counselors work to help clients prioritize their goals and evaluate the costs/benefits of their current actions with relation to those goals. For example, if an individual is suffering from pain, complete termination of opioid use may be less effective when compared to a harm reduction method that may change the prescription, lower the dosage, or alter the frequency of ingestion. More information on harm reduction techniques can be found at www.harmreduction.org. Each of the three counseling approaches discussed here (PET, MI, and harm reduction) aim to increase client awareness of the problem and help the client take responsibility for making the decisions to stop using. The lack of knowledge and understanding of the risks of prescription opioid use highlights the dire needs for counselors to utilize not only educational techniques with clients, but also to seek out their own knowledge on the prescription opioid pandemic.

Conclusion

The prescription opioid pandemic is a growing concern and efforts are being made to combat its devastating grasp on society. Legislative strides, such as prescription drug monitoring programs, have been made to address, highlight, and decrease misuse and abuse. However, it is too early to determine the efficacy of such programs (Garcia, 2013; Reifler et al., 2012; Smith, 2012). Further, due to other channels of nonmedical prescription drug use, it is difficult to discern the breadth of prescription opioid use, misuse, and abuse (United States Government Accountability Office, 2002). Counselors can play a vital role in combating the prescription opioid problem. Counselors should be aware of the national pandemic, knowledgeable about implications for users and society, and familiar with and skilled in the necessary methods of assisting clients with dependence on opioid painkillers.

References

Adams, T. (2013). *Opiate addiction: The painkiller addiction epidemic, heroin addiction and the way out*. St. Petersburg, FL: Rapid Response Press.

Bell, J. (2010). The global diversion of pharmaceutical drugs: Opiate treatment and the diversion of pharmaceutical opiates. *Addiction, 105*(9), 1531-1537.

Birnbaum, H. G., White, A. G., Schiller, M., Waldman, T., Cleveland, J. M., & Roland, C. L. (2011). Societal costs of prescription opioid abuse, dependence, and misuse in the United States. *Pain Medicine, 12*(4), 657-667. doi:10.1111/j.1526-4637.2011.01075.x

Bryant, C. D., Zaki, P. A., Carroll, F. I., & Evans, C. J. (2005). Opioids and addiction: Emerging pharmaceutical strategies for reducing reward and opponent processes. *Clinical Neuroscience Research, 5*, 103-115.

Center for Lawful Access and Abuse Deterrence. (2011). *The National Prescription Drug Abuse Prevention Strategy*. Retrieved from http://claad.org/

Centers for Disease Control and Prevention (CDC). (2011). *Prescription painkiller overdoses in US*. Retrieved from http://www.cdc.gov/drugoverdose/data/overdose.html

Cepeda, M., Fife, D., Wing, C., Mastrogiovanni, G., & Henderson, S. C. (2012). Assessing opioid shopping behaviour. *Drug Safety, 35*(4), 325-334.

Cleeland, C. S., Cesario, S. K., McFarlane, J., Nava, A., Gilroy, H., & Maddoux, J. (2014). Brief Pain Inventory. [Formerly denoted: Wisconsin Brief Pain Questionnaire]. *Clinical Journal of Oncology Nursing, 18*(1), 65-73.

Davis, M., Walsh, D., Lagman, R., & LeGrand, S. (2005). Controversies in pharmacotherapy of pain management. *Lancet Oncology, 6*(9), 696-704.

De Vries, T. J., & Shippenberg, T. S. (2002). Neural systems underlying opiate addiction. *The Journal of Neuroscience, 22*(9), 3321-3325.

Florida Department of Health. (2011). *User guide for the controlled substances reporting system*. Retrieved from http://www.myfloridalicense.com/dbpr/ddc/documents/UserGuide.pdf

Foundation for a Drug-Free World. (2015). *The truth about painkillers*. Retrieved from http://www.drugfreeworld.org/drugfacts

Frauger, E., Nordmann, S., Orleans, V., Pradel, V., Pauly, V., Thirion, X., . . . Reseau, C. (2012). Which psychoactive prescription drugs are illegally obtained and through which ways of acquisition? About OPPIDUM survey. *Fundamental & Clinical Pharmacology, 26*(4), 549-556.

Garcia, A. (2013). State laws regulating prescribing of controlled substances: Balancing the public health problems of chronic pain and prescription painkiller abuse and overdose. *Journal of Law, Medicine & Ethics, 41*, 42-45.

Garland, E.L., Froeliger, B., Passik, S., & Howard, M.O. (2013). Attentional bias for prescription opioid cues among opioid-dependent chronic pain patients. *Journal of Behavioral Medicine, 36*(6), 611-620. doi:10.1007/s10865-012-9455-8

Greenwald, M. K., Stitzer, M. L., & Haberny, K. A. (1997). Human pharmacology of the opioid neuropeptide dynorphin A(1-13). *Journal of Pharmacology and Experimental Therapeutics, 281*(3), 1154-1163.

Hanson, K. (2010). A pill problem. *State Legislatures, 36*(3), 22-25.

Holman, J. E., Stoddard, G. J., & Higgins, T. F. (2013). Rates of prescription opiate use before and after injury in patients with orthopaedic trauma and the risk factors for prolonged opiate use. *The Journal of Bone & Joint Surgery, 95*(12), 1075-1080. doi:10.2106/JBJS.L.00619

Institute of Medicine. (2011). *Relieving pain in America a blueprint for transforming prevention, care, education, and research.* Washington, DC: Author.

Jones, B. A., Fullwood, H., & Hawthorn, M. (2012). Preventing prescription drug abuse in adolescence: A collaborative approach. *The Prevention Researcher, 19*(1), 13-16.

King, A. C, Ho. A., & Schluger J. (1999). Acute subjective effects of dynorphin A(1-13) infusion in normal healthy subjects. *Drug and Alcohol Dependence, 54,* 87-90.

Kreek, M. J, Schluger, J., & Borg L. (1999). Dynorphin A1-13 causes elevation of serum levels of prolactin through an opioid receptor mechanism in humans: Gender differences and implications for modulations of dopaminergic tone in the treatment of addictions. *Journal of Pharmacology and Experimental Therapeutics, 288,* 260-269.

Kuehn, B. M. (2014). CDC: Major disparities in opioid prescribing among states. *Journal of the American Medical Association, 312*(7), 684-686.

Lushin, V., & Anastas, J. W. (2011). Harm reduction in substance abuse treatment: Pragmatism as an epistemology for social work practice. *Journal of Social Work Practice in the Addictions, 11*(1), 96-100. doi:10.1080/1533256X.2011.546205

Mandalà, M., Moro, C., Labianca, R., Cremonesi, M., & Barni, S. (2006). Optimizing use of opiates in the management of cancer pain. *Therapeutics and Clinical Risk Management, 2*(4), 447-453.

Mars, S., Bourgois, P., Karandinos, G., Montero, F., & Ciccarone, D. (2014). "Every 'never' I ever said came true": Transitions from opioid pills to heroin injecting. *International Journal of Drug Policy, 25*(2), 257-266.

Mayo Clinic (2015). *Prescription drug abuse.* Retrieved from http://www.mayoclinic.org/diseases-conditions/prescription-drug-abuse/

McCabe, S., & Boyd, C. J. (2012). Do motives matter? Nonmedical use of prescription medications among adolescents. *The Prevention Researcher, 19*(1), 10-12.

Miller, W. R., & Rollnick, S. (1991). *Motivational interviewing: Preparing people to change addictive behavior.* New York, NY: Guilford Press.

National Institute on Drug Abuse. (2011). *Analysis of opioid prescription practices finds areas of concern.* Retrieved from https://www.drugabuse.gov/news-events/news-releases/2011/04/analysis-opioid-prescription-practices-finds-areas-concern

National Institute on Drug Abuse. (2014). *American Psychiatric Association Adapted NIDA Modified ASSIST Tools.* Retrieved from www.drugabuse.gov/nidamed-medical-health-professionals/tool-resources-your-practice/screening-assessment-drug-testing-resources/american-psychiatric-association-adapted-nida

Office of the National Drug Control Policy. (2011). *Epidemic: Responding to America's prescription drug abuse crisis.* Retrieved from https://www.whitehouse.gov/sites/default/files/ondcp/policy-and-research/rx_abuse_plan.pdf

Peavy, K., Banta-Green, C. J., Kingston, S., Hanrahan, M., Merrill, J. O., & Coffin, P. O. (2012). "Hooked on" prescription-type opiates prior to using heroin: Results from a survey of syringe exchange clients. *Journal of Psychoactive Drugs, 44*(3), 259-265. doi:10.1080/02791072.2012.704591

Pollack, M. H., Penava, S. A., Bolton, E., Worthington, J., Allen, G., Farach, F. J., & Otto, M. W. (2002). A novel cognitive-behavioral approach for treatment-resistant drug dependence. *Journal of Substance Abuse Treatment, 23*(4), 335-342. doi:10.1016/S0740-5472(02)00298-2

Preston, J., O'Neal, J., & Talaga, M. C. (2013). *Handbook of clinical psychopharmacology for therapists.* Oakland, CA: New Harbinger Publications.

Prochaska, J. O., & DiClemente, C. C. (1982). Transtheoretical therapy: Toward a more integrative model of change. *Psychotherapy: Theory, Research & Practice, 19*(3), 276-288. doi:10.1037/h0088437

Prochaska, J.O., Norcross, J.C. & DiClemente, C.C. (1994). *Changing for good.* New York: Morrow.

Reifler, L. M., Droz, D., Bailey, J., Schnoll, S. H., Fant, R., Dart, R. C., & Bucher Bartelson, B. (2012). Do prescription monitoring programs impact state trends in opioid abuse/misuse? *Pain Medicine, 13*(3), 434-442. doi:10.1111/j.1526-4637.2012.01327.x

Rigg, K. K., March, S. J., & Inciardi, J. A. (2010). Prescription drug abuse & diversion: Role of the pain clinic. *Journal of Drug Issues, 40*(3), 681-701.

Rosenblatt, A. B., & Mekhail, N. A. (2005). Management of pain in addicted/illicit and legal substance abusing patients. *Pain Practice, 5*(1), 2-10. doi:10.1111/j.1533-2500.2005.05102.x

Sadock, B. J., Sadock, V. A., & Ruiz, P. (2009). *Kaplan and Sadock's Comprehensive Textbook of Psychiatry* (9th ed). Philadelphia: Lippincott Williams & Wilkins.

Schmidt, C. C., Bischof, G. G., Harting, M. M., & Rumpf, H. J. (2009). Motivation to change and readiness for counseling in prescription-drug-dependent patients in a general hospital population. *Addiction Research & Theory, 17*(2), 186-190. doi:10.1080/16066350802447082

Skinner, H. A. (1982). The Drug Abuse Screening Test. *Addictive Behaviors, 7*(4), 363-371.

Smith, D. E. (2012). Prescribing practices and the prescription drug epidemic: Physician intervention strategies. *Journal of Psychoactive Drugs, 44*(1), 68-71.

Stahl, S. M. (2013). *Stahl's essential psychopharmacology: Neuroscientific basis and practical application.* New York, NY: Cambridge University Press.

Stimmel, B. (2007). Buprenorphine misuse, abuse, and diversion: When will we ever learn? *Journal of Addictive Diseases, 26*(3), 1-3. doi:10.1300/J069v26n03_01

Substance Abuse and Mental Health Services Administration. (2011). *Treatment episode data set (TEDS) (1999—2009). National admissions to substance abuse treatment services.* Retrieved from http://wwwdasis.samhsa.gov/teds09/TEDS2k9NWeb.pdf

Substance Abuse and Mental Health Services Administration. (2014). *Prescription drug misuse and abuse.* Retrieved from http://www.samhsa.gov/prescription-drug-misuse-abuse

Trust for America's Health. (2013). *Prescription drug abuse: Strategies to stop the epidemic.* Retrieved from http://healthyamericans.org/reports/drugabuse2013/TFAH2013RxDrugAbuseRpt12_no_embargo.pdf

Unick, G., Rosenblum, D., Mars, S., & Ciccarone, D. (2013). Intertwined epidemics: National demographic trends in hospitalizations for heroin and opioid-related overdoses, 1993-2009. *PloS ONE, 8*(2), 1-8. doi:10.1371/journal.pone.0054496

United States Government Accountability Office. (2002). *Prescription drugs: State monitoring programs provide useful tool to reduce diversion.* Retrieved from www.gao.gov

Volkow, N. D., Frieden, T. R., Hyde, P. S., & Cha, S. S. (2014). Medication-assisted therapies: Tackling the opioid-overdose epidemic. *The New England Journal of Medicine, 370*(22), 2063-2066. doi:10.1056/NEJMp1402780

Webster, L. R., & Webster, R. M. (2005). Predicting aberrant behaviors in opioid-treated patients: Preliminary validation of the opioid risk tool. *Pain Medicine, 6*(6), 432-442. doi:10.1111/j.1526-4637.2005.00072.x

Wesson, D. R., & Ling, W. (2003). The clinical opiate withdrawal scale (COWS). *Journal of Psychoactive Drugs, 35*(2), 253-259. doi:10.1080/02791072.2003.10400007

4

Social Skills Training for Male Youth in Treatment for Substance Use Disorder

---

OKSANA KRAVETS AND JENEPHER LENNOX TERRION[1]

In an effort to explain the relationship between social competence and substance use disorder (SUD), Terrion (2015) argues that there is a direct link between the quality of young people's relationships, their ability to create healthy relationships through their communication skills, and the likelihood of problematic substance use. Terrion's communication model of relational pathways of SUD is based on an assumption that a gap exists in the ability of adolescents at risk for SUD to build healthy interpersonal relationships because they lack the social competence to build these relationships and that healthy, pro-social relationships are a protective factor against SUD. This paper explores the research on adolescent substance abuse, gender differences in substance use and the role of social skills in treatment for SUD. It then analyzes approaches to social skills training for adolescents, in particular males, in order to recommend

---

1. Oksana Kravets and Jenepher Lennox Terrion, Department of Communication, University of Ottawa. Correspondence concerning this article should be addressed to Jenepher Lennox Terrion, Ph.D., Department of Communication, University of Ottawa, 11121-55 Laurier Avenue, Ottawa, Ontario, Canada K1N 6N5, 613-562-5800 (2517) Email: jlennoxt@uottawa.ca

training approaches and techniques to be used by counselors in substance abuse treatment programs.

There is no question that experimentation with alcohol and other drugs, while included in a list of "normal feelings and behaviors of the middle school and early high school adolescent" (American Academy of Child and Adolescent Psychiatry, 2011, para 1), warrants attention when it evolves into SUD. In this regard, Bukstein et al. (2005) report that some 9.8% of American 17—to 19-year-olds struggle with problematic substance use. Recent Canadian statistics suggest that one-in-eight (13%) students aged 12 to 17 report symptoms of SUD, with 12th-graders most at risk for a drug use problem other than alcohol (Paglia-Boak, Adlaf, & Mann, 2011). Furthermore, some 4.6 % of young people in the United States aged 12-17 needed treatment for SUD in 2000 (Office of Applied Studies, 2002). In Canada, 1% of students of this same age group reported in 2011 that they had been in a treatment program during the past year because of their alcohol and/or other drug use (Paglia-Boak et al., 2011).

Studies of SUD consistently point to gender as an important factor (Substance Abuse and Mental Health Services Administration, 2012; 2013; 2014b). For example, in their extensive review of gender and substance use, Kloos, Weller, Chan, and Weller (2009) cite the 2006 Substance Abuse and Mental Health Statistics National Survey finding that problematic substance use among adults and adolescents 12 years of age and older was two times greater in males than females (12.3% vs 6.3%). Kloos et al. cite other studies that conclude that males are more likely than females to report marijuana and alcohol use (Cotto et al., 2010; Greenfield, Back, Lawson, & Brady, 2010). Likewise, Leatherdale and Burkhalter (2012), in their study of the prevalence of substance use among 45,425 adolescents in Canada, found significant gender differences with males more likely than females to report marijuana use only and both alcohol and marijuana use. Kuhn (2015), in her comprehensive analysis of factors contributing to gender differences in substance use, points out that many important differences between boys and girls emerge during adolescence and that they are moderated by sexual differentiation of the brain. She concludes that in addition to these biologic factors, psychiatric co-morbidities as well as personality and the environment present gender-specific risks as adolescents begin to initiate substance use.

Interestingly, differences in substance use patterns among men and women vary by age. According to the 2011 National Survey on Drug Use and Health, men aged 18 or older have almost twice the rate of SUD as adult women, but among youths aged 12 to 17, the rate of SUD for both genders is the same (6.9 percent) (cited in Substance Abuse and Mental Health Services Administration, 2014b). This difference points to the importance of targeting young people, particularly males, in drug prevention strategies and interventions.

In terms of gender differences in treatment of SUD, a recent report using the Treatment Episode Data Set (TEDS), an administrative data system that provides descriptive information about the national flow of admissions aged 12 or older to providers of addiction treatment, reported that in 2011 about 1.23 million (66.9 percent) of the 1.84 million admissions to substance use treatment in the U.S. were male while 609,000 were female (33.1 percent) (Substance Abuse and Mental Health Services Administration, 2014b). The authors concluded that there are "important differences in primary substance of abuse between males and females admitted to substance abuse treatment" (p. 5) and suggest that these findings may be "useful to those responsible for the design of outreach, prevention, and treatment programs" (p. 1).

There are "many forces at play to make one person more likely to abuse substances than another, including genetics, brain abnormalities, behavior, personality styles and the environment at home and at school" (Leyton & Stewart, 2014, p. 2). As well, because research and practice have demonstrated that the risk of SUD, its consequences, and the processes for treatment and recovery differ by race and ethnicity (Center for Substance Abuse Treatment, 2009), "the role of culture should be considered during initial intakes and interviews, in screening and assessment processes, and in the development of treatment planning" (Substance Abuse and Mental Health Services Administration, 2014a).

In addition to these factors, deficits in social competence have been identified as a risk factor for SUD in youth (Gaffney, Thorpe, Young, Collett, & Occhipinti, 1998; Hover & Gaffney, 1991; Webb & Baer, 1995; Wekerle, Leung, Goldstein, Thornton, & Tonmyr, 2009). In their study of social competence and substance use, Griffin and colleagues (2001) concluded that youth with less social competence may turn to substance use as a way to make friends, seem grown up, and appear "cool" to other adolescents. In support of this conclusion, Griffin et al. cite Jackson and her colleagues (1997), who found that elementary school students who scored poorly on self-reported and teacher-rated measures of social competence were more likely to initiate substance use early (p. 487).

Social competence, often referred to as communication skill, is a complex, multidimensional construct that includes both social skills and peer relationships (Merrell & Calderella, 2008). Merrell (2008) argues that the outcomes of socially competent behaviors are healthy relationships and the achievement of desirable goals. Thus social competence is composed of social skills and peer relations. Social skills, as an essential aspect of social competence, are defined by Merrell (2008) as specific behaviors that "when initiated, lead to desirable social outcomes for the person initiating them" (p. 381). In children and adolescents, Merrell provides the following examples of these behaviors: academic and task-related competence (e.g., success in school and in developmentally appropriate activities); cooperation with peers (e.g., getting along with others); reinforcement of peers' behaviors (e.g., behaviors that encourage others to continue what they are doing); and social initiation behaviors (e.g., inviting others to interact).

As Terrion, O'Rielly, and Rocchi, (2016) conclude in their exploratory study of the social competence of adolescents in addiction treatment, a lack of social competence can lead to negative outcomes for youth in treatment for two main reasons. First, there is an increased likelihood that they will be removed from treatment (or choose to withdraw on their own) because of their difficulty in getting along with others. Second, a lack of social competence can contribute to a reduced ability to connect positively with therapists and treatment center staff, with other residents and, upon completion of treatment, with pro-social members of the community. These relationships are critical to both treatment adherence and relapse prevention (Ritter et al., 2002; von Braun, 2013). This conclusion has been supported by other researchers who also argue that social skills training is necessary to help participants in addiction treatment build healthy relationships with staff in order to enhance the likelihood of remaining in treatment (Moos, Moos, & Andrassy, 1999).

While an absence of social competence has been identified as a risk factor for SUD, it has also been shown to be a protective factor against SUD and other problem behaviors. Specifically, research has shown the protective nature of social competence in that socially competent youth have lower rates of substance use, depression, delinquency, and aggression (Botvin, 1983; Griffin, Epstein, Botvin, & Spoth, 2001; Gundersen, 2010; Pentz, 1983; Segrin, 2000; Vorobjov, Saat, & Kull, 2014).

In terms of gender and social competence, it has been argued that differences exist in the social skills of boys and girls because gender differences exist in the social experiences and behavior of boys and girls (Crombie, 1988). Crombie suggests that there are clinical implications of these differences and that, specifically, it may be more difficult to address social skill deficits in boys than in girls through interventions because boys often are not as developmentally advanced as girls. More importantly, she argues that boys may be less motivated to develop their social skills compared to girls, because girls see social competence as essential to their ability to form relationships and get along with others. This argument is supported by Jean Baker Miller's *Relational Theory* (1976), which assumes that interpersonal connection is a basic human need and that this need is especially central to the communication patterns and motivation of women, who are "more attuned to connection while males are more attuned to differentiation" (Covington, 2007, p. 139).

Interestingly, Terrion et al. (2016), in their study of social competence of adolescents in addiction treatment, found that while girls in treatment did not differ from a normed sample of youth, boys in treatment differed significantly from the normed sample, with lower scores in social competence and, particularly, in peer relations or the ability to get along with others. These authors concluded that addiction treatment should offer social skills training, where participants are taught to interact more effectively with their friends, peers, family members, and/or other members of society, and that it was especially important to provide this training to male participants.

Group-based skills training, in which participants are taught social skills to help them develop healthier relationships and negotiate difficult situations (Kazdin, 1997), is a typical approach for addressing behavior problems and building social competence (Ang & Hughes, 2001). Whether delivered in residential or inpatient settings or offered on an outpatient basis, effective treatments for adolescents primarily consist of some form of behavioral therapy (for a review of a therapeutic interventions, see National Institute on Drug Abuse, 2014). Behavioral therapy is most effective if it takes "into account the needs of the whole person—including his or her developmental stage and cognitive abilities and the influence of family, friends, and others in the person's life, as well as any additional mental or physical health conditions (National Institute on Drug Abuse, 2014, p. 6). As the National Institute on Drug Abuse (2014) suggests, behavioral therapies include elements such as "providing incentives for abstinence, building skills to resist and refuse substances and deal with triggers or craving, replacing drug use with constructive and rewarding activities, improving problem-solving skills, and facilitating better interpersonal relationships" (p. 10).

Purpose Statement

Given that male youth are more at risk for substance use and for lower social competence than adolescent females, this paper seeks to identify the means by which social skills training might be most effective with male youth (defined here as ages 12-24, following the definition proposed by the Canadian Centre on Substance Abuse, 2007) in treatment for SUD. The goal of this paper is not to suggest content for social skills training programs, but rather to identify overarching approaches and techniques to build social competence of male adolescents who struggle with SUD.

Theoretical Framework

This paper will draw upon social learning theory, and more specifically the concept of self-efficacy, or a person's perception of being able to perform or abstain from particular actions (Bandura, 1997). While there is substantial research to support the role of self-efficacy as both a predictor and a mediator of treatment outcomes (e.g., Brown, Carrello, Vik, & Porter, 1998; De Weert-Van Oene, Breteler, Schippers, & Schrijvers, 2000; DiClemente, Fairhurst, & Piotrowski, 1995; Powledge, 1999), this concept has yet to become a significant factor in the development of psychosocial treatments (Kadden & Litt, 2011). Self-efficacy is particularly important to consider when working with adolescents, for it is during the teen years that youth arrive at realistic evaluations of their own abilities and limits (Jacobson, 2001). Such evaluations are shaped by adolescents' relationships, experiences and contexts; when youth view themselves as having low control over their behavior or limited ability to adopt a healthy lifestyle, they may fall into maladaptive behavioral patterns and harmful habits (Schwarzer & Luszczynska, 2005). For instance, research indicates that adolescent substance use may stem from low levels of perceived self-efficacy to refuse substances that are offered by friends (Miller, Alberts, Hecht, Trost, & Krizek, 2000). To increase adolescents' self-efficacy to resist social pressure to use drugs, the following methods could be helpful: modeling, skill training, guided practice with feedback, and reinforcement (Bartholomew, Parcel, Kok, Gottlieb, & Fernandez, 2011).

In a similar vein, adolescents with poor social competence have low levels of social self-efficacy, which means that they consider themselves ill-equipped to perform social behaviors (Connolly, 1989). Accordingly, adolescents who possess both problems (substance use and poor social skills) may suffer from associated deficits in several types of efficacy, leading to low levels of global (overall) self-efficacy. It is important, therefore, to take self-efficacy into account when designing social skill interventions for troubled male youth. Throughout this paper, methods for organizing and administering social skills training will be explored, in part, based on their likelihood of enhancing participants' self-efficacy.

Participant Involvement and Self Efficacy

Participant involvement in negotiating curriculum. Efficacy-based models of therapy gradually increase clients' autonomy and responsibility while reducing their dependence on therapist assistance (Bandura, Adams, Hardy, & Howells, 1980). This is often done progressively, in response to clients' increasing skills and coping abilities, but skills-training programs can also apply this principle at the outset of the training process. Goldstein and McGinnis (1997), for instance, advise counselors to negotiate the training curriculum (the specific skills to be taught) with participants before training sessions begin. This type of involvement is likely to improve self-efficacy in male adolescents because it encourages participants to reflect upon their social functioning and to take part in developing an action plan tailored to their own needs, thus contributing to their personal capacity building. Moreover, these authors suggest that this participative approach is likely to deliver confidence-boosting increases in participants' social skills, because skills training is most effective when it targets behaviors that participants themselves wish to improve.

This approach follows Miller and Rollnick's (2002) Motivational Interviewing (MI) technique, a "directive, patient-centered counseling style that aims to help patients explore and resolve their ambivalence about behavior change" (Treasure, 2004, p. 331). As Treasure points out, central to the approach is the belief that a client's "motivation to change is enhanced if there is a gentle process of negotiation in which the patient, not the practitioner, articulates the benefits and costs involved" (p. 331). In sum, this approach is focused and goal directed and, most important, engages clients in their own learning.

Involvement in instruction. Participant involvement can also be extended to the instruction components of skills-training sessions. Instead of presenting skills in a one-to-many, lecture-style manner, counsellors can take a discussion-based approach by asking interesting questions about trainees' experiences that will enable them to answer easily. Even the modeling of the skill (by the counsellor and his or her assistants, or through a videotape) may be presented in an interactive manner: the counsellor, for instance, may pause the modeling skit at various points and ask participants questions like, "What do you think this character might do next? What consequences might result if the character does that?"

Furthermore, many social skills-training programs "are erroneously based on the assumption that all participants have acquisition deficits" (or either unaware of or cannot perform a behavior) when, in fact, participants may already know about appropriate social behaviors but fail to perform these behaviors due to a lack of motivation or reinforcement (Gresham, Cook, Crews, & Kern, 2004, p. 43). By using participant-instructor interaction to tap into participants' existing knowledge of social skills, programs can strike an appropriate balance between instructional activities like "modeling, coaching, [or] direct instruction" and "remediation strategies for performance deficits (e.g., prompting, shaping, direct reinforcement)" (Gresham et al., 2004, p. 43).

These interactive, participant-involving approaches to skill instruction may help to enhance self-efficacy in two ways. First, a Socratic-style method—one in which the instructor teaches by asking questions and stimulating dialectical discussion—allows participants to reach conclusions about desirable social behaviors on their own, instead of accepting these conclusions from an authority figure. For adolescent males in treatment in particular, for whom authority figures may trigger resistance, a

Socratic-style method may lead to more compliance in training. Second, as noted by adult learning theorist Robert Smith (1982), training is particularly effective when it validates participants' existing knowledge of the topic and acknowledges the past experiences from which they draw this knowledge. This principle can be applied to adolescent skills training through the participatory approaches outlined above: although they are not yet adults, adolescents nevertheless possess a wide range of experiences upon which they can build new skills. By encouraging the sharing of such experiences, programs can contextualize the skill curriculum within participants' lived social realities, making it appear more realistic, more relevant, and potentially more applicable to their daily lives. For example, participants could be asked to brainstorm examples of conflicts they have had with friends, roommates or family members in the recent past. These specific examples, and how they were handled, could be used to illustrate a discussion of conflict resolution processes and strategies.

Participant involvement in skill practice. Just as it is important to give participants a measure of autonomy in determining the content of their training sessions, programs should also provide participants with freedom to choose *how* they learn and practice the skills that they have selected. Despite their stated objectives to improve social self-efficacy, traditional skills-training protocols may inadvertently reduce participants' sense of autonomy and competence by employing rigid or 'one-size-fits-all' training procedures. Rigid training designs are common because many programs are developed specifically for experimental research, and giving participants freedom to deviate from the protocol would make it difficult for researchers to draw causal inferences between training techniques and participant outcomes. Nevertheless, adolescent males might benefit from opportunities to determine other aspects of the training process aside from the skills being taught.

To understand this proposition, we may consider the example of role-playing, a widely used technique for rehearsing social skills that requires participants to perform a short skit before their peers and receive peer and instructor feedback on their performance. A potential problem with role plays, however, lies in the fact that "not all students enjoy learning in public" (Frick-Helms, 2008, p. 177). Some youth may "feel embarrassed or inadequate when asked to role-play" in front of their peers (Frick-Helms, p. 177); forcing them to role-play against their wishes may cause them to feel that they cannot perform social skills in a natural, comfortable manner.

This is particularly problematic because many skills-training programs require participants and instructors to provide feedback based on these role-plays (e.g., Gresham & Nagle, 1980). As Donohue, Van Hasselt, Hersen, and Perrin (1998) point out, while role-plays are among the most commonly used methods to assess social skill development, one of their disadvantages is the difficulty of determining whether observed behaviors are simply the result of being performed under observation in the lab. In other words, these authors question whether participants could or would transfer these behaviors to real life.

Furthermore, such programs treat role-plays as assessments of participants' social skills when, in fact, role-plays may simply demonstrate how well participants can act out a fictional scenario in front of an audience. If a shy or socially anxious participant cannot properly express himself during a role-play and receives negative feedback, he may attribute this feedback to the skill performance rather than to the artificial nature of the role-play, and may lose confidence in his ability to acquire the skill. Such a scenario is especially plausible among adolescent males who require social skill interventions: poor social skills are correlated with shyness and social anxiety in young people (La Greca & Lopez, 1998; Wenzel, Graff-Dolezal, Macho, & Brendle, 2005) and thus these adolescents may be too shy to comfortably perform in front of a group. Role-playing may be particularly unsuitable for teenage boys with a history of SUD, because shyness has been linked to substance use among young males (Page, 1990).

Integrating options and variety. While role-playing is an appropriate approach in certain situations and with certain participants, the above discussion illustrates the danger of uniformly applying any one skills-training method to an entire group of individuals. Instead, programs could offer a variety of activities to reinforce the social skills being taught—activities that correspond with different types of intelligence (Gardner, 2006) to which instruction may be tailored (See Brys, 2013, for an excellent practical resource of experiential therapies designed to address multiple intelligences). Spatial activities, for instance, appeal to those who learn by forming mental images such as drawings and visualizations (Miller & Stoeckel, 2011). In a social-skill training environment, instructors could ask participants to pair up and create comics or collages that illustrate the skill being learned—this approach would simultaneously allow participants to reflect upon the skill and to apply it in a real teamwork situation. Conversely, a bodily-kinesthetic approach, which appeals to those who are adept at expressing emotion, playing games, and inventing (Miller & Stoeckel, 2011), could involve learning social skills through sports, performing arts, construction, or strategy games. As Henley, Schweizer, de Gara, and Vetter (2007) have argued, sport and play provides opportunities for participants "to feel comfortable and in control of their feelings by allowing the expression of emotions in acceptable ways" (para. 4) while at the same time enabling the opportunity to negotiate and resolve conflict (para 4). These authors conclude that sport and play allow young people to "address a myriad of social and psychological challenges simultaneously in gentle and non-intrusive ways through accessing the natural predilection to play" (para 4). For male adolescents, in particular, physical activity may be essential to the ability to focus on learning.

By giving participants the freedom to choose activities that fit their strengths, interests, and learning styles, skills-training programs can help adolescents feel more confident and comfortable during the skill-learning process. Social skill interventions could accommodate this variety in one of two ways: training sessions could cycle between different types of activities over the course of the program (e.g., asking participants to role play one week, to draw the next, to play sports the next, and so on), or programs could offer unstructured practice time during which participants break off into small groups and choose preferred activities while the instructor circles between groups to provide feedback and keep participants on task.

Regardless of the approach, it is important to note that variety does not negate the need for structure in skills-training programs. Psychotherapists often work to develop familiar treatment routines that offer adolescents the opportunity to establish meaningful rituals with adults—something that they may not be able to do at home (Taffel, 2005). Because predictability and routine may make skills-training sessions more comfortable and significant for adolescents, program developers can provide activity options while keeping the overall structure and schedule of training sessions fairly uniform: for instance, instructors can preface unstructured practice times with skill instruction and follow these practice times with periods of sharing or reflection.

Male adolescents in substance abuse treatment may be used to receiving commands or reprimands from authorities (Goldstein & McGinnis, 1997), so the ability to choose some aspects of their own skills-training experience can offer them much-needed encouragement to exercise their autonomy in a prosocial activity. Goldstein and McGinnis advise counsellors to treat their skill lessons not as substitutes for the participants' present behavior, but as repertoires of alternative behaviors from which the adolescents may select. This approach enhances participants' self-efficacy by reminding them that skills training widens, rather than narrows, their range of behaviors, and that they retain the power to choose their own actions. It also teaches adolescents that expectations for social behaviors are rarely black and white; rather, as will be discussed below, some behavioral alternatives are more appropriate in certain contexts than others.

Creative Repetition: An Alternative to Over-Learning

Research on social skill development recommends that participants 'overlearn' social skills through repeated practice and review until the skills are mastered and become nearly automatic (Bellack, Mueser, Gingerich, & Agresta, 2004). This technique, however, appears to be incompatible with the personality characteristics typical of adolescents who have a history of substance abuse, in particular male youths. Lerman, Patterson, and Shields (2003), in their review of genetic factors that contribute to substance use, concluded that substance-using adolescents may have a high need for novelty and sensation that drives them to experiment with alcohol and other drugs. In principle, these adolescents would be unlikely to respond favorably to the lack of stimulation and variety that repetitive lessons provide. Moreover, many substance-abusing teens report feeling a low sense of self-efficacy to refuse substances when they are bored (Fishbein et al., 2002). Repetitive training sessions may produce boredom in participants and evoke accompanying feelings of helplessness and vulnerability to social pressure. These feelings may in turn interfere with the improvements in social self-efficacy that the skills-training sessions attempt to produce.

It may be advisable for counsellors to adopt a more comprehensive, context-based approach to skill instruction. One such method, employed in Feuerstein et al.'s (1985) groundbreaking Instrumental Enrichment program (IE), involves learning through progressive, "creative repetition" (p. 54) whereby students experience the same cognitive processes but in different learning contexts. Although IE mainly targets childhood cognitive skills, its principles can also be applied to adolescent social skills training. For instance, instead of requiring static, repetitive instruction and practice, programs can encourage participants to "rediscover [. . .] rules that are embedded in new content or couched in a new modality, so that the boredom and rigidity associated with overlearning and redundancy are avoided" (Feuerstein et al., 1985, p. 54). In other words, counsellors can reiterate concepts by extending rather than repeating them—already-learned skills may be applied to new situations, taught using new methods, or re-interpreted with the help of "questioning and interpretive feedback" from the counsellor (p. 54).

Social competence is "context-dependent," and thus "behaviors which are effective in one context may not have similar success in another" (Rose-Krasnor, 1997, p. 120). Creative repetition therefore encourages participants to consider how social behavior ideals may differ depending on where they are carried out and with whom. Instructors' questioning and feedback can further enhance this skill generalization, providing participants with the insight they need to generalize their social skill learning to the unique, complex contexts that they encounter outside of training sessions (Feuerstein et al., 1985). In addition to adequately preparing participants for a range of real-world situations, creative repetition acknowledges participants' objectives by teaching them that the success of "social competence is relative to specific goals" (Rose-Krasnor, 1997, p. 120) such as getting along with a teacher or helping a friend. By validating the goals that drive male adolescents' social interactions, this approach raises self-efficacy: it treats participants as autonomous individuals with complex personal motivations, rather than as passive performers expected to adhere to certain social scripts.

Reinforcing Desirable Behavior

Operant conditioning. Much classroom education has been founded on the idea of reinforcing learning through operant conditioning, or systematic rewarding and punishing of skill performances in order to maintain appropriate or desirable behaviors (Zirpoli & Melloy, 1993).

Reinforcement can take the form of positive feedback and direct rewards or it may be administered through a token economy—an arrangement in which participants are rewarded with tokens that can be exchanged for prizes or privileges (e.g., Kazdin, Bass, Siegel, & Thomas, 1989). Rewards can also take the form of negative reinforcement, or the performance of a desired behavior to avoid a negative stimulus (e.g., putting on sunscreen to avoid a sunburn). Punishment can involve withdrawing these rewards (e.g., Forman, 1980) or issuing aversive consequences like chores.

At first glance, given the emphasis on participant autonomy in this paper, one might assume that operant conditioning reduces participants' self-efficacy by making their behavior contingent on outside rewards and punishments. It is true that operant conditioning modifies behavior based on an external locus of control, or on sources outside of the individual. In principle, then, an over-reliance on operant conditioning may undermine a person's ability to choose a course of action and take responsibility for its consequences. However, one cannot overlook the vital role that rewards and punishment play for substance-using male youth. Adolescents use alcohol and other drugs in part because these substances stimulate pleasurable neurochemical responses, offer external (e.g., social) rewards, and reduce negative experiences like stress or substance 'crash' and withdrawal symptoms (Durand & Barlow, 2010).

Reinforcement may also encourage undesirable behaviors: youth might behave antagonistically because "aggression is an effective, albeit unpleasant, means of achieving a goal" (Davison, Blankstein, Flett, & Neale, 2010, p. 522). It is important, therefore, for training programs to counteract these easily accessible, maladaptive sources of reinforcement by providing rewards for positive behaviors—rewards that may not be readily available within substance-using adolescents' usual environments. Examples of these kinds of rewards might be gift cards for coffee or burgers, toiletries, privileges (e.g., watching a movie), or healthy but appealing snacks (e.g., granola bars). Rewards for desirable behavior need to occur immediately and consistently (i.e., by both the counsellor and other important figures in participants' lives), and should be neither too large (as this may reduce further reward-seeking) nor too small (as this may make desirable behavior not worth the effort).

Despite its potential links to external control and personal irresponsibility, reinforcement does not necessarily reduce self-efficacy. In fact, as Bandura (1997) points out, self-efficacy rises when one completes a task successfully because this success constitutes a desirable outcome, and it falls when one is unsuccessful because this denotes an undesirable outcome. In other words, reinforcement processes—the desirable and undesirable outcomes inherent in completing tasks successfully or unsuccessfully—are precisely what determine self-efficacy: people feel more confident about attempting tasks which they have previously found to be rewarding. Moreover, according to Schwarzer and Warner (2013), even in the case of failure, one's attributions (cognitive explanations) mediate the influence of that failure on self-efficacy. If, for instance, failure is attributed to low personal effort, self-efficacy remains undamaged; it is only when people believe that they are entirely unable to succeed—regardless of how much effort they apply—that self-efficacy may suffer. Skills-training programs, therefore, can use operant conditioning in conjunction with cognitive restructuring techniques to help participants alter the maladaptive, defeatist attributions that might arise upon failure and punishment (for an explanation of cognitive restructuring, see Davison et al., 2010, p. 53; for an example of its application in skills-training, see Forman, 1980).

It appears, therefore, that there is little harm in employing operant conditioning techniques to reinforce male adolescents' structured (assignment-based, role-played) and unstructured (spontaneous, participant-instructor or between-participant) interactions within skills-training sessions. Environments that are low in predictable and preferred contingencies have been found to lead to decreased self-efficacy and maladjustment (Benjamin et al., 2011) so it makes sense to reward appropriate behaviors in a consistent, predictable, and satisfying manner in order to improve young peoples' self-efficacy. Counsellors can enhance this predictability by asking participants to sign a contract that clearly outlines the consequences associated with desirable and undesirable behaviors.

Many existing social skill programs use positive reinforcement or response cost (the removal of reinforcers) (Goldstein & McGinnis, 1997), but most appear to stop short of using positive punishment (the presentation of aversive stimuli such as being required to run laps, complete difficult math problems, or perform chores, for example). These authors suggest that positive punishment be limited only to verbal reprimands and used sparingly, as it does not teach new behaviors and may lead to undesirable side-effects like aggressive responses, labeling, and good behavior that is contingent on surveillance. If punishment is absolutely necessary, Goldstein and McGinnis advise counsellors to combine the technique with another means of teaching desirable behavior. For instance, counsellors may pair it with overcorrection, requiring disruptive participants to apologize for and repair the damage that their behavior has produced; this can raise participants' self-efficacy by treating them as active agents of positive change rather than passive recipients of discipline. Counsellors are also advised to hypothesize about the causes of participant misbehavior. If participants are included in this problem-diagnosis process (i.e., if counsellors take noncompliant participants aside and try to collaboratively diagnose the root cause of their actions), this may prevent participants from feeling helpless and attributing their failures to some global, stable, internal impairment (for an explanation of attribution theory, see Davison et al., 2010, p. 254).

From extrinsic to intrinsic rewards. Over time, counsellors can gradually replace participants' reliance on external or tangible rewards with more realistic sources of reinforcement. At first, counsellors may pair material prizes with verbal praise, so that the praise becomes associated with reward. With time, verbal praise takes on reinforcing power, and counsellors can begin to use it in lieu of direct rewards. The reinforcement system thus comes to approximate more closely the types of rewards that adolescents are likely to encounter in their real lives, and may enhance the generalization of learned skills to real-world contexts.

However, skills-training programs should also encourage participants to develop intrinsic sources of reward to motivate prosocial behaviors. Because intrinsic motivation is correlated with self-efficacy (Niehaus, Rudasill, & Adelson, 2012) efforts to foster intrinsic rewards may help to enhance self-efficacy. One way to increase intrinsic motivation involves integrating motivational training directly into skills-training sessions. As mentioned in the previous section, programs can use cognitive restructuring techniques to teach participants to identify and modify negative, pessimistic cognitions. Reshaping attitudes regarding personal responsibility and control can go a long way towards enhancing learning: according to McCombs (1984), research has shown that instructors can promote learning by teaching students "that they cause their behavior and can influence future behaviors" (p. 210). Another approach for improving intrinsic motivation may involve assigning meaningful, action-based homework that introduces participants to the natural rewards stemming from appropriate interpersonal behavior. As participants apply learned skills to their own lives, they may recognize the rewards inherent in prosocial behavior, such as "positive interpersonal outcomes [. . .] in interactions with family, peers, or significant others," and feel motivated to continue acting in this way (Goldstein & McGinnis, 1997, p. 130).

Conclusion

The goal of this paper was to identify training approaches and techniques to be used by counsellors to help build the social competence of male adolescents in treatment for substance use disorder. Future research could evaluate the effectiveness of the approaches that have been proposed here and compare different instructional methods. While it was not the goal of this paper to suggest content for social skills training programs, further research could also be conducted to explore the curriculum of social skills training programs for adolescent males in treatment for SUD.

To summarize the findings of this paper, it appears that three main conclusions can be drawn. First, it is clear that involving participants in their learning is essential to building self-efficacy and thus social competence. As was seen, encouraging participants to negotiate the training curriculum (the specific skills to be taught) and providing training through a discussion and activity based approach (rather than a lecture format which implies a one-way transfer of information) serve to maintain interest, engage learners and demonstrate respect for the knowledge, skills and experiences that they already possess. These interactive approaches may help to enhance self-efficacy in two ways: by encouraging participants to reflect on problems and come to conclusions themselves (rather than being told the correct answers), and by validating existing knowledge and past experiences as important.

Second, it was seen that offering flexible or customized approaches depending on the learning styles and interests of participants could engage learners and build self-efficacy and social competence. This approach may conflict with the protocols of packaged training programs that, often for program evaluation purposes, are meant to be offered in the same way to every participant. However, by giving participants the freedom to choose activities that fit their strengths, interests, and learning styles, skills-training programs can help participants feel more confident and comfortable during the skill-learning process. It is important to note that flexibility in program offering is not the same as a lack of routine and predictability, since these are necessary for a comfortable and safe learning environment.

Third, we discussed the importance of reinforcing desirable behaviors, whether with positive feedback or rewards (such as points or tokens) or with negative reinforcement (the performance of a desired behavior to avoid a negative stimulus). As was seen, it may seem counterintuitive to suggest offering rewards while also attempting to build self-efficacy. However, as noted, self-efficacy increases when we enjoy a positive result from our behaviors, and it falls when we are unsuccessful because of the negative experience of failure. Thus, being rewarded for desirable behaviors can serve to increase confidence (and motivation) to attempt activities that have proven positive in the past. As discussed, it is desirable to eventually replace extrinsic rewards with intrinsic reinforcement and this can be done through the design of training—such that it helps participants to explore and reshape their own attitudes regarding personal responsibility and control—and through having participants engage in meaningful, concrete and action-based activities and homework which reflect the reality of their lives and relationships.

This paper has shown that social skills training programs may be beneficial for male adolescents with deficiencies in social competence who struggle with substance abuse, but many procedural factors moderate the potential effectiveness of such interventions. This paper has identified training approaches that may engage adolescent participants and can provide male youth with a sense of responsibility and confidence. In general, this paper has promoted a customized, contextualized, personalized, and integrated approach to program design. The recommendations advanced herein hold promise for breaking the cycle of poor social relationships, substance use, and low self-efficacy that keeps many male youth from engaging more deeply with society and reaching their full personal potential.

References

American Academy of Child & Adolescent Psychiatry. (2011). Normal Adolescent Development Part I. *Facts for Families, 57.* Retrieved from http://www.aacap.org/AACAP/ Families_and_Youth/Facts_for_Families/FFF-Guide/Normal-Adolescent-Development-Part-I-057.aspx

Ang, R. P., & Hughes, J. N. (2001). Differential benefits of skills training with antisocial youth based on group composition: A meta-analytic investigation. *Social Psychology Review, 31*(2), 164-185.

Bandura, A. (1997). *Self-efficacy: The exercise of control.* New York: W. H. Freeman.

Bandura, A., Adams, N. E., Hardy, A. B., & Howells, G. N. (1980). Tests of the generality of self-efficacy theory. *Cognitive Therapy and Research, 4*(1), 39-66. doi:0147-5916/80/0300-0039503.00/0

Bartholomew, L. K., Parcel, G. S., Kok, G., Gottlieb, N. H., & Fernandez, M. E. (2011). *Planning health promotion programs: An intervention mapping approach* (3rd ed.). San Francisco, CA: Wiley.

Bellack, A. S., Mueser, K., Gingerich, S., & Agresta, J. (2004). *Social skills training for schizophrenia: A step by step guide* (2nd ed.). New York, NY: Guilford Press.

Benjamin, C. L., Puleo, C. M., Settipani, C. A., Brodman, D. M., Edmunds, J. M., Cummings, C. M., & Kendall, P. C. (2011). History of cognitive-behavioural therapy (CBT) in youth. *Child and Adolescent Psychiatric Clinics of North America 20*(2), 179-189. doi:10.1016/j.chc.2011.01.011

Botvin, G. J. (1983). Prevention of adolescent substance abuse through the development of personal and social competence. In T. J. Glynn, C. G. Leukefeld & J. P. Ludford (Eds.), *Preventing adolescent drug abuse: Intervention strategies.* Rockville, MD: National Institute on Drug Abuse.

Brown, S. A., Carrello, P. D., Vik, P. W., & Porter, R. J. (1998). Change in alcohol effect and self-efficacy expectancies during addiction treatment. *Substance Abuse, 19,* 155–167. doi:10.1080/08897079809511384

Brys, S. (2013). Dropping defenses through experiential therapy. *Addiction Professional.* Retrieved from http://www.addictionpro.com/article/dropping-defenses-through-experiential-therapy

Bukstein, O. G., Bernet, W., Arnold, V., Beitchman, J., Shaw, J., & Benson, R. S. (2005). Practice parameter for the assessment and treatment of children and adolescents with substance use disorders. *Journal of the American Academy of Child and Adolescent Psychiatry, 44,* 609-621. doi:10.1097/01.chi.0000159135.33706.37

Canadian Centre on Substance Abuse. (2007). *Substance abuse in Canada: Youth in focus.* Ottawa, ON: Canadian Centre on Substance Abuse.

Center for Substance Abuse Treatment. (2009). *Substance Abuse Treatment: Addressing the Specific Needs of Women.* (Treatment Improvement Protocol (TIP) Series, No. 51.) Chapter 6: Substance Abuse Among Specific Population Groups and Settings. Rockville (MD): Substance Abuse and Mental Health Services Administration (US). Retrieved from: http://www.ncbi.nlm.nih.gov/books/NBK83240

Connolly, J. (1989). Social self-efficacy in adolescence: Relations with self-concept, social adjustment, and mental health. *Canadian Journal of Behavioural Science, 21*(3), 258-269. doi:10.1037/h0079809

Cotto, J. H., Davis, E., Dowling, G. J., Elcano, J. C., Stanton, A. B., & Weiss, S. R. B. (2010). Gender effects on drug use, abuse, and dependence: A special analysis of results from the National Survey on Drug Use and Health. *Gender Medicine, 7*(5), 402-413. doi:10.1016/j.genm.2010.09.004

Covington, S. (2007). The relational theory of women's psychological development: Implications for the criminal justice system. In R. Zaplin (Ed.) *Female offenders: critical perspectives and effective interventions* (2nd ed.). (pp. 135-164). Sudbury, MA: Jones & Bartlett Publishers.

Crombie, G. (1988) Gender differences: Implications for social skills assessment and training, *Journal of Clinical Child Psychology, 17,* 116-120. doi:10.1207/s15374424jccp1702_2

Davison, G. C., Blankstein, K. R., Flett, G. L., & Neale, J. M. (2010). *Abnormal psychology* (4th ed.). Mississauga, ON: Wiley Publishers.

De Weert-Van Oene, G., Breteler, M. Schippers, G., & Schrijvers, A. (2000). The validity of the self-efficacy list for drug users. *Addictive Behaviors, 25*(4), 599-605. doi:10.1016/S0306-4603(99)00028-3

DiClemente, C., Fairhurst, S., & Piotrowski, N. (1995). Self-efficacy and addictive behaviors. In J. Maddux (Ed.), *Self-efficacy, adaptation, and adjustment: Theory, research, and application* (pp. 109-141). New York: Plenum Press.

Donohue, B., Van Hasselt, V. B., Hersen, M., & Perrin, S. (1998). Role-play assessment of social skills in conduct disordered and substance abusing adolescents: An empirical review. *Journal of Child and Adolescent Substance Abuse, 8*(2), 1-28. doi:10.1300/J029v08n02_01

Durand, V. M., & Barlow, D. H. (2010). *Essentials of abnormal psychology* (5th ed.). Belmont, CA: Wadsworth.

Feuerstein, R., Hoffman, M. B., Rand, Y., Jensen, M. R., Tzuriel, D., & Hoffman, D. B. (1985). Learning to learn: Mediated learning experiences and instrumental enrichment. *Special Services in the Schools, 3*(1-2), 49-82. doi:10.1300/J008v03n01_05

Fishbein, M., Cappella, J., Hornik, R., Sayeed, S., Yzer, M., & Ahern, R. K. (2002). The role of theory in developing effective anti-drug public service announcements. In W. D. Crano & M. Burgoon (Eds.), *Mass media and drug prevention: Classic and contemporary theories and research* (pp. 89-118). Mahwah, NJ: Lawrence Erlbaum & Associates.

Forman, S. G. (1980). A comparison of cognitive training and response cost procedures in modifying aggressive behavior of elementary school children. *Behavior Therapy, 11*(4), 594-600. doi:0005-7894/80/0594--060051

Frick-Helms, S. (2008). Enhancing role play activities in play therapy supervision groups. In A. A. Drewes & J. M. Mullen (Eds.), *Supervision can be playful: Techniques for child and play therapist supervisors* (pp. 173-190). Lanham, MD: Rowman & Littlefield Publishers.

Gaffney, L. R., Thorpe, K., Young, R., Collett, R., & Occhipinti, S. (1998). Social skills, expectancies, and drinking in adolescents. *Addictive Behaviors, 23*(5), 587-599. doi:10.1016/S0306-4603(98)00025-2

Gardner, H. (2006). *Multiple intelligences: New horizons.* New York, NY: Basic Books.

Goldstein, A. P., & McGinnis, E. (1997). *Skillstreaming the adolescent: New strategies and perspectives for teaching prosocial skills* (2nd ed., Vol. 1). Champaign, IL: Research Press.

Greenfield, S. F., Back, S. E., Lawson, K., & Brady, K. T. (2010). Substance abuse in women. *Psychiatric Clinics of North America, 33*(2), 339-355. doi:10.1016/j.psc.2010.01.004

Gresham, F. M., Cook, C. R., Crews, S. D., & Kern, L. (2004). Social skills training for children and youth with emotional and behavioral disorders: Validity considerations and future directions. *Behavioural Disorders, 30*(1), 32-46.

Gresham, F. M., & Nagle, R. J. (1980). Social skills training with children: Responsiveness to modeling and coaching as a function of peer orientation. *Journal of Consulting and Clinical Psychology, 48*(6), 718-729. 729. doi:10.1037/0022-006X.48.6.718

Griffin, K. W., Epstein, J. A., Botvin, G. J., & Spoth, R. L. (2001). Social competence and substance use among rural youth: Mediating role of social benefit expectancies of use. *Journal of Youth and Adolescence, 30*(4), 485-498. doi:10.1023/A:1010449300990

Gundersen, K. K. (2010). Reducing behaviour problems in young people through social competence programmes. *International Journal of Emotional Education, 2*(2), 48-62. Retrieved from https://brage.bibsys.no/xmlui//bitstream/handle/11250/98887/ENSECV2I2P4.pdf?sequence=1

Henley, R., Schweizer, I., de Gara, F., & Vetter, S. (2007). How psychosocial sport and play programs help youth manage adversity: A review of what we know and what we should research. *International Journal of Psychosocial Rehabilitation. 12*(1), 51-58. Retrieved from http://www.psychosocial.com/IJPR_12/Psychological_Sport_and_Play_Henley.html

Hover, S., & Gaffney, L. R. (1991). The relationship between social skills and adolescent drinking. *Alcohol and Alcoholism, 26*, 207-214.

Jackson, C., Henriksen, L., Dickinson, D., & Levine, D. W. (1997). The early use of alcohol and tobacco: Its relation to children's competence and parents' behavior. *American Journal of Public Health, 87*(3), 359-364.

Jacobson, L. P. (2001). Sports and adolescents. In J. V. Lerner & R. Lerner (Eds.), *Adolescence in America: An encyclopedia, volume 2* (pp. 700-711). Santa Barbra, CA: ABC-CLIO.

Kadden, R. M., & Litt, M.D . (2011). The role of self-efficacy in the treatment of substance use disorders. *Addictive Behaviors, 36*(12), 1120-6. doi:10.1016/j.addbeh.2011.07.032

Kazdin, A. E. (1997), Practitioner review: Psychosocial treatments for conduct disorder in children. *Journal of Child Psychology and Psychiatry, 38*, 161–178. doi:10.1111/j.1469-7610.1997.tb01851.x

Kazdin, A. E., Bass, D., Siegel, T., & Thomas, C. (1989). Cognitive-behavioural therapy and relationship therapy in the treatment of children referred for antisocial behavior. *Journal of Consulting and Clinical Psychology, 57*(4), 522-535. doi:10.1037/0022-006X.57.4.522

Kloos, A., Weller, R. A., Chan, R., & Weller, E. B. (2009). Gender differences in adolescent substance abuse. *Current Psychiatry Reports, 11*, 120–126. doi:10.1007/s11920-009-0019-8

Kuhn, C. (2015). Emergence of sex differences in the development of substance use and abuse during adolescence, *Pharmacology and Therapeutics, 153*, 55-78. doi:10.1016/j.pharmthera.2015.06.003

La Greca, A. M., & Lopez, N. (1998). Social anxiety among adolescents: Linkages with peer relations and friendships. *Journal of Abnormal Child Psychology, 26*(2), 83-94. doi:0091-0627/98/0400-0083$15.00/0

Leatherdale, S. T., & Burkhalter, R. (2012). The substance use profile of Canadian youth: Exploring the prevalence of alcohol, drug and tobacco use by gender and grade. *Addictive Behaviors, 37*(3), 318-322. doi:10.1016/j.addbeh.2011.10.007

Lerman, C., Patterson, F., & Shields, A. (2003). Genetic basis of substance use and dependence: Implications for prevention in high-risk youth. In D. Romer (Ed.), *Reducing adolescent risk: Toward an integrated approach* (pp. 149-164). Thousand Oaks, CA: Sage Publications, Inc.

Leyton, M., & Stewart, S. (Eds.). (2014). *Substance abuse in Canada: Childhood and adolescent pathways to substance use disorders.* Ottawa, ON: Canadian Centre on Substance Abuse.

McCombs, B. L. (1984). Processes and skills underlying continuing intrinsic motivation to learn: Toward a definition of motivational skills training interventions. *Educational Psychologist, 19*(4), 199-218. doi:10.1080/00461528409529297

Merrell, K. W. (2008). *Behavioral, social, and emotional assessment of children and adolescents.* Mahwah, NJ: Lawrence Erlbaum Associates.

Merrell, K. W., & Calderella, P. (2008). *HCSBS Home and Community Social Behavior Scales users guide.* Baltimore, MD: Paul H. Brookes Publishing Co.

Miller, J. B. (1976). *Toward a new psychology of women.* Boston, MA: Beacon Press.

Miller, M., Alberts, J. K., Hecht, M. L., Trost, M. R., & Krizek, R. L. (2000). *Adolescent relationships and drug use.* Mahwah, NJ: Lawrence Erlbaum Associates Publishing

Miller, M. A., & Stoeckel, P. R. (2011). *Client education: Theory and practice.* Sudbury, MA: Jones and Bartlett Publishers.

Miller, W. R., & Rollnick, S. (2002). *Motivational interviewing: Preparing people for change* (2nd ed.). New York, NY: Guilford Press.

Moos, R. H., Moos, B. S., & Andrassy, J. M. (1999). Outcomes of four treatment approaches in community residential programs for patients with substance use disorders. *Psychiatric Services, 50*(12), 1577-1583. doi:10.1176/ps.50.12.1577

National Institute on Drug Abuse (2014). *Principles of adolescent substance use disorder treatment: A research-based guide.* Retrieved from https://www.drugabuse.gov/publications/principles-adolescent-substance-use-disorder-treatment-research-based-guide/

Niehaus, K., Rudasill, K. M., & Adelson, J. L. (2012). Self-efficacy, intrinsic motivation, and academic outcomes among Latino middle school students participating in an after-school program. *Educational Psychology Papers and Publications.* Paper 156. Retrieved from http://digitalcommons.unl.edu/edpsychpapers/156

Office of Applied Studies (2002). *National and state estimates of the drug abuse treatment gap: 2000 national household survey on drug abuse.* Rockville, MD: Substance Abuse and Mental Health Services Administration.

Page, R. M. (1990). Shyness and sociability: A dangerous combination for illicit substance use in adolescent males? *Adolescence, 25*(100), 803-806.

Paglia-Boak, A., Adlaf, E. M., & Mann, R. E. (2011). *Drug use among Ontario students, 1977-2011: Detailed OSDUHS findings (CAMH Research Document Series No. 32).* Toronto, ON: Centre for Addiction and Mental Health.

Pentz, M. A. (1983). Prevention of adolescent substance abuse through social skill development. In T. J. Glynn, C. G. Leukefeld, & J. P. Ludford (Eds.), *Preventing adolescent drug abuse: Intervention strategies* (pp. 195-232). Rockville, MD: National Institute on Drug Abuse.

Powledge, T. (1999). Addiction and the brain. *BioScience, 49*, 513-519.

Ritter, A., Bowden, S., Murray, T., Ross, P., Greeley, J., & Pead, J. (2002), The influence of the therapeutic relationship in treatment for alcohol dependency. *Drug and Alcohol Review, 21*, 261–268. doi:10.1080/0959523021000002723

Rose-Krasnor, L. (1997). The nature of social competence: A theoretical review. *Social Development, 6*(1), 111-135. doi:10.1111/j.1467-9507.1997.tb00097.x

Schwarzer, R., & Luszczynska, A. (2005). Self-efficacy, adolescents' risk-taking behaviors, and health. In F. Pajares, & T. C. Urdan (Eds.), *Self-efficacy beliefs of adolescents* (pp. 139-159). Greenwich, CT: Information Age Publishing.

Schwarzer, R., & Warner, L. M. (2013). Perceived self-efficacy and its relationship to resilience. In S. Prince-Embury & D. H. Saklofske (Eds.), *Resilience in children, adolescents, and adults* (pp. 139-150). New York, NY: Springer.

Segrin, C. (2000). Social skills deficits associated with depression. *Clinical Psychology Review, 20*(3), 379-403. doi:10.1016/S0272-7358(98)00104-4

Substance Abuse and Mental Health Services Administration, Center for Behavioral Health Statistics and Quality. (2012). *Results from the 2011 National Survey on Drug Use and Health: Summary of national findings* (HHS Publication No. SMA 12-4713, NSDUH Series H-44). Rockville, MD: Substance Abuse and Mental Health Services Administration. Retrieved from http://www.samhsa.gov/data/sites/default/files/Revised2k11NSDUHSummNatFindings/Revised2k11NSDUHSummNatFindings/NSDUHresults2011.htm

Substance Abuse and Mental Health Services Administration, Center for Behavioral Health Statistics and Quality. (2013). *Treatment Episode Data Set (TEDS): 2001-2011*. National admissions to substance abuse treatment services (HHS Publication No. SMA 13-4772, DASIS Series S-65). Rockville, MD: Substance Abuse and Mental Health Services Administration. Retrieved from http://www.samhsa.gov/data/sites/default/files/TEDS2011St_Web/TEDS2011St_Web/TEDS2011St_Web.pdf

Substance Abuse and Mental Health Services Administration. (2014a). *Improving Cultural Competence*. Treatment Improvement Protocol (TIP) Series No. 59. HHS Publication No. (SMA) 14-4849. Rockville, MD: Substance Abuse and Mental Health Services Administration. Retrieved from http://store.samhsa.gov/shin/content/SMA14-4849/SMA14-4849.pdf

Substance Abuse and Mental Health Services Administration, Center for Behavioral Health Statistics and Quality. (2014b). *The TEDS Report: Gender differences in primary substance of abuse across age groups*. Rockville, MD. Retrieved from http://archive.samhsa.gov/data/2k14/TEDS077/sr077-gender-differences-2014.htm

Smith, R. (1982). *Learning how to learn: Applied theory for adults*. Chicago, IL: Follett Publishing Company.

Taffel, R. (2005). *Breaking through to teens: Psychotherapy for the new adolescence*. New York, NY: The Guilford Press.

Terrion, J. L. (2015). A communication model of relational pathways into and out of adolescent substance use disorder. *Journal of Child & Adolescent Substance Abuse, 24*(1), pp. 54-65. doi:10.1080/1067828X.2012.761168

Terrion, J., O'Rielly, S., & Rocchi, M. (2016). Social competence of adolescents in residential substance abuse treatment. *Journal of Child and Adolescent Substance Abuse, 25*(4), 280-191. doi:10.1080/1067828X.2015.1037515

Treasure, J. (2004). Motivational interviewing. *Advances in Psychiatric Treatment, 10*, 331-337. doi:10.1192/apt.10.5.331

von Braun, T. (2013). Chapter 12. Therapists' narratives of therapeutic relationships in the treatment of drug-dependent patients. *Substance Use & Misuse, 48*(13), 1416-1433, doi:10.3109/10826084.2013.815017

Vorobjov, S., Saat, H., & Kull, M. (2014). Social skills and their relationship to drug use among 15-16-year-old students in Estonia: An analysis based on the ESPAD data. *Nordic Studies on Alcohol and Drugs, 31*(4), 401-412. doi:10.2478/nsad-2014-0031

Webb, J. A., & Baer, P. E. (1995). Influence of family disharmony and parental alcohol use on adolescent social skills, self-efficacy, and alcohol use. *Addictive Behaviors, 20*(1), 127-135. doi:10.1016/0306-4603(94)00054-3

Wekerle, C., Leung, E., Goldstein, A., Thornton, T., & Tonmyr, L. (2009). *Substance use among adolescents in child welfare versus adolescents in the general population: A comparison of the Maltreatment and Adolescent Pathways (MAP) longitudinal study and the Ontario Student Drug Use Survey (OSDUS) datasets.* London, ON: University of Western Ontario. Retrieved from http://cwrp.ca/sites/default/files/publications/en/Report-MAP_2010EN.pdf

Wenzel, A., Graff-Dolezal, J., Macho, M., & Brendle, J. R. (2005). Communication and social skills in socially anxious and nonanxious individuals in the context of romantic relationships. *Behaviour Research and Therapy, 43*(4), 505–519. doi:10.1016/j.brat.2004.03.010

Zirpoli, T. J., & Melloy K. J. (1993). *Behavior management: Applications for teachers and parents.* New York, NY: MacMillan Publishing Company.

5

Promoting Resilience in Children of Alcoholics
A Family Perspective

Shaywanna Harris and S. Kent Butler[1]

According to the National Council on Alcohol and Drug Dependence (2012), approximately 1 in 10 children in the United States live with an alcoholic parent. These statistics are startling considering the research on negative effects of parental alcoholism. For example, according to Bijttebier and Goethals (2006), children of alcoholic parents (COAs) are more likely to possess lower self-worth. Park and Schepp (2014) found aggressive behavior, low academic and cognitive performance, high suicide risk, mental disorders—such as Attention Deficit Hyperactivity Disorder (ADHD), anxiety, and eating disorders—to be among the myriad of negative effects COAs face. Researchers have also found correlations between COAs and difficulties in social functioning, physical distress (e.g., back pain), and behavior control (Jacob, Windle, Seilhamer, & Bost, 1999; Jacob & Windle 2000; Pecukonis, 2004).

---

1. Shaywanna Harris and Kent Butler, College of Education and Human Performance, Department of Child, Family, and Community Sciences, University of Central Florida. Correspondence regarding this article should be sent to: Shaywanna Harris, College of Education and Human Performance, Department of Child, Family, and Community Sciences, University of Central Florida, Orlando, Florida, 32816-1250. Email: s.harris@knights.ucf.edu

Although previous researchers have focused on pathology among COAs, there has been a recent shift to resilience-based conceptualizations and treatments for this population. Resilience is understood as the ability to become strong, healthy, or successful again after adverse life experiences (Merriam-Webster, 2014). In similar terms, Masten, Best, and Garmezy (1990) defined resilience in children as a "dynamic process encompassing positive adaptation within the context of significant adversity" (p. 425). The interest in resilience among authors has changed the focus from identifying vulnerabilities among COAs to fostering strengths and preventing negative outcomes. For instance, Carle and Chassin (2004) proffered that COAs who are highly competent socially and resilient have increased positive affect and lower internalization. Likewise, Park and Schepp (2014) indicated that resilient COAs are older, have high self-esteem, self-regulation, academic and cognitive ability, flexibility, and possess an optimistic temperament.

In addition to this attention to individual-level variables among COAs, authors have begun exploring systemic variables that promote resilience. This point of focus is particularly important, given that childhood resilience is theorized to develop through familial and social supports, as children are dependent on parental and sibling relationships for moral, social, and emotional development (Coyle, 2009; McCubbin & McCubbin, 1988). McCubbin and McCubbin (1988), for example, explored the concept of resilience from a systemic perspective. They conceptualized resilience as a multidimensional concept within the family that is influenced by three major factors, including the length of time the family faces adversity, the life cycle stage at which the family encounters the adverse situation, and the sources of support the family uses during the situation. Moreover, Walsh (2002) addressed resilience within the family context and designed models to identify resilient characteristics and promote flexibility and adjustment. Walsh also identified adversity as a potential opportunity for personal and relational growth within the family, allowing individuals to build upon each other's strengths and emerge from a difficult situation stronger and more resourceful.

Specific to COAs, Ulrich, Stopsack, and Barnow (2010) reported that resilient COAs are exposed to a higher level of warm parenting styles. Indeed, family coping skills have been shown to increase communication skills leading to effective parenting and improved self-worth of COAs (Bjittebier & Goethals, 2006; Coyle, 2009). Similarly, Park and Schepp

(2014) suggested that secure attachment, positive parent-child relationships, consistent and positive parenting, high family cohesion and adaptability, and low violence and conflicts are major protective factors in COAs.

Despite this growing understanding of resilience among COAs, more exploration is needed of family systems treatment models that leverage the systemic aspect of resilience. Interventions in the past targeted individual-level resilience in COAs, especially within school settings (Lambie & Sias, 2005; Roosa, Gensheimer, Short, Ayers, & Shell, 1989; Emshoff & Valentine, 2006; Dies & Burghardt, 1991), with little research focused on the family system as an intervention for promoting resilience. While family systems may have been identified as contributing to resilience in COAs (Coyle, 2009; O'Farrell, 2012; Park & Schepp, 2014), the family is seldom identified as a point of intervention. The purpose of this book chapter is to present a guiding framework of systemic variables that promote resilience in COAs. The framework utilized here is the Family Resilience Framework by Walsh (1998, 2003). Secondly, we intend to identify systemic interventions that exemplify attention to each aspect of the framework.

Family Resilience Framework

The family resilience framework (Walsh, 1996, 2003) contributed to extant family resilience literature that individuals are best understood and nurtured within the context of the family and social world to which they belong. This premise differs from other structures in its focus on the family's influence on individual resilience. That is, the family resilience framework focuses on viewing the family system as an impactful tool in influencing individuals. Walsh added that all families have the potential for resilience and it may be fostered by identifying strengths within the family and building upon them. Walsh categorized family strengths into three realms: belief systems, organization, and communication processes. Furthermore, Walsh expressed that resilience within the family may be fostered within the context of beliefs—how the family views and approaches a crisis (i.e., a family's beliefs about their ability to face an adverse experience), organization—how a family connects and is flexible (i.e., a family's structure, level of connection, and adaptability to an adverse experience), and communication processes—how a family fosters trust and mutual respect (i.e., a family's communication patterns surrounding an adverse experience). A resilient family is able to make meaning of adversity, has a positive outlook, is flexible and open to change, communicates clearly, and collaborates on problem solving (Walsh, 2003).

The family resilience framework as used in practice shifts focus from problems to strengths and functioning. The emphasis is not placed on how problems originated, rather, on how a family uses inherent strengths to ensure they are solved. This framework promotes resilience by addressing meaning making; how a family views adversity and the meaning they assign to adverse situations. Families may approach difficult situations believing that they cannot handle the problem with the resources already possessed. The family resilience framework focuses on the system's strength to promote positivity and collaborative problem solving amongst members (Walsh, 2013). Other tenets of this framework include spirituality, positivity, connectedness, and flexibility; all of these factors are vital to the promotion of resilience within the family (Walsh, 2003). In the following sections, we introduce treatment models that exemplify Walsh's emphases on family beliefs, organization, and communication.

Treatment Model for Family Beliefs: Resilience Focused Brief Family Therapy

According to the family resilience framework, as described above, family beliefs about adversity are a potential point of intervention for fostering family resilience. It would behoove counselors to consider therapeutic models and interventions specific to assessing and building on family beliefs. One such therapeutic model is Resilience-Focused Brief Family Therapy (RFBFT); this model is beneficial in fostering resilience in families by identifying a family's beliefs and building on the strengths inherent in the family. What follows is an overview of the model and how it specifically relates to and addresses family beliefs.

Based on resilience research, positive psychology, and family development, counselors utilize RFBFT to promote resilience systemically to decrease symptomatic behaviors amongst members (Nicoll, 2011). Among other objectives, RFBFT targets a family's belief systems to promote resilience within the family. This emphasis arises, in particular, during the later stages of the seven stages of RFBFT (Nicoll, 2011). The first stage includes the counselor educating the client on the counseling process. The counselor works as a guide and helps the family to clarify what they would like to work on in therapy. The second stage is to connect with the family system. The counselor asks questions that elicit descriptive responses from the family such as "What would be important for me to know about your family?" (p. 214). This allows the counselor to assess how each family member views the system and define his or her role. After the initial assessment through the lens of each member, the counselor focuses on the presenting issue. In the third stage, the questions shift to focus on what the family would like to change or improve with therapy. Nicholl notes that it is important for the counselor to ask questions that focus on describing the concern in a relational context to reduce blaming and allow members to view their roles in creating or maintaining the conflict. The fourth stage of RFBFT focuses on gaining information about family rules, roles, and beliefs. The counselor may ask for descriptions of a typical day to assess how the family is addressing the maintenance tasks. Stage five focuses on recognizing the ability to create change by accenting the strengths of each member and reframing conflicts to focus on the family's competence in each of the maintenance tasks. After the family has addressed shared perceptions, the counselor prescribes new behavioral tasks as the sixth stage. The stage addresses the maintenance tasks the family lacks. When the family addresses these tasks and improves, the counselor may shift into the last stage of therapy which is termination. In RFBFT, the family does not officially terminate sessions, rather, the sessions are suspended and the family returns for follow-up sessions as needed.

The RFBFT model addresses many key factors in promoting resilience in COAs. Many of the maintenance tasks of this model promote positive parent-child interactions, and family cohesion which are important in the development of resilience (McCubbin & McCubbin, 1988; Ulrich, et al., 2010). Moreover, the fourth stage of this model focuses primarily on family beliefs which directly relates to the Walsh model of family resilience.

Additional resources. Currently, counselors use a myriad of interventions to help identify and develop positive beliefs and expectations regarding family strengths. transgenerational trauma and resilience genogram, boat-storm-lighthouse, and the balloon bounce game may be introduced into most therapeutic work with alcoholic families to promote resilience and adjust thinking about family resources and opportunities during difficulties associated with alcohol abuse.

Transgenerational Trauma and Resilience Genogram. Goodman (2013) provides an intervention specifically geared towards healing and resilience in families that have experienced transgenerational trauma; focusing on how a family has overcome obstacles or helped others overcome obstacles in the past or present. Genograms are commonly used in family therapy as an assessment tool for counselors and provide a visual multigenerational representation of family relationships. Focusing on how these families overcome obstacles may help them identify their strengths, thereby adjusting beliefs about accessible resources for the family, and build upon these strengths to become more resilient.

Boat-Storm-Lighthouse. The boat-storm-lighthouse (Lowenstein, 2011) intervention begins with families drawing a picture of a boat, a storm and a lighthouse on a piece of paper. Once it is drawn, family members write a story pertaining to the picture. The counselor processes by allowing members to read their story aloud, guiding a discussion on feelings being on the boat with their family before, during, and after the storm. This intervention promotes family strength as the disclosures highlight family members' beliefs about adversity and how they may face storms as a family.

The Balloon Bounce Game. This intervention involves family members writing a question on an inflated balloon to stimulate conversation. The counselor provides sample questions to the family that focus on positive attributes of family members and strengths of the family. Lowenstein and Hertlein (2012) suggest questions like "Tell me about a time your family did something fun together" or "What do you appreciate most about your family" (p. 65). The family then tries to keep each balloon in the air for one minute. When a balloon falls, one family member is selected to pick it up and answer the question. This intervention promotes positive interactions as well as allows members to express family strengths.

Treatment Model for Family Organization: Behavioral Couples Therapy

Family organization and cohesion combined is another major construct in the family resilience framework. According to Walsh (2003) family structure and organization are integral in fostering resilience. A model that focuses on family structure and organization is behavioral couple's therapy (BCT). This model addresses couples dealing with alcoholism in order to promote more family cohesion. BCT involves incorporating behavioral interventions to promote abstinence and relationship functioning in couples with an alcohol abusing individual (O'Farrell & Schein, 2000). It also focuses on communication and overall positive feelings toward the relationship to help increase the likelihood that an individual will remain abstinent. These factors not only promote abstinence in the alcohol abusing family member, but also increase overall positive family functioning (Kelley & Fals-Stewart, 2002). BCT has been shown as effective in reducing significant impairment in children of couples with an alcohol abusing parent (Kelley & Fals-Stewart, 2002).

A clear emphasis is placed upon strengthening and supporting the couple subsystem, an important aspect of functional family organization. The first step in BCT is to assess the alcohol abuse in the couple subsystem and overall relationship functioning. Once the couple is committed to starting the process, the counselor and couple arrange a daily Recovery Contract. The agreement commits the couple to proactively discontinue the alcohol abuse; either by intent to not drink or being a source of moral support. The couple then reviews this contract and has a "trust discussion" everyday promising not to discuss the past or fears of future drinking behaviors. At the beginning of each session, the counselor and the couple review the Recovery Contract to ensure compliance (O'Farrell & Schein, 2000).

Once the couple has successfully adapted to the Recovery Contract routine, the counselor shifts emphasis to relational interventions; utilizing BCT to increase positive interactions and improving communication skills. Interventions may include assigning homework activities like "Catch Your Partner Doing Something Nice" where the counselor provides a sheet to record one nice thing each partner does each day (O'Farrell & Schein, 2000). This intervention allows the couple to recognize each person's positive actions rather than focusing on the negative ones. Other BCT interventions promoting positive couple activities include the processes of assisting couples in planning shared activities and assigning partners to provide each other special caring days in between therapy sessions. These interventions are also effective in promoting family cohesion and positive interactions (O'Farrell & Schein, 2000).

Another focus of BCT is teaching communication skills. The counselor affords the couple time to enhance their listening skills by allowing them to practice giving and receiving messages during session. One partner speaks while the other repeats what they heard to ensure clarity of the intended message and its meaning. This is important as miscommunication has been identified as a contributing factor to family and couple dysfunction (Walsh, 2002). The counselor and couple also practice skills involving feeling expression and negotiating requests. Feeling expression consists of having partners take responsibility of their feelings by learning to express them without blaming each other. Negotiating requests involves having the couple practice making specific requests and coming to agreements through compromise. These interventions help to strengthen communication patterns commonly weak in couples with alcohol abusing partners.

The last step of BCT involves maintenance of skills and prevention of relapse. The counselor and couple make a Continuing Recovery Plan with specific behaviors to utilize in the future. The intervention will also be inclusive of a plan for the alcohol abusing partner to avoid high risk situations and develop coping skills for potential relapses. These maintenance steps are important and afford the alcohol abusing partner an incentive to sustain abstinence as well as providing an atmosphere that enhances positive interactions and family cohesion.

BCT has proven to be effective and beneficial with couples and children of couples; Children whose parents were in BCT showed improved functioning in the year after therapy was completed (Kelley & Fals-Stewart, 2002). This improvement in children may be due to the emphasis on positive interpersonal communication, increased family activities, and more positive parenting. Each of the above stated factors successfully promotes resilience and family cohesion in COAs.

Additional resources. Family cohesion is an important factor in the development and maintenance of resilience in COAs. Family cohesion refers to the relationships and bonds amongst family members. Counselors may use many creative family interventions to promote cohesion. Two such interventions include "our family life scavenger hunt" and the "rappin' family puppet interview."

Our Family Life Scavenger Hunt. The "our life family scavenger hunt" (Cavett, 2010) involves providing a list of items that the family is to collect and bring into the next therapeutic session. Suggested items for scavenger hunt include pictures from a family vacation, homemade keepsakes, representations of family's culture, and representations of love within the family (Lowenstein & Hertlein, 2012). After the list of items are introduced, the family discusses how they will be obtained. The family may collectively choose to split the list, decide which items they will bring, or some other method of completing the task. In the subsequent session, the counselor facilitates discussion on participation in the scavenger hunt and how the family worked together. This activity enhances communication between family members and allows a common goal to be achieved together. The scavenger hunt also promotes cohesion, through the provision of opportunities to reflect on positive experiences and the overall strengths of the family.

Rappin' Family Puppet Interview. The rappin' family puppet interview (Sori, 2010) is adapted from Irwin and Malloy's (1975) Family Puppet Interview. In the Rappin' Family Puppet Interview, the counselor instructs members to select a puppet and create a story about their family in the form of a rap. The family then practices the rap until they are ready to perform it—allowing the counselor to observe how the family interacts to achieve a goal. The rap lyrics also provide insight into how family members view themselves individually and as a system. This intervention allows families to work together, problem solve, and improve communication skills important in maintaining family cohesion.

Treatment Model for Family Communication: Multidimensional Family Prevention

The family resilience framework suggests that open and positive communication is important in the promotion of resilience in COAs. Multidimensional Family Prevention (MDFP; Liddle & Hogue, 2000) is a model of therapy designed to reduce alcoholism and delinquency in adolescents through numerous avenues. One of these avenues includes family communication processes. MDFP promotes resilience in COAs by increasing positive communication between family members. What follows is an overview of MDFP and how it specifically relates to family communication.

MDFP is an intervention used to prevent drug and alcohol use as well as delinquency in at risk adolescents (Liddle & Hogue, 2000). The framework is based on risk and protection theory, developmental psychopathology, and ecological theory. Risk and protection theory focuses on the balance between factors that predispose an individual to negative outcomes and protective factors, which foster positive outcomes. Developmental psychopathology conceptualizes behaviors through the lens of an individual's stage of development distinguishing maladaptive behavior from expected behaviors. Ecological theory asserts that relationships within and outside of the family are influential to human development. Thus, it is at the intersection of these three theories that MDFP promotes change. MDFP focuses on decreasing risks and increasing protective factors through the adolescents' attachments to his or her family, and the family's connections to social institutions, all of which are important in promoting positive outcomes and resilience (Walsh, 2002).

MDFP is grounded on seven main domains that influence therapeutic intervention. Relationships, school involvement, prosocial activities, peer relationships, drug issues, cultural themes, and adolescent health and sexuality are assessed throughout therapy and allow the counselor to identify problematic areas within the family. Counselors using MDFP must set the prevention agenda, or plan for therapy, in the beginning stages of the therapeutic relationship. Counselors do this by first stressing the importance of the parents' roles in treatment and then by assessing the family's level of functioning in each of the domains to identify specific issues to address in therapy. The counselor assesses the family's risk and protective factors in each domain by gathering a non-structured oral history from the family to determine which domains have the highest risk and will be the focus of therapy.

This family prevention program was formed as a means to prevent negative outcomes in at-risk adolescents. As COAs are identified as at risk for a myriad of reasons, this intervention's focus on familial change to foster resilience in adolescents is relevant. MDFP contains five modules of intervention; first, the model focuses on the adolescent as an individual within the context of the family system as well as other social systems (e.g., school, peer relationships). Within this adolescent module of intervention, the goal is to identify personal strengths and support systems in order to build upon them and decrease the risk factors. MDFP also includes a parenting skills module of intervention which has been found to serve as a protective factor in COAs (Werner & Johnson, 2004). Additionally, in the familial aspect of promoting resilience, the interactional module addresses family communication patterns and relationships. The counselor facilitates positive interactions and promotes problem-solving skills between family members. From the ecological perspective, the extended-family and extrafamilial modules foster communication with extended family members and other social support systems such as the adolescent's school and their peers. This is important when promoting resilience in COAs as social supports and positive mentors are protective factors within this population (Hall, 2007). MDFP promotes resilience in COAs through numerous modules, the familial module specifically addresses communication patterns by facilitating positive interactions amongst family members and providing an atmosphere conducive to family trust and mutual respect.

Additional resources. Positive communication patterns are common in resilient families and have been identified as a protective factor in COAs. Family counselors use many interventions to promote positive communication skills in couples and families; examples include toss the ball and family survivor.

Toss the Ball. This intervention encourages positive communications while decreasing possible family tension through play. The counselor provides a small ball explaining that the family members will toss the ball to one another complimenting the recipient. After each person has had a turn, the counselor asks what it was like to hear nice things from their family (Lowenstein, 2011). This intervention provides family members the opportunity to practice positive communication as well as build on family cohesion.

Family Survivor. Family survivor (Community Based Education in Nurturing Parenting, 2011) identifies interactional patterns that family members may not be aware of and alters them to promote positive communication. The counselor first assigns family members a card they cannot see and must stick on their forehead for the rest of the family to see. The cards each have a phrase dictating how to communicate with the person wearing the card. The cards may say phrases such as "I'm always wrong", "I'm always right", "Laugh at everything I say", or "Ignore everything I say". The counselor then provides a list of approximately 20 potential survival items (e.g. toilet paper, water, pocket knife, first aid kit, cell phone, matches, playing cards, sewing kit, etc.) to the family and tells them they must work together, taking into consideration the phrases on the cards, to pick five of the listed items that they would need if stranded on a deserted island. The counselor then allows members to discuss their reactions to how they were treated and process how they view the communication patterns within the family system. This intervention allows the family to experience and identify negative interactions within the system and develop positive alternative methods of intermingling.

Conclusion

Alcoholism is a major issue in the United States and the negative outcomes of COAs dominate the literature, however, recent studies have provided protective factors and possible interventions that may be beneficial to the well-being of COAs. Furthermore, the family has been identified as a major contributing factor to resilience in COAs and as a result, family therapy models have been formed to promote resilience within the family.

Resilience based family therapy models provide a crucial backdrop for counselors working with COAs. The family therapy models described within this book chapter provide a framework for counselors to practice building resilience within the family through the promotion of cohesion, communication, and overall positive relationships. As a result, these models promote individual resilience within each family member. Empirical evidence exists in support of BCT's impact on COAs (Kelley & Fals-Stewart, 2002), stating that children of couples involved in BCT show improvement in functioning. Alternatively, MDFP and RFBFT both lack empirical support for use specifically with families in which alcoholism is a concern. Further research on the efficacy of these family models with these particular families is needed to provide best practices guidelines for promoting resilience. Ultimately, RFBFT, MDFP, and BCT focus on promoting skills within families that may lead to resilience in COAs. To be successful, counselors should understand the importance of promoting positive interactions within the family, identifying and building on family strengths, and encouraging family cohesion in therapy. Counselors may address these themes by integrating a myriad of different interventions. The interventions and therapy models provided allow counselors to assess family functioning and offer evidenced-based opportunities for families to build and maintain resilience, especially as they relate to COAs.

References

Bijttebier, P., & Goethals, E. (2006). Parental drinking as a risk factor for children's maladjustment: The mediating role of family environment. *Psychology of Addictive Behaviors, 20*(2), 126. doi:10.1037/0893-164X.20.2.126

Carle, A. C., & Chassin, L. (2004). Resilience in a community sample of children of alcoholics: Its prevalence and relation to internalizing symptomatology and positive affect. *Applied Developmental Psychology, 25,* 577-595. doi:10.1016/j.appdev.2004.08.005

Cavett, A. M. (2010). *Structured Play-Based Interventions for Engaging Children and Adolescents in Therapy.* Infinity Publishing: West Conshohocken, Pennsylvania.

Community Based Education in Nurturing Parenting. (2011). *10 Individual Parenting Lessons for Promoting a Community Philosophy of Nurturing for the Primary Prevention of Child Abuse and Neglect.* [CD]. Available from: http://www.nurturingparenting.com/ ecommerce/product

Coyle, J. P., Nochajski, T., Maguin, E., Safyer, A., DeWit, D., & Macdonald, S. (2009). An exploratory study of the nature of family resilience in families affected by parental alcohol abuse. Journal of Family Issues, 30(12), 1606-1623. doi: 10.1177/0192513X09339478

Dies, R. R., & Burghardt, K. (1991). Group interventions for children of alcoholics: Prevention and treatment in the schools. *Journal of Child and Adolescent Group Therapy, 1*(3), 219-234.

Emshoff, J., & Valentine, L. (2006). Supporting adolescent children of alcoholics. *Prevention Researcher, 13*(4), 18-20.

Garmezy, N. (1993). Children in poverty: Resilience despite risk. *Psychiatry, 56*(1), 127-130.

Goodman, R. D. (2013). The transgenerational trauma and resilience genogram. *Counselling Psychology Quarterly, 26*(3-4), 386-405. doi:10.1080/09515070.2013.820172

Hall-Lande, J. A., Eisenberg, M. E., Christenson, S. L., & Neumark-Sztainer, D. (2007). Social isolation, psychological health, and protective factors in adolescence. *Adolescence, 42*(166), 265.

Hipke, K. N., Wolchik, S. A., Sandler, I. N., & Brauer, S. L. (2002). Predictors of children's intervention-induced resilience in a parenting program for divorced mothers. *Family Relations, 51*(2), 121-129.

Irwin, E. C., & Malloy, E. S. (1975). Family puppet interview. *Family Process, 14*(2), 179-191. doi:10.1111/j.1545-5300.1975.00179.x

Jacob, T., & Windle, M. (2000). Young adult children of alcoholic, depressed and nondistressed parents. *Journal of Studies on Alcohol and Drugs, 61*(6), 836.

Jacob, T., Windle, M., Seilhamer, R. A., & Bost, J. (1999). Adult children of alcoholics: Drinking, psychiatric, and psychosocial status. *Psychology of Addictive Behaviors, 13*(1), 3. doi:10.1037/0893-164X.13.1.3

Kelley, M. L., & Fals-Stewart, W. (2002). Couples-versus individual-based therapy for alcohol and drug abuse: Effects on children's psychosocial functioning. Journal of Consulting and Clinical Psychology, 70(2), 417. doi:10.1037/0022-006X.70.2.417

Lambie, G. W., & Sias, S. M. (2005). Children of alcoholics: Implications for professional school counseling. *Professional School Counseling, 8*(3), 266.

Liddle, H. A., & Hogue, A. (2000). A family-based, developmental-ecological preventive intervention for high-risk adolescents. *Journal of Marital and Family Therapy, 26,* 265–279.

Lowenstein, L., & Hertlein, K. (2012). Engaging children in family sessions: Three creative interventions. *Journal of Family Psychotherapy*, 23(1), 62-66. doi: 10.1080/08975353.2012.654090

Lowenstein, L. (2011). *Favorite Therapeutic Activities for Children, Adolescents, and Families: Practitioners Share Their Most Effective Interventions.* Champion Press: Toronto, Ontario, Canada

Masten, A. S., Best, K. M., & Garmezy, N. (1990). Resilience and development: Contributions from the study of children who overcome adversity. *Development and Psychopathology*, 2(4), 425-444.

McCubbin, H. I., McCubbin, M. A., Thompson, A. I., Sae-Young, H., & Allen, C. T. (1997). Families under stress: What makes them resilient. *Journal of Family and Consumer Sciences*, 89(3), 2.

McCubbin, H. I., & McCubbin, M. A. (1988). Typologies of resilient families: Emerging roles of social class and ethnicity. *Family relations*, 37(3), 247-254.

Merriam Webster's collegiate dictionary (11th ed.). (2014). Merriam-Webster, Inc.

Nicoll, W. G. (2011). Resilience-focused brief family therapy: An Adlerian approach. Journal of Individual Psychology, 67(3).

O'Farrell, T. J., & Schein, A. Z. (2011). Behavioral couples therapy for alcoholism and drug abuse. Journal of Family Psychotherapy, 22(3), 193-215. doi: 10.1080/08975353.2011.602615

Park, S., & Schepp, K. G. (2014). A systematic review of research on children of alcoholics: Their inherent resilience and vulnerability. *Journal of Child and Family Studies*, 24 1222-1231. doi:10.1007/s10826-014-9930-7

Patterson, J. M. (2002). Understanding family resilience. *Journal of Clinical Psychology*, 58(3), 233–246.

Pecukonis, E. V. (2004). Female children of alcoholics and chronic back pain. *Pain Medicine*, 5(2), 196-201. doi:10.1111/j.1526-4637.2004.04024.x

Roosa, M. W., Gensheimer, L. K., Short, J. L., Ayers, T. S., & Shell, R. (1989). A preventive intervention for children in alcoholic families: Results of a pilot study. *Family Relations*, 38(3) 295-300. doi:10.2307/585055

Simon, J. B., Murphy, J. J., & Smith, S. M. (2005). Understanding and fostering family resilience. *The Family Journal*, 13(4), 427-436. doi:10.1177/1066480705278724

Sori, C. F. (2010). Rappin' family puppet interview. *Creative family therapy techniques: Play, art, and expressive activities to engage children in family sessions*, 63-66.

Taylor, E. R., & Karcher, M. (2009). Cultural and developmental variations in the resiliencies promoted by school counselors. *Journal of Professional Counseling: Practice, Theory and Research*, 37(2), 66-88.

Ulrich, I., Stopsack, M., & Barnow, S. (2010). Risk and resilience factors of adolescent children of alcoholics: Results of the greifswald family study. *Diskurs Kindheits—und Jugendforschung*, 5(1), 47-61.

Walsh, F. (2013). Community-based practice applications of a family resilience framework. In D. Becvar (Ed.), *Handbook of family resilience* (pp. 82-65). NY: Springer New York.

Walsh, F. (2002). A family resilience framework: Innovative practice applications. *Family Relations*, 51(2), 130-137.

Walsh, F. (2003). Family resilience: A framework for clinical practice. *Family process*, 42(1), 1-18.

Walsh, F. (1996). The concept of family resilience: Crisis and challenge. *Family process*, 35(3), 261-281.

Werner, E. E., & Johnson, J. L. (2004). The role of caring adults in the lives of children of alcoholics. *Substance Use & Misuse, 39*(5), 699-720. doi:10.1081/JA-120034012

Werner, E. E., & Smith, R. S. (2001). *Journeys from childhood to midlife: Risk, resilience, and recovery.* Ithaca, NY: Cornell University Press.

West, M. O., & Prinz, R. J. (1987). Parental alcoholism and childhood psychopathology. *Psychological Bulletin, 102*(2), 204.

White, J. M., & Klein, D. M. (2008). *Family theories.* Los Angeles, CA: Sage.

6

The Professionals and Procedures Involved in Drug Courts

John T. Petko[1]

History of Drug Courts in America (How It All Started)

Drug-related crimes have increased over time. Traditional judicial methods (e.g. increased incarcerations and court cases) were proving to be ineffective deterrents against drug-related crimes. Additionally, the increased use of crack also played a role in the development of drug courts. Drug courts were also started in response to repeat drug offenders, an effort to reduce drug-related crimes. The first drug court was started in Miami, Florida in 1989. The cities of Oakland, California and Portland, Oregon started after the success in the program in Miami (National Association of Drug Court Professionals Drug Court Standards Committee; NADCP: DCSC, 2013; Roget & Fisher, 2009; Terry, 1999). Studies have shown that drug courts reduce administration costs of the judicial system since individuals' upkeep (i.e. housing, food costs, etc.) are maintained by the individual (or his/her respective families) and not by the criminal justice system (Roper, 2007). The reduction of costs to the

---

1. Correspondence concerning this article should be addressed John T. Petko, 741 Hawks Ridge Rd. Port Orange, Fl 32127. Email: jpetko2009@knights.ucf.edu

criminal justice system reduces the burden of taxpayers (Alonso, 2009). Additionally, studies have shown that drug courts produce savings for the client's ($3000 to $13,000) due to reduced prison costs and court appearances (NADCP, 2013). Drug courts have also been shown to reduce recidivism rates (Thrasher, 2007). Another important development was President Obama's administration which was very supportive of drug courts and related courts. The president's 2012 fiscal year budget request included funding for courts that are problem solving in nature with drug courts being an example. There are over 2,500 drug courts in operation today throughout the United States with more programs being developed each year (Office of National Drug Control Policy, ONDCP, 2011).

After drug courts proved to have success, the legal system developed other types of drug treatment courts such as family drug courts, juvenile drug courts and driving under the influence/driving while intoxicated (DWI/DUI) courts. Family drug courts work with individuals and their respective families and juvenile drug courts work with the juvenile offender and their respective families. The DWI/DUI courts work with offenders whose charges are vehicle-related (i.e. involve a DWI/DUI). The DWI/DUI drug courts differ from traditional drug courts by their focus and participants. The DWI/DUI drug courts focus on keeping the highways safe and all DWI/DUI participants have driving-related arrests. The juvenile, family and DWI/DUI drug courts all follow the same model as the original drug courts (Gwinnell & Adamec, 2006; Narag, Maxwell, & Lee, 2013; Roget & Fisher, 2009). As of December 31, 2011, the total number of drug courts comprised in the United States are: (a) 1,435 Adult Drug Courts of which, 406 are hybrid DWI/DUI courts; (b) 787 Family and Juvenile Drug Courts; (c) 192 designated DWI/DUI courts; and (d) a total of 276 various Drug Courts (National Institute of Justice, 2012).

What is a Drug Court?

Drug courts were created with the intention of reducing recidivism rates of repeat drug offenders (Lurigio, 2008). A drug court is first and foremost a judiciary program with the focus on drug treatment. Individuals in drug treatment programs are held accountable to court imposed sanctions and are expected to adhere to treatment requirements as they are supervised by the court system (Mackinem & Higgins, 2007; Terry, 1999). According to Harrison and Scarpitti (2002), the "Drug treatment courts couple drug treatment with intensive supervision and the sanctions available to the court" (p. 1447). "Drug courts target a very specific yet growing offender population that accounts for a significant percentage of prison populations" (Nored & Carlan, 2008, p. 330). Drug courts typically last between 12 to 18 months for the participants. Extenuating circumstances can extend participants' time in a drug court (e.g. payment of court fees) if it is determined that continued participation won't prohibit a participant from completing probation which typically runs concurrent with their drug court stay (Huddleston & Marlowe, 2011). Participants in drug courts have regular status hearings with the court to review their progress in the program. The status hearings for the participants serve two functions. The primary function is to ensure the participants are meeting the judicial requirements. The second function is to ensure that the participants are meeting all their treatment requirements (Marlowe, Festinger, & Lee, 2004).

The NADCP (1997), as part of a grant developed 10 key components of drug courts. The 10 key components are:

- drug courts integrate alcohol and other drug treatment services with justice system case processing;
- using a nonadversarial approach, prosecution and defense counsel promote public safety while protecting participants' due process rights;
- eligible participants are identified early and promptly placed in the drug court program;
- drug courts provide access to a continuum of alcohol, drug, and other related treatment and rehabilitation services;
- abstinence is monitored by frequent alcohol and other drug testing;
- a coordinated strategy governs drug court responses to participants' compliance;
- ongoing judicial interaction with each drug court participant is essential;
- monitoring and evaluation measure the achievement of program goals and gauge effectiveness;

- continuing interdisciplinary education promotes effective drug court planning, implementation, and operations; and
- forging partnerships among drug courts, public agencies, and community-based organizations generates local support and enhances drug court program effectiveness.

According to Siedler (2000), the author states that "What distinguishes drug courts from traditional compulsory treatment is the role of the members of the drug court in overseeing and monitoring the client's progress in treatment" (p.8). The drug court model is essentially a therapeutic jurisprudent model where the legal system and the therapeutic system work together for the betterment of society and the participants (Hora, Schma, & Rosenthal, 1999). To be considered a successful graduate of the program, participants must meet all program requirements and typically have abstained from substances for at least 6 months or more (Huddleston & Marlowe, 2011).

The Process of Drug Courts

The screening process and admission.

According to Mackinem & Higgins (2008), success of participants in drug courts should be determined by the screening process. Mackinem & Higgins contend that individuals should not be admitted into a drug court program until they have been appropriately screened. From a judicial standpoint, the prosecution will make referrals to the drug court based on legal eligibility (Belenko, Fabrikant, & Wolf, 2011). In addition to criminal histories of individuals, mental health histories should be reviewed prior to admission into a drug treatment program in order to reduce recidivism rates. Further considerations to take into account in the screening process are the severity of the participants' addiction. Individuals who have addictions requiring medical interventions would not be good candidates for a drug court (Alonso, 2009). Promoting participant success is essential for program staff (Evans, Huang, & Hser, 2011). The NADCP's (1997) key component number 3 recommends identifying eligible participants early and promptly. Once individuals are determined fit for a drug court program, it is important to inform them early of the program requirements and expectations of the drug court program (Roget & Fisher, 2009).

The therapeutic process.

Individuals entering drug treatment programs tend to be highly resistant. Treatment programs need to have treatment aspects that not only address the individual's resistance but also instill a sense of responsibility for their actions (Little & Robinson, 1988). Participant success in Drug Treatment programs is very dependent on the judicial process. While judiciary processes and therapeutic processes run independent, each component reinforces the other (DeVall, 2008). The therapeutic process in drug courts often involves the participants' attendance in 12-step meetings. Attendance in 12-step meetings helps to reinforce addiction therapy and provide a support group for the participants (Gebelein, 2000). According to Mateyoke-Scrivner, Webster, Staton, and Leukefeld (2004), encouraging participants to become gainfully employed promotes graduation rates among drug court participants. Part of the therapeutic process begins at the screening process. Mental health counselors and addiction counselors should carefully screen potential participants prior to the beginning of starting treatment to be able to account for additional medical or mental health problems that may interfere with successful graduation. Many participants entering a drug court also have a dual mental health diagnosis that needs to be accounted for (Belenko et al., 2011; Gray & Saum, 2005). Lay and King (2007), recommend a multi-modal approach to therapy with drug court participants. Lay and King advocate approaches that include motivational interviewing counseling and cognitive behavioral counseling methods. Lay and King also recommend the use of individual, group and family counseling. A therapy program in a drug court needs to be structured and consistent in order to facilitate progress. Inconsistency in a program can lead to client's relapsing and possible failure at graduating from a program (Mackinem & Higgins, 2008). To monitor abstinence in a drug court program, on-going drug testing has to be conducted (Alonso, 2009; Auerbach, 2007; Miller & Shutt, 2001).

Ongoing drug testing.

An essential part of an effective drug court is drug testing. For example, "Drug testing and monitoring comprise the heart of a drug treatment court program. Testing and monitoring of participants holds them accountable for their behavior and provides a concrete basis for sanctions" (Alonso, 2009, p. 20). Drug court programs should use drug testing methods that are well-tested and reliable in drug courts in order to be able to appropriately screen participants and address positive drug tests if and when they come up (Miller & Shutt, 2001). When drug tests are administered, staff conducting the drug test needs to be aware of adulterations of samples and substitutions of samples. A common method of adulterants is to dilute the sample with water. Typical methods for dilution are drinking large amounts of water prior to taking a urine test. Confirmation of all drug tests should be conducted following receipt of a urine drug test prior to accepting results as positive or negative. A drug court that receives a questionable drug test can send the specimen to an outside laboratory to confirm the results (Auerbach, 2007). Positive drug tests, program infractions and progress need to be monitored and enforced (e.g., Lindquist, Krebs, & Lattimore, 2006). Sanctions and rewards are discussed in the next section.

Imposed sanctions and rewards.

Imposed legal and treatment noncompliance consequences should be discussed among the members of the drug court team. The decision of legal sanctions falls under the jurisdiction of the criminal justice staff (i.e. judges, lawyers and probation). Decisions on treatment consequences and recommendations can be discussed and agreed upon by all members of the drug court team. The treatment staff needs to advocate that the treatment decisions are therapeutic in nature (Arabia, Fox, Caughie, Marlowe, & Festinger, 2008). There is limited research on the use of sanctions and rewards in drug courts (Lindquist et al., 2006). According to Longshore et al. (2001), the authors suggest that imposed sanctions need to be clear and consistent and incremental (i.e. not using the same sanction for repeated infractions). Guastaferro and Daigle (2012) recommend that a sanction should be imposed soon after the infraction occurs in order to maximize behavioral change. While there is limited research on the use of sanctions and rewards, Lindquist et al., 2006 recommend that program infractions should have sanctions imposed and reward participants accordingly. Lindquist et al., also contend that while sanctions need to be consistent among drug court participants, considerations need to be made if the imposed sanction can cause undo family hardships. Judges may be more lenient on a participant regarding a sanction if the participant admitted to the infraction prior to the imposed sanction. The judge will use discretion as to whether or not the infraction warrants further action depending on the severity of the infraction. Ultimately, sanctions need to be consistent with participants' rights (Burns & Peyrot, 2008). Imposed sanctions and rewarding of participants are discussed amongst the drug court team prior to informing the participants of the judicial status hearing (e.g. Marlowe et al., 2003).

Judicial status hearings.

In a drug court program where participant progress is closely monitored, judicial status hearings are part of the review process. In drug court programs where progress is dependent on participants completing requirements for a phase, status hearing may typically be more frequent for participants who are in the early stages of the program. More frequent judicial status hearing for participants in the early stages tends to lead to greater program success (Carey, Finigan, & Pukstas, 2008; Festinger et al., 2002; Marlowe et al., 2004). According to Marlowe et al., 2004), regular judicial status hearings lead to better performance for drug court participants and was especially beneficial for participants who were considered high-risk (e.g. had anti-social behaviors or failed at previous attempts at substance abuse treatment). Marlowe et al. (2003) suggest that frequent judicial hearings works better for participants over a long period of time as opposed to the initial stages of treatment. Festinger et al. (2002), argue that status hearings need to be targeted to those participants who it would benefit the most since the cost of status hearings can be expensive. The next section discusses the members of the drug court team and their function in the drug court.

The Drug Court Team

An effective drug court team is collaborative in nature relying on the cooperation of the legal professionals (e.g. judges, lawyers and probation) and the treatment professionals (Terry, 1999; Wenzel, Turner, & Ridgely, 2004). Drug court team members are fully invested in the progress of the individual participants in the drug court program (Siedler, 2000). The policies for legal sanctions, program expectations and treatment protocols should be written and clearly defined and made readily available to all drug court team members and individual participants (Roper & Lessenger, 2007). The following sections will discuss each member of the drug court team from the drug court managers/administrators, judges, lawyers (e.g. district attorneys and defense lawyers), probation officers and treatment providers.

Drug court managers/administrators.

Drug Court managers' responsibilities vary from state to state and within each respective county. The primary responsibility of drug court managers is to maintain the day to day operations of the drug court. Day to day operations can include managing communications between all members of the drug court team, monitoring funding and expenditures of the drug court program itself (Mackinem & Higgins, 2008). Drug court managers/administrators have close ties with other government officials (both elected and appointed). It is important that they have a good relationship with those officials to both promote their respective programs and to gain support from government officials (Nored & Carlan, 2008). Essentially, drug court managers/administrators serve as the liaison between the judicial system and treatment providers and the drug court members and the political world (Wenzel, Turner, & Ridgely, 2004). The next section discusses the role of judges in drug courts.

Judges.

Judges in drug courts serve as the lead member of the drug court professional team. While judges follow recommendations made by the other drug court professionals, the judge makes the final decision concerning any legal sanctions. Drug Court judges provide both the praise and criticism for the drug court participants during status hearings (Mackinem & Higgins, 2008; Marlowe et al., 2004). With regard to research on specific behaviors of drug court judges, "there appears to be no empirical research on the role and behavior of the judge in terms of approach behavior, experience, and training" (Siedler, 2000, p.17). While empirical research on specific judicial behaviors of judges in drug courts is limited, the idea for the judges' role in drug courts arose from the mental health field that jurisprudence can have a therapeutic effect either positive or negative. The concept of therapeutic jurisprudence started developing in the late 1980's and was introduced as a reasonable theory around 1999. One of the essential principles of therapeutic jurisprudence is that the consequences of legal sanctions can have therapeutic impacts (Hora et al., 1999; Hora, 2002). While judges are not counselors, they need to have some understanding of addiction. Judges need to uphold the law but also account for issues that participants might have due to their addictions (Burns & Peyrot, 2008; National Institute of Justice (NIJ), 2006; Roper and Lessenger 2007),

According to Roper and Lessenger (2007), judges need to be aware of the addiction process and the rehabilitation process while making judicial decisions. Roper and Lessenger contend that judges that are more knowledgeable about the addictive process can make better legal decisions that hold participants accountable and also have therapeutic value. According to NIJ (2006), judges are integral to the success of the participants in drug courts. The NIJ also asserts that in the drug court model, it " presumes that effectiveness depends on the judge's nontraditional style (informal, hands-on, and flexible), the non-adversarial nature of proceedings, the frequency of required hearings, and the opportunity for direct communication between defendants and the bench" (p.9). Since the drug court serves as a continual entity in the judicial system, judges in drug courts are assigned bailiffs, court clerks and other related officials on a permanent basis for continuity purposes (Roper & Lessenger, 2007). Judges make the final decision in drug courts and they have to make sure that decisions are consistent with participants' rights (Burns & Peyrot, 2008). The next two sections describe the role of the prosecution and defense attorneys in a drug court.

Prosecutors.

The prosecution in a drug court team has a unique stance compared to their other drug court team members. Prosecutors' primary concern is society's safety. Drug court prosecutors agree with other team members that the reduction of recidivism is important. One of the key differences for prosecutors is the accountability of the participants (in this case the defendants) to be responsible and face penalties for their violations of the laws. Prosecutors also have to review criminal case records of the participants to make certain that there are no pending long-term incarcerations that would prohibit successful completion of a drug court program (Mackinem & Higgins, 2008; Roget & Fisher, 2009). The overall role of the prosecution in drug courts is to serve as the legal gatekeeper for the program (Hora, 2002).

Public defender/private attorney.

Defense attorneys on the drug court team have a slightly different role than their counterparts in the prosecution (Tobin, 2012). While defense attorneys share the same goals of other members of the drug court team (e.g. reducing recidivism and treating addiction), they are generally the initial drug court team members to advocate their clients admission into a drug court program. Defense attorneys also have to ensure that their clients' rights are protected (Mackinem & Higgins, 2008). The defense attorneys serve as the participants' key legal advocate. Defense attorneys may be the first to request that their clients be admitted to the drug court program. Defense attorneys also need to advise their clients on the advantages of entering a drug court program as well as alternatives. Defense attorneys also have to advise clients the need to maintain sobriety and the potential consequences for failing the drug court program (Roget & Fisher, 2009). Defense attorneys' ultimate role as the legal advisor for the participant is to assist their clients in determining if it is in their best interest to be a participant in a drug court program. This process needs to be done diligently so that their clients' rights are being considered (Hora, 2002). Next is the role of the probation officers in drug courts.

Probation officers.

One of the key functions of the drug court probation officers is monitoring clients to ensure that they are being abstinent from substance use and following the conditions of their court order which may include restitution fees and community service hours. Part of this monitoring may include regular drug testing in conjunction with the treatment provider and home visits (Rodriguez & Webb, 2007; Thrasher, 2007). If a violation occurs, a probation officer has to report the violation to the court and other members of the drug court team (Anderson, 2003). According to Rodriguez and Webb (2007), the judiciary members of the drug court team depend a great deal on recommendations from the probation department since they regularly see the participants. It is not uncommon for the judges in drug courts to rely on the recommendations made by the probation officers (Leifker & Sample, 2011).

Treatment providers.

According to Roper and Lessenger (2007, p. 286-287), treatment providers need to have five things in place when running a drug court. They are: (a) written protocols; (b) appropriate certification and state licensure, if required; (c) a method of accountability to the court; (d) availability to the clients in terms of hours of operation and geographic location; and (e) adherence to the drug court requirements and protocols for treatment and reports. Roper and Lessenger contend that counselors in treatment programs need to have sufficient training and accountability to the court since they are part of the drug court treatment team.

When it comes to honesty, counselors are aware that many of the participants in drug court programs are addicts and that dishonesty is part of the disease of addiction. Counselors understand that continued dishonesty on behalf of the participants also indicates that they may not be committed to the process of change (Mackinem & Higgins, 2007). Counselors are also pivotal in the screening process of participants. The counselors' role in screening is to identify possible additional mental health concerns or severity of participants' addiction. Participants with severe mental health concerns or serious addictions may not successfully complete drug court if those concerns are not addressed (Alonso, 2009; Evans, Huang, & Hser, 2011; Roget & Fisher, 2009). Counselors in drug courts need to keep the other members of the drug court team informed of participants' progress (Roget & Fisher, 2009).

Counselors in drug court programs have similar responsibilities as do other counselors in nondrug court programs but there are apparent differences. The one major difference is the complexity that a drug court participant can present to a counselor. This complexity of the participants (e.g. compounding legal issues and possible health and mental health issues), create the necessity of drug court counselors to frequently review participants cases. If and when an issue arises during the time a participant is in drug court, a drug court counselor should amend the treatment plans accordingly. Another difference is that drug court counselors are in constant communication with the legal system whereas their non-drug court counselors do not have as much frequent interaction (Mackinem & Higgins, 2008; Roper & Lessenger, 2007).

Like other drug counselors, counselors in drug court programs understand that their respective client is resistant to change. Using proven strategies (e.g. motivational interviewing, family counseling, group counseling, etc.) can help clients work through the resistance and change and build meaningful lives (Lay & King, 2007). Taxman and Bouffard (2005) recommend using cognitive-behavioral strategies when working with drug court participants. Counselors must develop a treatment plan that is tailored to the needs of the individual client. Treatment plans should be holistic in order to be able to address the various concerns that a participant may have (Huddleston & Marlowe, 2011). Integrating therapy with the judicial team members is essential for counselors since the treatment team is part of the drug court process. Strong professional relationships with the other drug court members are essential for the treatment team members because the other treatment team members will reinforce the therapy intentions (Fletcher et al., 2009).

Treatment providers need to be aware of various influences that can impact whether or not a participant successfully completes a drug court program. Among these influences can include: (a) drug of choice and frequency of usage (West, 2008); (b) mental health issues (Belenko et al., 2011; Gray & Saum, 2005); and (c) education and legal history of participants (Gill, 2012). Most importantly, counselors need to have good therapeutic relationships with their clients since they see clients more often than the rest of the drug court team (Mackinem & Higgins, 2008). In addition to having good therapeutic relationships with clients, treatment providers also need to provide good support services to clients to aid in success due to the complexity that a drug court participant can present (Carey, Mackin, & Finigan, 2012). The goal of counselors in drug court for their respective clients is the successful completion of the program (Mackinem & Higgins, 2008). The next section provides some examples of some useful resources for counselors in a drug treatment team.

Resources for Counselors

Resources and the sharing of resources are somewhat limited among drug court professionals. Resources for counselors and other professionals working in drug courts are vital in order to maintain best practices within the community (Wenzel et al., 2004). One such resource is the National Association of Drug Court Professionals (NADCP). The NADCP was established in 1994 and is a nonprofit organization. The NADCP's goal is to help reduce recidivism and drug-related crimes. Additionally, the NADCP works with other organization and drug courts in training for drug court professionals. The NADCP helped to establish the National Drug Court Institute (NDCI) which assists in training and research in drug courts (NADCP, 2013). The NDCI provides 130 trainings each year to both individual professionals and treatment providers. The NDCI is considered to be a service branch of the NADCP. The NDCI is funded through the Bureau of Justice Assistance (BJA) and is aimed at improving the drug court process through research and collaboration (Huddleston & Marlowe, 2011). The Substance Abuse and Mental Health Administration (SAMSHA) (2013) is an agency within the U.S. Department of Health and Human Services. SAMSHA's "mission is to reduce the impact of substance abuse and mental illness on America's communities" (para. 1). SAMSHA provides publications on mental health and substance abuse. Some of these publications can be downloaded in pdf format free of charge.

Discussion

Drug courts have shown to be have positive results for their respective participants, but there is still room for improvement. Part of the improvement is consistency between the drug courts throughout the country

(Banks & Gottfredson, 2003). The counselors in drug courts have a unique position compared to other drug counselors. Drug court counselors have to communicate frequently with court officers and members of the drug court team. One of the functions of the counselor is to not only serve as the facilitator of treatment, but as a liaison between the program participants and the other members of the drug court team to report on the progress of the participants. The counselors also must be an advocate for their clients which is a role of counselors (Mackinem & Higgins, 2008; Roper & Lessenger, 2007).

Drug court counselors need not only be adequately trained as counselors, they need to have training specific to working in drug courts (Roper and Lessenger, 2007). While counselors may prescribe to their own theoretical orientation, they need to accept that counseling is an ever developing field and they need to constantly develop their field of vision to be effective (Lay & King, 2007). It is important that counselors utilize counseling strategies that hold drug court participants accountable and promote changes in behavior (Lay & King, 2007; Little & Robinson, 1988). Having a strong professional relationship with other members of the drug court team is essential for the overall success of the program (Carey et al., 2012).

The purpose of this article was to describe in brief, the responsibilities of each member of a drug court team and stress the importance of the function of counselors in a drug court. Drug court counselors have a precarious role compared to counselors in programs that are not judicially monitored. Treatment programs need to keep their staff training current since the drug courts are constantly evolving (Lurigio, 2008; Roper & Lessenger, 2007). Treatment team providers need to be aware of different factors that can affect successful completion of a drug court program such as drug use history, mental health history, education and legal history

(Belenko et al., 2011; Gill, 2012; Gray & Saum, 2005; West, 2008). It is imperative that treatment providers keep updated on training their counselors and staff in order to be effective members of the drug court team (Roper & Lessenger, 2007).

References

Alonso, A. (2009). *"Best practices" for drug courts*. (Doctoral dissertation) Retrieved from ProQuest Dissertations and Theses, (78).

Anderson, P. (2003). Treatment with teeth. *American Prospect, 11,* 45-48. Retrieved from http://jpo.wrlc.org/bitstream/handle/11204/82/110.pdf?sequence=1

Arabia, P.L., Fox, G., Caughie, J., Marlowe, D.B., & Festinger, D.S. (2008). Sanctioning practices in an adult felony drug court. *Drug Court Review, 6,* 1-31. Retrieved from http://www.ndci.org/sites/default/files/ndci/DCRVolume6_1.pdf

Auerbach, K. (2007). Drug testing methods. In J.E. Lessenger & G.F. Roper (Eds.), *Drug courts: A new approach to treatment and rehabilitation* (pp.230-233). New York: Springer.

Banks, D. & Gottfredson, D.C. (2003). The effects of drug treatment and supervision on time to rearrest among drug treatment court participants. *Journal of Drug Issues, 33,* 385-412. doi:10.1177/002204260303300206

Belenko, S., Fabrikant, N., & Wolf, N. (2011). The long road to treatment: Models of screening and admission into Drug Courts. *Criminal Justice and Behavior, 38,* 1222—1243. doi:10.1177/0093854811424690

Burns, S.L. & Peyrot, M. (2008). Reclaiming discretion: Judicial sanctioning strategy in court-supervised drug treatment. *Journal of Contemporary Ethnography, 37,* 720-744. doi:10.1177/0891241607310705

Carey, S. M., Finigan, M. W., & Pukstas, K. (2008). *Exploring the key components of drug courts: A comparative study of 18 adult drug courts on practices, outcomes and costs.* Portland, OR: NPC Research. Retrieved from https://www.ncjrs.gov/pdffiles1/nij/grants/223853.pdf

Carey, S.M., Mackin, J.R., & Finigan, M.W. (2012). What works? The ten key components of drug court: Research-based best practices. *Drug Court Review, 8,* 6-42. Retrieved from http://live-ndci.gotpantheon.com/sites/default/files/nadcp/DCR_best-practices-in-drug-courts.pdf

DeVall, K. E. (2008). *The theory and practice of drug courts: Wolves in sheep clothing?* (Doctoral Dissertation). Retrieved from http://scholarworks.wmich.edu/dissertations/763.

Evans, E., Huang, D., & Hser, Y. (2011). High-risk offenders participating in court-supervised substance abuse treatment: Characteristics, treatment received, and factors associated with recidivism. *Journal of Behavioral Health Services & Research, 38,* 510-525. doi:10.1007/s11414-011-9241-3

Festinger, D. S., Marlowe, D. B., Lee, P. A., Kirby, K. C., Bovasso, G., & McLellan, A. T. (2002). Status hearings in drug court: When more is less and less is more. *Drug and Alcohol Dependence, 68,* 151–157. doi:10.1016/s0376-8716(02)00187-4

Fletcher, B. W., Lehman, W. E., Wexler, H. K., Melnick, G., Taxman, F. S., & Young, D. W. (2009). Measuring collaboration and integration activities in criminal justice and substance abuse treatment agencies. *Drug and Alcohol Dependence, 103,* S54-S64. doi:10.1016/j.drugalcdep.2009.01.001

Gebelein, R. S. (2000). *Rebirth of Rehabilitation: Promise and perils of drug courts.* National Institute of Justice. Retrieved from https://www.ncjrs.gov/pdffiles1/nij/181412.pdf

Gill, M. E. (2012). *Predictors of Drug Court Client Graduation* (Doctoral dissertation) Retrieved from http://etd.uthsc.edu/WORLD-ACCESS/Gill_Marie/2012-039-Gill.pdf

Gray, A.R. & Saum, C.A. (2005). Mental health, gender and drug court completion. *American Journal of Criminal Justice, 30,* 55-69. doi:10.1007/BF02885881

Guastaferro, W.P. & Daigle, L.E. (2012). Linking noncompliant behaviors and programmatic responses: The use of graduated sanctions in a felony-level drug court. *Journal of Drug Issues, 42*, 396-419. doi:10.1177/0022042612461773

Gwinnell, E., & Adamec, C. A. (2006). *Encyclopedia of Addictions and Addictive Behaviors*. New York, NY: Facts On File, Inc.

Harrison, L. D., & Scarpitti, F. R. (2002). Introduction: Progress and issues in Drug Treatment Courts. *Substance Use & Misuse, 37*(12-13), 1441. doi:10.1081/JA-120014418

Hora, H. (2002). A dozen years of drug treatment courts: uncovering our theoretical foundation and the construction of a mainstream paradigm. *Substance Use & Misuse, 37*, 1469-1488. doi:10.1081/JA-120014419

Hora, P.F., Schma, W.G., & Rosenthal, J.T. (1999). Therapeutic jurisprudence and the drug treatment court movement: Revolutionizing the criminal justice system's response to drug abuse and crime in America. *Notre Dame Law Review, 74*, 439–538. Retrieved from http://www.ndci.org/sites/default/files/ndci/NotreDame.Hora_.pdf

Huddleston, C. W., & Marlowe, D. B. (2011). *Painting the current picture: A national report on drug courts and other problem-solving court programs in the United States*. Washington, DC: National Drug Court Institute.

Lay, K.R. & King, L.J. (2007). Counseling strategies. In J. E. Lessenger & G. F. Roper. (Eds.), *Drug courts: a new approach to treatment and rehabilitation* (pp.166-182). New York: Springer.

Leifker, D. & Sample, L.L. (2011). Probation recommendations and sentences received: The association between the two and the factors that affect recommendations. *Criminal Justice Policy Review, 22*, 494-517. doi:10.1177/0887403411388405

Lindquist, C.H., Krebs, C.P., Lattimore, P.K. (2006). Sanctions and rewards in drug court programs: Implementation, perceived efficacy, and decision making. *The Journal of Drug Issues, 36*, 119-146. doi:10.1177/002204260603600106

Little, G.L. & Robinson, K.D. (1988). Moral Reconation Therapy: A systematic step-by-step treatment for treatment resistent clients. *Psychological Reports, 62*, 135-151. doi:10.2466/pro.1988.62.1.135

Longshore, D., Turner, S., Wenzel, S., Morral, A., Harrell, A., McBride, D.,. . . Iguchi, M. (2001). Drug courts: A conceptual framework. *Journal of Drug Issues, 31*, 7-26. doi:10.1177/002204260103100103

Lurigio, A. (2008). The first 20 Years of drug treatment courts: A brief description of their history and impact. *Federal Probation, 72*, 13-17. Retrieved from http://www.uscourts.gov/viewer.aspx?doc=/uscourts/FederalCourts/PPS/Fedprob/2008—06/20_index.html

Mackinem, M.B. & Higgins, P. (2007). Tell me about the test: The construction of truth and lies in drug court. *Journal of Contemporary Ethnography, 36*, 223-251. doi:10.1177/0891241606287417

Mackinem, M. B., & Higgins, P. (2008). *Drug Court: Constructing the Moral Identity of Drug Offenders*. Springfield: Charles C Thomas Publisher, LTD.

Marlowe, D. B., Festinger, D. S., & Lee, P. A. (2004). The Judge is a key component of drug court. *Drug Court Review, 4*, 1-34. Retrieved from http://www.ndci.org/sites/default/files/ndci/DCR.IV2_.pdf

Marlowe, D.B., Festinger, D.S., Lee, P.A., Schepise, M.M., Hazzard, J.E.R., Merrill, J.C.,. . . McLellan, A.T. (2003). Are judicial status hearings a key component of drug court? During treatment data from a randomized trial. *Criminal Justice and Behavior, 30*, 141-162. doi:10.1177/0093854802250997

Mateyoke-Scrivner, A., Webster. J.M., Staton, M., & Leukefeld, C. (2004). Treatment retention predictors of drug court participants in a rural state. *The American Journal of Drug and Alcohol Abuse, 30*, 605-625. doi:10.1081/ADA-200032304

Miller, J.M. & Shutt, J.E. (2001). Considering the need for empirically grounded drug court screening mechanisms. *Journal of Drug Issues, 31*, 91-106. doi: 10.1177/002204260103100106

Narag, R. E., Maxwell, S.R., & Lee, B. (2013). A phenomenological approach to assessing a DUI/DWI program. *International Journal of Offender Therapy and Comparative Criminology, 57*, 229-250. doi:10.1177/0306624X11431685

National Association of Drug Court Professionals, Drug Court Standards Committee. (1997). *Defining drug courts: The key components*. Washington, DC: U.S. Department of Justice Office of Justice Programs Bureau of Justice Assistance.

National Association of Drug Court Professionals. (2013). *What are drug courts?* Retrieved from http://www.nadcp.org/learn/what-are-drug-courts

National Institute of Justice. (2006). *Drug Courts: The second decade*. Washington, DC: US Department of Justice Programs, National Institute of Justice.

National Institute of Justice. (2012). *Drug Courts*. Retrieved from http://www.nij.gov/topics/courts/drug-courts/

Nored, L. S., & Carlan, P. E. (2008). Success of drug court programs: Examination of the perceptions of drug court personnel. *Criminal Justice Review, 33*, 329-342. doi:10.1177/0734016808322050

Office of National Drug Control Policy (ONDCP) (2011). Drug Courts: A smart approach to criminal justice. Retrieved from http://www.whitehouse.gov/sites/default/files/ondcp/Fact_Sheets/drug_courts_fact_sheet_5-31-11.pdf

Rodriguez, N. & Webb, V.J. (2007). Probation violations, revocations, and imprisonment: The decisions of probation officers, prosecutors and judges pre—and post-mandatory drug treatment. *Criminal Justice Policy Review, 18*, 3-30. doi:10.1177/0887403406292956

Roget, N. A., & Fisher, G. L. (2009). *Encyclopedia of Substance Abuse Prevention, Treatment, & Recovery*. Los Angeles, CA: SAGE.

Roper, G.F. (2007). Introduction to drug courts. In J.E. Lessenger & G.F. Roper (Eds.), *Drug courts: a new approach to treatment and rehabilitation* (pp.1-22). New York: Springer.

Roper, G.F. & Lessenger, J.E. (2007). Drug Court Organizations and operations. In J.E. Lessenger & G.F. Roper (Eds.), *Drug courts: a new approach to treatment and Rehabilitation* (pp.284-300). New York: Springer.

Siedler, H. M. (2000). *Therapeutic jurisprudence: the role of perceived empathy of drug court judges and its effects on therapeutic outcome* (Doctoral dissertation). Retrieved from Dissertation Abstracts International, (61)

Substance Abuse and Mental Health Administration. (2013). *About us*. Retrieved from http://beta.samhsa.gov/about-us

Taxman, F. S., & Bouffard, J. A. (2005). Treatment as part of drug court: The impact on graduation rates. *Journal of Offender Rehabilitation, 42*, 23-50. doi:10.1300/J076v42n01_02

Terry, W. (1999). *The Early Drug Courts: Case Studies in Judicial Innovation*. Thousand Oaks, CA: Sage Publications.

Thrasher, R.R. (2007). Law enforcement and drug courts. In Roper, G. F., & Lessenger, J. E. (Eds.), *Drug courts: a new approach to treatment and rehabilitation (pp.389-400)*. New York: Springer.

Tobin, M. (2012). Participation of defense attorneys in drug courts. *Drug Court Review, 8*, 96-130. Retrieved from http://live-ndci.gotpantheon.com/sites/default/files/ nadcp/DCR_best-practices-in-drug-courts.pdf

Wenzel, S.L., Turner, S.F., & Ridgely, M.S. (2004). Collaboration between drug courts and service providers: Characteristics and challenges. *Journal of Criminal Justice, 32*, 253-263. doi:10.1016/j.jcrimjus.2004.02.005

West, R. M. (2008). *Predictors of successful completion of family treatment drug court programs: An archival investigation.* (Doctoral dissertation). Retrieved from http://etd.fcla.edu/UF/UFE0022556/west_r.pdf

7

Avatar Assisted Therapy

A Novel Technology Based Intervention to Treat Substance Use Disorders

MICHAEL S. GORDON, STEVEN B. CARSWELL, ERICA N. PETERS,
SUSAN TANGIRES, TIMOTHY W. KINLOCK, FRANK J. VOCCI, AND
LAUREN RESTIVO[1]

Substance use disorders among individuals 12 years of age or older continue to be one of the most serious public health problems in the US (Center for Substance Abuse Treatment, 2004; Substance Abuse and Mental Health Services Administration [SAMHSA], 2011). Substance use is associated with impaired academic and career performance and social functioning (The National Center on Addiction and Substance Abuse [CASA], 2011a-c; Cox, Zhang, Johnson, & Bender, 2007); mental and physical health problems (CASA, 2011a-c; Clark, Lynch, Donovan, & Block, 2001; Kaminer & Bukstein, 2008); increased participation in risky

---

1. Michael S. Gordon and Steven B. Carswell, Friends Research Institute; Erica N. Peters, Battelle Memorial Institute; Susan Tangires, Friends Research Institute; Timothy W. Kinlock, School of Criminal Justice in the College of Public Affairs, University of Baltimore; Frank J. Vocci, Friends Research Institute; Lauren Restivo, ICF International. Correspondence concerning this article should be addressed to Michael S. Gordon, Friends Research Institute, Inc., 1040 Park Avenue, Suite 103, Baltimore, MD 21201. E-mail: mgordon@friendsresearch.org

sexual behaviors, including early age of sexual initiation and multiple partners (Carswell, Hanlon, O'Grady, & Watts, 2012; CASA, 2011a-c; Lee, McNeely, & Gourevitch, 2011); involvement in criminal activities resulting in arrest and incarceration (CASA, 2011a-c; Dembo & Sullivan, 2009; Mulvey, Schubert, & Chassin, 2010); and premature death (CASA, 2011a-c; Lee, McNeely, & Gourevitch, 2011).

Unfortunately, only 18% of individuals with a diagnosable substance use disorder (SUD) receive substance abuse treatment (SAMHSA, 2011). Empirically supported substance abuse treatment typically involves cognitive behavioral, motivational enhancement, and contingency management interventions and has been found to be efficacious in engendering abstinence (Dutra et al., 2008; Kinlock & Gordon, 2006). However, retention in treatment remains problematic (Coviello et al., 2012; Katz, Sears, Adams, Battjes, & Epoch Counseling Center, 2003; Williams & Chang, 2000). Less than half of admitted clients nationwide successfully complete substance abuse treatment and approximately 50% drop out of treatment after the first month (White, 2008). Quantitative and qualitative data suggest low treatment completion rates can be attributed to a wide variety of factors including lack of motivation, incarceration, schedule conflicts, geographic move, transportation issues, treatment costs, and a lower perceived need for treatment (CASA, 2011a-c; Kaminer, Burleson, & Burke, 2008; Katz et al., 2003). As such, new and innovative treatment strategies are needed to increase access to treatment services and to improve retention in substance abuse treatment.

Technology based interventions have the potential to improve access, delivery, dissemination, and effectiveness for individuals in need of substance abuse treatment (Marsch, 2011; Ondersma, Grekin, & Svikis, 2011) and have grown in popularity in recent years (Marsch, 2011; VanDeMark et al., 2010). From the treatment provider perspective, this growth in use of technology based interventions is driven primarily by the potential to: (a) increase treatment access, retention, and completion rates; (b) provide customized intervention content to clients; (c) enable widespread dissemination; and (d) reach individuals who typically may be difficult to engage in treatment (Marsch, 2011; Noar, Black, & Pierce, 2009). Moreover, through the use of technology based interventions, novel treatment approaches can be provided to individuals within and outside of traditional systems of care (e.g., criminal justice and medical facilities, home, schools). In addition, such treatment can be provided at relatively low costs, as primary expenses are related to the initial development of such technology with limited cost for implementation thereafter (Copeland, 2011; Marsch, 2011; Ondersma et al., 2011; VanDeMark et al., 2010). From the clients perspective, the growth in use of technology based interventions may be particularly appealing based on: (a) general familiarity and comfort using emerging technologies, especially among youth and young adults; (b) convenience; (c) ease of access; and (d) the ability to be anonymous (Marsch, 2011; Nunes et al., 2010). Given the stigma applied to people who struggle with SUDs, the opportunity for total anonymity may be especially appealing.

The Present Study

In this paper, the authors describe avatar assisted therapy (AAT), an innovative, technology based intervention via the Internet with the potential to improve access, retention, and outcomes in substance abuse treatment. AAT has only recently been implemented in substance abuse treatment, yet has shown promise due to its ability to overcome common barriers associated with traditional, in person treatment. Here the authors provide a detailed description of AAT, as well as the strengths and limitations that characterize this novel treatment modality. The authors present findings from a cross-sectional survey of current clients in one community based treatment program regarding their ability to consistently access the Internet (i.e., and thus the web-based AAT platform) and interest in receiving AAT as an alternative to the traditional in-person treatment format. The authors describe the development of a pilot study to evaluate AAT and provide considerations for future research studies that utilize AAT.

Description of Avatar Assisted Therapy

AAT is an emerging technology that has recently been used to treat individuals with SUDs. AAT uses the Internet to enable counselors and clients to interact from separate and remote locations in real time through the use of avatars, which are digital self-representations within virtual environments (Lee & Park, 2011; Nunes et al., 2010). Individuals participating in AAT must have access to a computer and consistent Internet service. Similar to a traditional, in person treatment format, AAT occurs at a regularly scheduled time and covers the same treatment content that would be provided in person. To initiate a treatment session at the appointed time, counselors and clients log into a secure web-based location, select an avatar to represent them, and take part in individual—or group-based treatment in virtual environments.

Strengths of AAT

Four essential features of AAT stand as strengths of this type of intervention relative to other technology-based interventions and in person treatment for SUDs. First, the relative ease of access to substance abuse treatment via Internet-based AAT enables the provision of treatment to clients who reside in remote geographic areas, or who may have transportation or scheduling issues that impede their ability to consistently attend in person treatment sessions (Dillon, 2011; Nagel & Anthony, 2011). Even for clients who live relatively close to their particular treatment program, travel to the program via public transportation may be time consuming, particularly when transfers from one bus to another are required. Clients may also lack sufficient funds to pay public transportation fares for weekly treatment sessions. Parents of youth in need of treatment may face difficulties transporting their children to and from weekly treatment sessions due to work schedules and may have safety concerns about them using public transportation. Other barriers to treatment that could be addressed through AAT may be gender-specific. For example, females may not desire to receive treatment in the same groups as men, perhaps because of trauma history, or may have more difficulty arranging for childcare in order to attend weekly treatment sessions. AAT can overcome these common barriers to traditional treatment access and delivery and may result in greater treatment engagement and retention.

Second, AAT is a unique technology-based intervention in that it allows counselors and clients to *interact* and *immerse* themselves in virtual environments—computer simulated, three dimensional representations of real or imagined places (Nagel & Anthony, 2011). Through avatars and virtual environments, AAT participants interact with one another in the same digital space by talking, walking, and gesturing. Participation in these types of interactive experiences stimulates a sense of connection with others and the virtual world, thereby creating the perception that AAT activities are reality (Blascovich & Bailenson, 2011; Nagel & Anthony, 2011; Rothbaum, Rizzo, & Difede, 2010). Treatment programs can design the virtual environment so that it closely resembles the actual physical space of their particular treatment program, with program logos, identical floor plans, and psychoeducational information that is posted on walls of treatment meeting rooms.

Third, and related to the above point, the virtual environment can be designed to resemble neighborhoods in which clients reside. Therefore, behavioral skills, such as drug refusal and effective communication skills can be enacted through AAT and translated to their day to day lives. That is, the use of virtual environments affords counselors the ability to repeatedly expose clients to life like drug related temptations and social situations, under controlled and safe conditions, in order to increase drug resistance and coping skills, and strengthen their capacity to engage in appropriate behavioral responses (Cho et al., 2008; Nagel & Anthony, 2011; Rothbaum et al., 2010). Such repeated exposure to drug related stimuli in order to reduce or eliminate ineffective responses forms the basis of cue exposure therapy. For example, this type of virtual environment treatment has been found to be efficacious in addressing tobacco use, especially when virtual environments were sufficiently complex in representing real places (e.g., bars, coffee shops, restaurants) and smoking related cues were evident (García-Rodríguez, Pericot-Valverde, Gutiérrez-Maldonado, Ferrer-García, & Secades-Villa, 2012). Other technology-based interventions, such as those delivered via teleconferencing or Skype, may lack the feeling of being in the same room as other individuals because of the use of single or multiple monitors. AAT, therefore, offers a distinct, deep sense of interaction and immersion that may especially promote treatment engagement.

Fourth, clients are able to maintain an unusual sense of anonymity in AAT. Although counselors are aware of clients' identities, clients receiving AAT are instructed to use pseudonyms and remain anonymous to one another, potentially increasing their comfort and the likelihood of them honestly reporting difficulties with abstinence and other sensitive issues (e.g., negative affect, illicit behaviors) (Dillon, 2011). Another reason why the anonymity afforded by AAT is so critical is because of the stigma facing people with SUDs; in fact, stigma may be so problematic that it can contribute to avoiding or delaying seeking treatment in a community setting. This may be particularly true for individuals who work in certain occupations (e.g., attorneys, doctors, police officers, public officials, and teachers); simply being seen entering the office of a substance abuse treatment program could be viewed as a personal disclosure for such individuals. Thus, potential clients who are concerned about privacy may be especially reluctant to initiate, engage, and/or attend in person treatment sessions. Individuals who feel stigmatized or have privacy concerns may prefer individual-based treatment. Yet, community-based treatment programs are predominated by group-based treatment, due to the cost effectiveness of this modality and limited staff resources. Hence, AAT may honor clients' preference for anonymity in a cost-effective manner.

Limitations of AAT

Although increased access to substance abuse treatment stands as a potential strength of the AAT platform, this increased access may be undermined by difficulties with consistent access to the Internet. Individuals with SUDs may not have sufficient income to afford consistent Internet access at their home or, due to chaotic living circumstances or transportation problems, may have difficulty consistently accessing the Internet in community locations such as public libraries, coffee shops, or restaurants. About 39-45% of clients in substance abuse treatment report having Internet access, although these rates appear to be higher for some individuals in treatment, such as those who are younger and who have higher education and income (Gandhi, Welsh, Bennett, Carreno & Himelhoch, 2009; McClure, Acquavita, Harding, & Stitzer, 2013).

Second, AAT may be limited by concerns about clients honestly presenting themselves for treatment in the virtual environment. Because counselors do not see the actual physical features of clients when immersed in the virtual environment, clients may not be physically present for the duration of an AAT-based treatment session or may ask others to participate in a treatment session. This would preclude clients from experiencing the full range of therapeutic benefits that may be provided by AAT. This may be particularly problematic for criminal justice clients who, based on their level of need and the severity of their involvement in substance abuse and criminal activity, could potentially benefit from the full complement of AAT treatment services. One solution for this potential problem is to have counselors periodically request that clients show a live "screen shot" of themselves. At treatment orientation, counselors can assist clients in creating a free account via Skype or another web-based calling service in which individuals can see each other. Clients can be required to log in to both the AAT virtual environment and Skype during a treatment session, and if any concerns about honest presentation occur, then counselors can request that clients show their faces to counselors via Skype. This screen shot is available to counselors only and thus preserves anonymity among clients.

Third, because the AAT platform occurs in a web-based virtual environment, there is a lack of face to face contact between counselors and clients. This lack of face to face contact may have untold consequences on therapeutic alliance and, potentially, treatment engagement. To minimize this concern, counselors may supplement AAT sessions with periodic in person treatment sessions. In fact, in person treatment sessions may be necessary for completing usual treatment requirements (e.g., reviewing and signing ongoing treatment plan reviews; performing urinalysis) and some specific sessions such as exit interviews. To preserve the essential AAT feature of anonymity, in person sessions can occur in an individual format.

Fourth, the handling of clinical emergencies, such as urgent suicidal ideation, in the AAT virtual environment may be a concern. For clients treated with AAT, emergencies are handled as if clients presented an emergency outside of an appointed in person treatment session. Depending on treatment program policies, this would entail the clinician calling 911 on behalf of the clients or recommending that the clients go to the nearest emergency room.

Finally, enthusiasm for AAT may be limited by the lack of available empirical data on its efficacy. Research on the efficacy of AAT to treat individuals with SUDs is growing, though findings have yet to be published in peer reviewed sources. Initial findings in non peer-reviewed sources, however, indicate promise for this type of technology-based intervention (Nagel & Anthony, 2011). One pilot study has been aimed at providing AAT to 70 rural youth in their homes (Dillon, 2011). These youth had difficulty attending in person treatment sessions because of distance, transportation, time, and/or money. Preliminary findings indicate that compared to youth who attended standard in person treatment sessions, youth who participated in AAT attended two and a half times more treatment sessions (Dillon, 2011). That is, youth who participated in standard treatment spent, on average, approximately six hours per month receiving substance abuse treatment, while AAT youth received, on average, five hours per week or approximately 20 hours per month of treatment (D. Dillon, personal communication, February 20, 2013). Importantly, the increased exposure to AAT translated to higher completion rates, with a significantly greater percentage of clients who received AAT completing treatment than those who received standard in person treatment (90% vs. 35%). Possible explanations for these positive findings may be related to the removal of barriers to attending in person treatment and greater interest of clients in the AAT platform. Data on the ability of AAT to produce substance abstinence have yet to be published in peer-reviewed scientific journals.

Ethical Considerations

The importance of reaching people struggling with SUDS who might not otherwise receive services in a traditional outpatient community-based treatment setting has led to the increased use and development of new technology-based interventions including AAT. Technology-based interventions bring potential benefits to both clients and clinicians. However, they also have significant legal and clinical considerations that need to be addressed prior to implementation, particularly if counseling services will be provided to clients across state jurisdictions (Baker & Ray, 2011; DeAngelis, 2012; Shaw & Shaw, 2006). Such concerns include issues regarding state jurisdiction, licensing requirements, restrictions on scope of practice, and legality. At the present time, no state specifically restricts the practice of AAT but it would be important for counselors contemplating AAT to recognize that they may be physically located in a different state than the clients receiving the services. In order to address such concerns, according to a national review of tele-health laws conducted by the American Psychological Association (APA, 2013), most states require that counselors be licensed in both their home state as well as the state in which their clients reside (DeAngelis, 2012). Some states, however, allow brief (10—to 30-day) counseling sessions under the "guest license provision" for out of state licensed counselors, but only on a temporary basis (APA, 2013). According to the APA, counselors are encouraged to collect information pertaining to their clients' states of residence prior to commencing treatment. If it is determined that a client resides in a different state than their counselor, the counselor would need to disclose this fact and address any differences in applicable state laws (American Counseling Association, 2014; National Board for Certified Counselors [NBCC], 2012). Further, in addition to meeting any qualifications required in the counselor's home state, if the counselor is not qualified to provide services in the state in which the potential client lives, a referral to a properly credentialed clinician in the client's home state should be provided (Shaw & Shaw, 2006).

There are clinical considerations that also need to be planned for in situations when AAT counseling services are provided from a distance using the Internet. It is important to plan for the possibility that a client may choose to switch from AAT to face to face counseling or that they may require a higher level of care. If the counselor does not maintain a physical location or is located too far from a client, referrals to other providers would need to be provided. Similarly, if a client experiences a clinical emergency or requires a transfer to a higher level of care, the counselor should have procedures in place to make appropriate referrals to providers who operate within a reasonable distance from the client. Prior to commencing AAT with any client, all of these issues should be explained as part of the treatment plan discussion.

With the emergence and increasing use of technology-based interventions in substance abuse treatment and associated research, new and unanticipated ethical dilemmas related to its use may impact human subject protection. Thus, researchers, practitioners, and institutional review boards may need to adapt and revise their standard policies and procedures to address issues related to: (a) privacy, (b) data transmission, and (c) HIPAA compliance. Moreover, clinic and research consent forms may need to incorporate technology related language that is understandable to both clients and research participants. Furthermore, if AAT is adopted by treatment clinics who receive referrals from the criminal justice system, it would be important to explain AAT and ensure that criminal justice partners are willing to accept AAT for clients who are court-ordered to complete treatment. In addition, appropriate procedures will need to be established to make certain that ongoing communication occurs between the two agencies to ensure that criminal justice clients are appropriately attending and receiving services.

AAT Pilot Study under Development

Because of the promise that AAT may hold for effectively addressing barriers to traditional in person substance abuse treatment, a pilot study to evaluate AAT is under development in one community-based outpatient substance abuse treatment program. Aims of the pilot study are to gather process data on clients' and clinicians' acceptance of AAT plus outcome data on treatment retention and abstinence. More broadly, aims are to gather sufficient evidence to justify offering AAT in other treatment programs and secure health insurance coverage for this type of intervention. Here, the authors report on the development of the AAT pilot study in this one treatment program.

Method

Description of Treatment Program

The treatment program is community-based (i.e., is not directly affiliated with an academic institution) and provides outpatient and intensive outpatient substance abuse behavioral treatment to youth and adults with SUDs. The treatment program operates in three locations, has been in operation for over 40 years, and is adjacent to a large metropolitan city in which there are high rates of substance abuse and criminal activity. The program provides evidence-based individual, group, and family treatment to clients, as well as mental health and anger management treatment. The program serves approximately 1,300 youth and adults per year, with approximately 60% percent of clients being uninsured at the time of admission and 85% having household incomes below $30,000. In 2011, approximately 70% of clients were male; 69% were White, 27% African American, and 4% Hispanic; and 17% were younger than 18, 32% were between 18-25 years of age, and 51% were 26 years of age or older. The most prevalent referral source was the criminal justice system (e.g., parole/probation, diversionary program, juvenile justice agency), constituting 76% of referrals. Other referral sources were healthcare providers (9%), employer or school (3%), and family members (1%); 10% were self-referred. Primary drugs of abuse were marijuana (45%), alcohol (33%), opiates/heroin (14%), cocaine (7%), and other (1%; e.g., benzodiazepines, PCP).

Initial Feasibility to Determine Interest in AAT

Although the treatment program had strong interest in offering AAT, documentation of clients' interest in AAT as well as clients' access to the Internet in order to effectively utilize AAT was critical before implementing the AAT pilot study. Therefore, a 7-item survey was administered to a convenience sample of youth and adults ($N = 164$) currently receiving outpatient treatment in the treatment program. The cross-sectional survey obtained self-report information regarding clients': (a) age and ethnicity, (b) parole/probation status, (c) barriers to engagement in standard in person outpatient treatment, and (d) consistent access to the Internet. The survey was administered over a one month period in January 2013. All survey procedures were approved by an accredited Institutional Review Board.

Table 1 presents results from the cross-sectional survey. Approximately one-fourth of the 164 clients, of which 121(71.9%) were under community supervision (i.e., probation or parole), reported they had difficulty attending treatment sessions because of employment and/or school obligations, lack of transportation, privacy/stigma, or other reasons. Overall, 69% of the participants indicated interest in receiving a computer-based treatment such as AAT. Moreover, access to the Internet was common, and slightly more than four fifths of those reporting interest in a computer based treatment such as AAT indicated that they had Internet access at home.

Pilot Study Participants

Based on initial feasibility findings with respect to AAT interest, the treatment is currently ongoing through a pilot study that is enrolling participants at the treatment program. To be eligible for participation in the AAT pilot study, individuals must: (a) be 18 years of age or older; (b) be a resident of the county where the treatment program is located; (c) provide no report of a current untreated psychiatric problem or suicidal ideation; and (d) report that they have Internet access at home or frequently access the Internet at a community location (e.g., public library). Individuals eligible for AAT were informed that participation in the study was completely voluntary and that, if they requested, they could be transferred to face to face counseling at the treatment center at any time. Individuals had to provide signed, informed consent to participate in the pilot study. Once enrolled in the study, AAT participants must meet the same requirements for successful treatment completion as clients receiving face to face treatment at the treatment program, including attendance in 16 treatment sessions, compliance with random drug urinalysis, and attendance in ancillary 12-step meetings.

From May 2013 through July 7, 2015, the AAT pilot study screened and acquired consent from 66 clients at two treatment sites. Of the 66 individuals who provided informed consent, 54 (81.8%) attended at least one AAT session and were enrolled in the ongoing pilot study.

Treatment Delivered

AAT is a technology-based platform through which evidence-based behavioral treatment is provided, that is, AAT provides the same treatment content that would be provided in person. The AAT manual developed for the pilot study is based on two sources. First, the AAT was aimed to be evidence-based, consistent with cognitive-behavioral treatment in the treatment program, and targeted to adults with cannabis use disorders. The first source was the treatment manual (Steinberg et al., 2005), developed for the Marijuana Treatment Project, the largest empirical study of behavioral treatments for cannabis use disorders to date (The Marijuana Treatment Project Research Group, 2004). Additional treatment sessions address topics regarding alcohol and tobacco; sex, drugs, and alcohol; sexually transmitted diseases; and nutrition and exercise from the evidence-based Living in Balance manual (Hoffman, Landrey & Caudill, 2003). AAT was provided in a group-based modality. All participants were given netbooks in order to effectively receive treatment through AAT.

Results

Participants ($N = 54$) were 75.5% male, 63.3% African American, and had a mean age of 26.7 years ($SD = 8.5$). In addition, 88.9% of participants were referred by the criminal justice system (primarily probation). They endorsed the following reasons to participate in AAT (reasons are not mutually exclusive): (a) transportation issues (73.5%); (b) interest in technology-based interventions (58.8%); (c) childcare issues (11.8%); and (d) preference for anonymity (8.8%). Of the 54 participants, six are currently receiving AAT treatment; thus, 48 participants (88.9%) are considered in the evaluable sample. Of the 48 participants, 43 (89.6%) attended at least three treatment sessions, which could be an indicator of early treatment engagement and the average total sessions to date is 11.3 (SD = 6.4). Only 52/184 (28.3%) urine specimens during treatment were positive for any illicit substance or alcohol; of which four clients accounted for 32.6% of those positive urine drug screens. Moreover, there were no reported new arrests or incarcerations during treatment.

Discussion

Research Considerations in Community-Based Treatment

In the process of developing the pilot study to evaluate AAT, several considerations of how to effectively implement AAT research in a community-based substance abuse treatment setting arose. These considerations included: adapting the treatment program's policies and procedures to the research study and to a non face to face intervention; conducting in person urinalysis (i.e., a required component of the treatment program) in the context of web-based treatment; conforming to regulating agencies' standards and contracts (e.g., probation and parole, drug courts); selecting and training counselors to deliver AAT; monitoring clinician fidelity to AAT treatment; and identifying and managing clients who lose equipment necessary to receive AAT (i.e., transitioning AAT clients to standard in person treatment if a loss of computer or consistent Internet access occurs). Although these considerations are not necessarily unique to the partnership between this research study and treatment program, they must be effectively resolved with input from both researchers and treatment program leadership before implementation of a randomized controlled trial can begin.

Although technology has been unevenly adopted in substance abuse treatment (Hogue, 2010; Johnson, Isham, Shah, & Gustafson, 2011), its use has recently been growing because of its potential to address pressing challenges faced by substance abuse treatment providers (Chiauzzi & Gammon, 2012; Marsch, 2011; VanDeMark et al., 2010). AAT is an emerging technology based intervention that may address barriers that typically undermine traditional, in person substance abuse treatment initiation, retention, and effectiveness. In immersive online environments, AAT participants interact with one another through the use of avatars. This innovative use of technology in substance abuse treatment enables wide spread dissemination of services and increased treatment access, and allows participants to remain anonymous during treatment sessions, potentially increasing honest disclosure of relapse or other treatment related difficulties.

However, AAT is not a technological panacea capable of mitigating all challenges faced by substance abuse treatment providers. AAT inherently has limitations related to: consistent Internet access and affordability; verification of clients' identity during treatment sessions; lack of face to face contact between counselors and clients and, during group based treatment, between clients themselves; and appropriate methods for handling clinical emergencies. Prior to the initiation of AAT in outpatient treatment settings, clinical protocols will need to be established and adapted to assess clients' treatment needs and determine those individuals best suited for participation in this type of web-based treatment. Notwithstanding these issues, AAT has the potential to dramatically alter the provision of therapeutic services to individuals in substance abuse treatment by reducing barriers to treatment that typically undermine optimal client outcomes.

Initial Evidence to Support ATT

Recent surveys of access to technology in substance abuse treatment clients (Gandhi et al., 2009; McClure et al., 2013) indicate that 39-45% of clients have Internet access. However, rates of Internet access were much higher in the current sample of clients receiving outpatient treatment in the treatment program in which AAT was implemented. Possible explanations for differences in rates of Internet access between the current study and that of prior studies may be differences in clients' age, education, and income, or differences in type of substance abuse treatment received (i.e., outpatient behavioral vs. opioid maintenance). In addition to evidence on clients' accessibility of AAT via the Internet, there was support for clients' acceptability of AAT. Surprisingly, few survey respondents indicated that barriers impacted treatment attendance. Survey respondents were clients already receiving in person treatment, which could account for having few reported problems attending in person sessions.

Implications for Future Research

Before dissemination of AAT can be considered, future studies are necessary to build the evidence base surrounding the acceptability, efficacy, and effectiveness of AAT. First, additional studies in other substance abuse treatment settings, through the use of randomized clinical trials, are needed to determine the feasibility and efficacy of AAT as compared to face to face treatment. Second, if AAT is reliably shown to be acceptable and efficacious in clients receiving substance abuse treatment, then further randomized clinical trials might compare AAT to other types of technology-based interventions (e.g., substance abuse treatment delivered via Skype). Research in varied settings, such as prisons, jails, community corrections (probation and parole), drug courts, hospitals, and schools, and in varied populations would attest to the generalizability of AAT findings. Finally, research may elucidate clients for whom AAT is most acceptable (e.g., clients with noted barriers to attending in person treatment) or least acceptable (e.g., clients with low computer literacy), plus counselors for whom AAT is most or least acceptable (i.e., depending on theoretical orientation).

Conclusion

ATT is an innovative delivery mechanism for evidence-based substance abuse treatment and may represent an important advancement in technology-based interventions for substance abuse. Although further research is needed, inherent strengths of AAT plus initial evidence on clients' interest in this type of intervention highlight the potential for AAT to become an effective, widespread substance abuse intervention. In addition, AAT might be attractive to criminal justice agencies and treatment providers serving individuals in rural geographical locations and clients who have transportation or anonymity concerns.

References

American Counseling Association. (2014). *ACA Code of Ethics*. Alexandria, VA: Author.

American Psychological Association. (2013). *Telepsychology 50-state review*. Legal & Regulatory Affairs. Retrieved from http://www.apapracticecentral.org/advocacy/state/telehealth-slides.pdf

Baker, K.D., & Ray, M. (2011). Brief communication: Online counseling: The good, the bad, and the possibilities. *Counseling Psychology Quarterly, 24*(4), 341-346.

Blascovich, J., & Bailenson, J. (2011). *Infinite Reality: Avatars, Eternal Life, New Worlds, and the Dawn of the Virtual Revolution*. New York: HarperCollins Publishers.

Carswell, S. B., Hanlon, T. E., O'Grady, K. E., & Watts, A. M. (2012, December 11). Correlates of risky sexual activity for urban African American youth in an alternative education program. *Education and Urban Society*. doi:10.1177/0013124512468005

Cho, S., Ku, J., Park, J., Han, K., Lee, H., Choim, Y. K., Shen, D. F. (2008). Development and verification of an alcohol craving–induction tool using virtual reality: Craving characteristics in social pressure situation. *CyberPsychology & Behavior, 11*, 302-309. doi:10.1089/cpb.2007.0149

Chiauzzi, E., & Gammon, J. (2012). *Recovery 2.0: Substance Abuse Treatment in a Technological World. Healthy Behavior Through Technology*. Newton, MA: Inflexxion, Inc.

Clark, D. B., Lynch, K. G., Donovan, J. E., & Block, G. D. (2001). Health problems in adolescents with alcohol use disorders: self-report, liver injury, and physical examination findings and correlates. *Alcoholism, Clinical & Experimental Research, 25*, 1350-1359. doi:10.1111/j.1530-0277.2001.tb02358.x

Copeland, J. (2011). Application of technology in the prevention and treatment of substance use disorders and related problems: Opportunities and challenges. *Substance Use & Misuse, 46*, 112-113. doi:10.3109/10826084.2011.521423

Coviello, D. M., Cornish, J. W., Lynch, K. G., Boney, T. Y., Clark, C. A., Lee, J. D., . . . O'Brien, C. P. (2012). A multisite pilot study of extended-release injectable naltrexone treatment for previously opioid-dependent parolees and probationers. *Substance Abuse, 33*, 48-59. doi:10.1080/08897077.2011.609438

Cox, R. G., Zhang, L., Johnson, W. D., & Bender, D. R. (2007). Academic performance and substance use: findings from a state survey of public high school students. *Journal of School Health, 77*, 109-115. doi:10.1111/j.1746-1561.2007.00179.x

DeAngelis, T. (2012). Practicing distance therapy, legally, and ethically. *American Psychological Association, 43*(3), 52. Retrieved from http://www.apa.org/monitor/2012/03/virtual.aspx

Dembo, R., & Sullivan, C. (2009). Cocaine use and delinquent behavior among high-risk youths: a growth model of parallel processes. *Journal of Child & Adolescent Substance Abuse, 18*, 274-301. doi:10.1080/10678280902973278

Dillon, D. (2011, July). Avatar Assisted Therapy: And other technological innovations shaping the future of treatment. Symposium conducted at the NIATx Summit and SAAS National Conference, Boston, MA.

Dutra, L., Stathopoulou, G., Basden, S. L., Leyro, T. M., Powers, M. B., & Otto, M. W. (2008). A meta-analytic review of psychosocial interventions for substance use disorders. *American Journal of Psychiatry, 165*, 179-187. doi:10.1176/appi.ajp.2007.06111851

Gandhi, D., Welsh, C., Bennett, M., Carreno, J., & Himelhoch, S. (2009). Acceptability of technology-based methods substance abuse counseling in office based buprenorphine maintenance for opioid dependence. *The American Journal on Addictions, 18,* 182-183. doi:10.1080/10550490902772553

Garcia-Rodriguez, O., Pericot-Valverde, I., Gutierrez-Maldonado, J., Ferrer-Garcia, M., & Secades-Villa, R. (2012). Validation of smoking-related virtual environments for cue exposure therapy. *Addictive Behaviors, 37,* 703-708. doi:10.1016/j.addbeh.2012.02.013

Hoffman, J., Landrey, M. J., & Caudill, B. (2003). *Living in Balance.* Center City, MN: Hazelden Foundation.

Hogue, A. (2010). When technology fails: getting back to nature. *Clinical Psychology: Sciences and Technology (New York), 17,* 77-81. doi:10.1111/j.1468-2850.2009.01196.x

Johnson, K., Isham, A., Shah, D. V., & Gustafson, D. H. (2011). Potential roles for new communication technologies in treatment of addiction. *Current Psychiatry Reports, 13,* 390-397. doi:10.1007/s11920-011-0218-y

Kaminer, Y., & Bukstein, O. G. (Eds.). (2008). *Adolescent Substance Abuse: Psychiatric Comorbidity and High-Risk Behaviors.* New York, NY: Routledge/Taylor & Francis.

Kaminer, Y., Burleson, J. A., & Burke, R. H. (2008). Efficacy of outpatient aftercare for adolescents with alcohol use disorders: a randomized controlled study. *Journal of the American Academy of Child & Adolescent Psychiatry, 47,* 1405-1412. doi: 10.1097/CHI.0b013e318189147c

Katz, E. C., Sears, E. A., Adams, C. A., Battjes, R. J., & The Epoch Counseling Center Adolescent Treatment Team. (2003). *Group-Based Treatment for Adolescent Substance Abuse.* Bloomington, IL: Chestnut Health Systems.

Kinlock, T. W., & Gordon, M. S. (2006). Substance abuse treatment: New research. In L. A. Bennett (Ed.), *New Topics in Substance Abuse Treatment* (pp. 73-111). Hauppauge, NY: Nova Science Publishers, Inc.

Lee, J. D., McNeely, J., & Gourevitch, M. N. (2011). Management of associated medical conditions. In P. Ruiz & E. Strain (Eds.), *Substance Abuse: A Comprehensive Textbook.* (5th ed.). Baltimore, MD: Lippincott Wiliams & Wilkins.

Marsch, L. A. (2011). Technology-based interventions targeting substance use disorders and related issues: an editorial. *Substance Use & Misuse, 46,* 1-3. doi: 10.3109/10826084.2011.521037

McClure, E. A., Acquavita, S. P., Harding, E., & Stitzer, M. L. (2013). Utilization of communication technology by patients enrolled in substance abuse treatment. *Drug and Alcohol Dependence, 129,* 145-150. doi:10.1016/j.drugalcdep.2012.10.003

McNicholas, L. (2004). Clinical Guidelines for the Use of Buprenorphine in the Treatment of Opioid Addiction (Treatment Improvement Protocol (TIP) Series 40). Rockville, MD: Center for Substance Abuse Treatment.

Mulvey, E. P., Schubert, C. A., & Chassin, L. (2010). *Substance Use and Delinquent Behavior Among Serious Adolescent Offenders.* Washington, DC: U.S. Department of Justice, Office of Juvenile Justice and Delinquency Prevention.

Nagel, D. M., & Anthony, K. (2011). Avatar therapy. *The Capa Quarterly, 3,* 6-9.

National Board for Certified Counselors (NBCC). (2012). *NBCC Policy Regarding the Provision of Distance Professional Services.* Retrieved from http://www.nbcc.org/Assets/Ethics/NBCCPolicyRegardingPracticeofDistanceCounselingBoard.pdf

Noar, S. M., Black, H. G., & Pierce, L. B. (2009). Efficacy of computer technology-based HIV prevention interventions: a meta-analysis. *AIDS, 23,* 107-115.

Nunes, D., Daly, B., Rao, K., Borntrager, C., Rohner, K., & Shrestha, S. (2010). *Technology and the Adolescent: Pairing Modern Mesia and Technology with Mental Health Practice*. Baltimore, MD: University of Maryland, Center for School Mental Health.

Ondersma, S. J., Grekin, E. R., & Svikis, D. (2011). The potential for technology in brief interventions for substance use, and during-session prediction of computer-delivered brief intervention response. *Substance Use & Misuse, 46*, 77-86. doi: 10.3109/10826084.2011.521372

Rothbaum, B. O., Rizzo, A. S., Difede, J. (2010). Virtual reality exposure therapy for combat-related posttraumatic stress disorder. *Annals of the New York Academy of Sciences, 1208*, 126-132. doi:10.1111/j.1749-6632.2010.05691.x

Shaw, H.E., & Shaw, S.F. (2006). *Journal of Counseling & Development, 84*, 41-53.

Steinberg, K. L., Roffman, R. A., Carroll, K. M., McRee, B., Babor, T. F., Miller, . . . Stephens, R. (2005). *Brief Counseling for Marijuana Dependence: A Manual for Treating Adults*. Rockville, MD: Center for Substance Abuse Treatment, Substance Abuse and Mental Health Services Administration.

Substance Abuse and Mental Health Administration (SAMHSA). (2011). *Results from the 2010 National Survey on Drug Use and Health: Summary of National Findings* [NSDUH Series H-41, HHS Publication No. (SMA) 11-4658]. Rockville, MD: SAMHSA.

The Marijuana Treatment Project Research Group. (2004). Brief treatments for cannabis dependence: findings from a randomized multisite trial. *Journal of Consulting and Clinical Psychology, 72*, 455-466. doi:10.1037/0022-006X.72.3.455

The National Center on Addiction and Substance Abuse (CASA) at Columbia University. (2011a). *Adolescent substance use: America's #1 public health problem*. New York: CASA.

The National Center on Addiction and Substance Abuse (CASA) at Columbia University. (2011b). *CASA analysis of the National Survey on Drug Use and Health (NSDUH), 2009* [Datafile]. Rockville, MD: U.S. Department of Health and Human Services, Substance Abuse and Mental Health Services Administration.

The National Center on Addiction and Substance Abuse (CASA) at Columbia University. (2011c). *National Survey of High School Students, Parents of High School Students, and High School Personnel*. New York: CASA.

VanDeMark, N. R., Burrell, N. R., Lamendola, W. F., Hoich, C. A., Berg, N. P., & Medina, E. (2010). An exploratory study of engagement in a technology-supported substance abuse intervention. *Substance Abuse Treatment, Prevention, and Policy, 5*, 10. doi: 10.1186/1747-597X-5-10

White, W. L. (2008). *Recovery Management and Recovery-Oriented Systems of Care: Scientific Rationale and Promising Practices* (Vol. 6). Chicago: Great Lakes Addiction Technology Transfer Center, Northeast Addiction Technology Transfer Center, and the Philadelphia Department of Behavioral Health/Mental Retardation Services.

Williams, R. J., & Chang, S. Y. (2000). A comprehensive and comparative review of adolescent substance abuse treatment outcome. *Clinical Psychology: Science and Practice, 7*, 138-166.

Table 1
Interest in and Access to Avatar Assisted Therapy

Characteristic	Total Sample (N = 164)
Race, n (%)	
African American	43 (26.5)
Caucasian	102 (63.0)
Other	17 (10.5)
Mean age (SD)	32.3 (11.9)
Age category, n (%)	
Less than 18	8 (4.9)
18-25	55 (34.0)
26+	99 (66.1)
On Probation/Parole, n (%)	121 (73.8)
Problems attending treatment, n (%)	42 (25.6)
Employment	21 (12.8)
Transportation	18 (11.0)
School	4 (2.4)
Privacy/Stigma	4 (2.4)
Other	14 (8.5)
Interest in computer-based treatment, n (%)	103 (68.7)
Consistent Internet access at home, n (%)	112 (74.7)
Internet access through local community resource, n (%)	76 (50.7)

Note. Two participants did not report race. Two participants did not report age. Reasons for other problems attending treatment: children, distance, do not like leaving home, family, medical, money, distance, Narcotics Anonymous commitments, and other appointments.

8

Best Practices in Counseling Gay Male Youth with Substance Use Disorders

Michael D. Brubaker and Michael P. Chaney[1]

Gay male youth have consistently reported higher rates of drug and alcohol use than heterosexual males within their same age cohort, using between two to five times higher across substances (Marshal et al., 2008). However, many counselors are not adequately trained to treat this population from a culturally responsive perspective. Thus, this article highlights best clinical practices to effectively counsel gay male youth with substance use disorders (SUDs). For the purposes of this article, the United Nations (2001) definition of youth will be used, which includes individuals who are between 15 and 24 years.

The odds of gay male youth using alcohol in the last 30 days are almost doubled as is binge drinking when compared to heterosexual male youth (Rosario et al., 2014). Higher alcohol usage rates persist as these youth continue into their college years (Hatzenbuehler, Corbin, & Fromme, 2008). Tobacco use is also significantly higher among sexual minority youth, with cigarette usage at 36% compared to 14% among heterosexual youth (Rosario et al., 2014). Gay and lesbian youth report

---

[1]. Michael D. Brubaker, School of Human Services, University of Cincinnati; Michael P. Chaney, Department of Counseling, Oakland University. Correspondence concerning this article should be addressed to Michael D. Brubaker, P.O. Box 210068, University of Cincinnati, Cincinnati, OH 45224. E-mail: michael.brubaker@uc.edu

smoking at a younger age and have a higher likelihood of ever having been a daily smoker (Corliss et al., 2014). Illicit drug use among gay male youth is also significantly higher with marijuana, ecstasy, cocaine, heroin, amphetamines, methamphetamine, ketamine, and LSD/mushrooms rates all exceeding those of heterosexual male youth (Corliss et al., 2010; Hegna & Rossow, 2007; Lampinen, McGhee, & Martin., 2006). In fact, among 12-17 year old males, the odds of using illicit drugs are over five times that of heterosexual males (Corliss et al., 2010). This higher risk begins to taper off into young adulthood (18-23 year olds), but still remains at twice that of their heterosexual counterparts (Corliss et al., 2010). These higher usage rates subsequently translate to increased risk for substance use disorders among gay youth (Fergusson, Horwood, & Beautrais, 1999; Noell & Ochs, 2001).

Although there remains a dearth of research on ethnic minority gay male youth, preliminary findings suggest that ethnic minority gay, lesbian, and bisexual youth populations also use at higher rates than their heterosexual counterparts. Newcomb, Birkett, Corliss, and Mustanski, (2014) found that Latino gay youth use illicit drugs at comparable rates to White gay youth, and African American youth who identify their sexual orientation as unsure or bisexual use at higher rates, closer to Whites, than do African American heterosexual youth. When examining the prevalence of alcohol use disorders by ethnicity, gay or bisexual youth met 12-month alcohol abuse or dependence criteria as follows: Black—4.2%, Latino—11.1%, White—12.3%, and Other—8.1%, (Burns, Ryan, Garofalo, Newcomb, & Mustanski, 2015). As found in other studies, being Black was associated with lower dependence rates (Burns et al., 2015). More research is needed to understand the broader SUD rates among ethnic minority gay males.

Recent substance use trends further underscore discrepancies between heterosexual and nonheterosexual male youth. For example, nonmedical prescription drug (NMPD) use has become a growing problem among the general population of youth, and use among gay male youth is even higher. Gay male youth have four times the risk of using NMPDs than their heterosexual cohort (Corliss et al., 2010). They initiate use of NMPDs at younger ages and as they get older, continue to use at higher rates than their heterosexual peers (Corliss et al., 2010), often obtaining these drugs from within their own households (Kecojevic et al., 2012).

Gay youth are not exempt from the common problems associated with substance use including diminished academic performance, mental health problems, reduced cognitive functioning, body image issues, auto accidents and death (Blashill & Safren, 2014; Goldstein, 2011; Jacobus, Bava, Cohen-Zion, Mahmood & Tapert, 2009; Pompili et al., 2012). Gay youth also report more risky sexual behavior, with a 2.5 times greater chance of having unprotected sex during their last sexual intercourse than heterosexual males (Rosario et al., 2014). They are also 1.6 times as likely to use drugs the last time they had intercourse (Rosario et al., 2014), a factor that may be leading to the greater odds of unprotected sex. The higher rates of substance use and related consequences for this population suggest the need for greater attention among counseling professionals.

Due to the disproportionate rates of substance use among gay male youth and the negative consequences associated with their use, it is crucial for counselors to be adequately prepared to treat this high-risk population. Therefore, the purpose of this article is to highlight substance use trends, identify underlying causes of increased usage, and to explore best practices to counsel gay youth needing treatment for substance use disorders. In order to illuminate these practices, the authors provide a case vignette of a gay male student who struggles with a SUD. The implications of using gay-affirming practices as well as future research are discussed.

Etiology of SUDs among Gay Male Youth

Professional literature is replete with studies and theories about the etiology of SUDs. Though a detailed description of all of the theories is beyond the scope of this article, briefly, two theories seem particularly relevant to gay male youth who abuse substances. Sociocultural theories posit that the interaction of social and cultural factors contribute to the etiology of SUDs (Stevens & Smith, 2013). These factors include environmental support of use, cultural attitudes and beliefs about use, and familial influences. Grounded in systems theory, the biopsychosocial systems model conceptualizes SUDs as resulting from the confluence of systemic, social, psychological, and biological factors (Buchman, Skinner, & Illes, 2010). This model takes macrosocial systems factors into consideration as contributing to the etiology of SUDs. It should also be noted that these factors are among the many that may contribute to substance use disorders and are not necessarily the sole cause. In the following sections, the aforementioned constructs are utilized as a framework to explicate substance use among gay male youth. Specifically, the influence of gay male identity development, minority stress and internalized heterosexism, gay male socialization, and sexual behavior is explored.

Gay Male Identity Development

As a young male comes into awareness of his identity as gay, certain markers along the gay male identity developmental process may contribute to the development of a SUD. Researchers have identified these milestones in previous studies as first awareness of one's sexual or affectional attractions to members of the same gender and initial sexual experiences emerge (Friedman, Marshal, Wright, & Stall, 2007; Marshal, Friedman, Stall, & Thompson, 2009). For many gay males, the aforementioned developmental milestones can be a great source of stress, anxiety, shame and fear. As a way to cope with these powerful emotions, some individuals may use mood-altering substances. Another noteworthy developmental event that may be associated with substance use is disclosure of sexual orientation to others. Carrion and Lock (1997) described the process of coming out as a combination of verbalizing one's sexual identity to others and also integrating one's sexual orientation into all other aspects of living and being. Research has underscored the relationship between sexual orientation disclosure issues and substance use. Rosario, Schrimshaw, and Hunter (2009) found that individuals who do not come out are at increased risk for developing a SUD. Other studies have shown that negative reactions from others postdisclosure to be related to substance use (Goldbach, Tanner-Smith, Bagwell, & Dunlap, 2014).

Minority Stress and Internalized Heterosexism

Physical and emotional stress associated with being a member of a historically stigmatized cultural group has been termed *minority stress* (DiPlacidio, 1998). Gay male youth are at increased risk for experiencing minority stress as a result of living in a heterosexist society. Meyer (2003) theorized that nonheterosexual individuals' emotional and social well-being is compromised as a result of heterosexist stressors. Negative experiences (discrimination, bullying, violence, etc.) and negative attitudes from others or towards oneself (internalized heterosexism, concealment of sexual orientation, etc.) are major sources of stress. Long-term psychological stress experienced by sexual minorities as a result of living in an oppressive culture might lead to impairments in the ability to regulate emotions, resulting in negative feelings (Hatzenbuehler, 2009). Due to the inability to self-regulate the negative affect, some gay male youth may develop unhealthy coping strategies such as substance use. Past studies support the argument that minority stress is linked to substance use among nonheterosexuals (Goldbach, Schrager, Dunlap, & Holloway, 2015; Goldbach et al., 2014). For example, in one of the largest studies focused on experiences of LGB youth, Goldbach et al. (2015) found that the minority stress model may partially explain increased marijuana use among this population. Additionally, a great deal of research has found relationships between internalized heterosexism, experiences of heterosexism, and substance use (Amadio, 2006; Szymanski & Gupta, 2009; Weber, 2008). Examples of heterosexist experiences that contribute to the development of substance use among gay male youth include bullying and familial rejection.

Bullying. The Gay, Lesbian, and Straight Education Network (GLSEN) conducts annual nationwide surveys to assess the school climate for sexual minority and gender nonconforming students. Consistent with prior years, their 2013 survey data illustrated how bullying is prevalent and creates the conditions that promote substance use among gay youth. For example, it was found that over the prior 12 months, 74.1% of LGBT students were verbally harassed because of their sexual orientation, 36.2% were physically harassed, 16.5% were physically assaulted, and 49% experienced electronic harassment (GLSEN, 2015). The survey also revealed that among LGBT students who experienced some form of bullying, almost 57% did not report the incident to school staff. An implication of not seeking help from others is that bullying experiences could result in youth feeling isolated, depressed, and helpless. Additionally, not seeking help from staff can result in continuation of the victimization. As a means to cope with ongoing victimization and stress associated with bullying, some gay male youth might turn to substance use (Bontempo & D'Augelli, 2002; Goldbach et al., 2014; Marshal et al., 2009).

Lack of familial support. For many gay males, disclosing one's sexual orientation to family members becomes part of integrating his sexual orientation into his overall identity. Not coming out has been found to lead to anxiety and lower self-esteem (Jordon & Deluty, 1998). However, many gay males choose not to come out due to fear of rejection from significant others. How others, particularly parents, respond to the disclosure can strongly influence substance use among gay male youth. For example, gay and bisexual males who had disclosed their sexual orientations to their parents and whose parents were not supportive, engaged in more binge drinking than gay and bisexual males whose parents were supportive (Rothman, Sullivan, Keyes, & Boehmer, 2012). This finding is consistent with other research that found parental negative reactions to sexual orientation disclosure had a significant negative effect on substance use. Specifically, lack of parental acceptance postdisclosure can increase the risk of substance use and mood disorders among gay and bisexual male youth (Padilla, Crisp, & Rew, 2010; Ryan, Huebner, Diaz, & Sanchez, 2009). The mere perception of having unsupportive parents may be related to higher levels of substance use among gay male youth. At the other extreme, negative reactions may come in the form of domestic violence, a predictive factor for many gay male youth who runaway from home and engage in higher rates of substance use (Rosario, Schrimshaw & Hunter, 2012).

Socio-Sexual Causes

In addition to the aforementioned causes of substance use among gay male youth, two additional variables may also contribute to high rates of SUD. First, the influence of gay male socialization likely influences substance use. Historically, there were limited places for gay men to connect and socialize. As a result, secret "underground" gathering places, clubs, and bars emerged, often in undesirable locations within urban areas. In the 1970s and 1980s, gay bars became more visible and a common socializing hub for many gay men. Today, gay bars and clubs continue to represent a safe space where gay men are able to socialize without negative repercussions (Chaney & Brubaker, 2014). According to Ghaziani and Cook (2005), gay bars not only represent a place for gay males to congregate, but gay bars are a place where gay cultural norms are learned. Because alcohol and other drugs are often consumed in the context of a gay bar or club, some gay males may view this behavior as a cultural norm. This rationale is consistent with findings from a study that found involvement with gay men and/or regular attendance at gay bars to be related to alcohol and poly-substance use (Lea, Reynolds, & de Wit, 2013).

These findings have implications for gay male youth. Though increasing, there continue to be few safe alcohol and drug-free social spaces in which gay male youth are able to gather. As a result, some youth may be drawn toward gay bars and clubs seeking out other members of the LGB communities. Frequenting bars and clubs may lead gay male youth to engage in alcohol and other drug use while in these venues (Goldbach & Steiker, 2011; Jordan, 2000). Moreover, initial involvement in gay-related activities such as attending events in gay bars and clubs increases the risk of youth engaging in alcohol and marijuana use (Rosario, Schrimshaw, & Hunter, 2004). Further, as gay male youth become more connected to the LGB communities and increase their LGB social networks, their risk of drug use also increases (Wright & Perry, 2006). This is due, in part, to more opportunities to engage in substance use as gay male youths' increase the number of LGB individuals in their social circles.

Another variable that may contribute to the high rates of substance use among gay male youth is related to the sexual behavior of this population. First, to help minimize feelings of anxiety, shame, and guilt associated with same-sex sexual desires and/or initial sexual experiences, some gay male youth may integrate drugs and alcohol into the sexual activity (Chaney & Brubaker, 2014). One negative consequence of incorporating drugs and alcohol into sexual activity is that some gay male youth engage risky behaviors in which they might not otherwise engage such as unprotected sexual activity. Recent reports show that among all males (13 years and older) newly diagnosed with HIV, gay and bisexual males represent 81% of these cases (Center for Disease Control and Prevention , 2015). A second sex-related factor that contributes to the high rates of substance use among gay male youth is sexual sensation seeking. Sexual sensation seeking, the proclivity to search for peak levels of sexual stimulation and to participate in new sexual behaviors, particularly among gay males, has been linked to substance use (Kalichman & Cain, 2004). A recent study found that among young (mean age 18.5 years) men seeking men (MSM), sensation seeking was related to alcohol and drug use prior to engaging in risky sexual behavior (Newcomb, Clerkin, & Mustanski, 2011). All of the aforementioned causes may influence substance use, and competent counselors must assess to what extent these dynamics exist within their own clients and how to effectively address such concerns in treatment.

Counseling Gay Male Youth

With higher substance usage rates, the need for effective substance abuse treatment is essential for gay male youth, but it is uncertain how many actually seek treatment. Among the general population of 12-17 year olds, utilization rates are exceptionally low with only 9.1% of those in need actually receiving treatment (Substance Abuse and Mental Health Services Administration, 2014). For gay male youth, this lower rate may be offset by the fact that adult gay male populations seek substance abuse treatment over their lifetimes at nearly twice the rate of heterosexual males (McCabe, West, Hughes, & Boyd, 2013). To date, studies on utilization rates among gay male youth do not exist.

Although there is great need for SUD treatment in the gay male community, there remains a lack of training among practitioners and supportive climates that protect LGBT clients from discrimination (Matthews, Selvidge, & Fisher, 2005). Gay and lesbian adults report that counselors and agencies are not affirming (Matthews & Selvidge, 2005) and commonly support discriminatory practices (Matthews, Lorah, & Fenton, 2006). Among 144 of the nation's adolescent treatment centers, Brannigan, Schackman, Falco and Millman (2004) found that only 12% were meeting the unique needs of gay and lesbian adolescent clients (e.g., specialized groups). Unsupportive treatment climates and a lack of cultural competence likely diminish treatment outcomes and may prevent initial utilization.

Out of the need to address the concerns of sexual minority populations, substance abuse treatment agencies have developed specialized services such as coming out groups, and in some cases creating whole centers that only serve LGBT individuals and families (Adam & Guttierrez, 2011). Chaney and Brubaker (2014) noted that such groups provide the advantage of normalizing the unique experiences of gay youth and the space for young men to critically evaluate heterosexism and minority stress in a safe environment with peer support. The prevalence of specialized services is difficult to pinpoint as most programs have overrepresented the availability of these services (Cochran, Peavy, & Robohm, 2007), and gay youth are commonly integrated into the general population with little to no specialized support. As a part of these specialized services, a few clinicians have attempted to modify evidence-based practices (EBPs) to better serve gay youth.

Adapting Evidence-Based Approaches for Gay Male Youth

Among three top national registries of EBP, including the National Registry of Evidence-Based Programs and Practices (NREPP), Evidence-Based Practices Substance Abuse Database, and Stop Underage Drinking, there are currently no programs identified as being effective with gay male youth. Steiker (2008) reported that some agencies serving LGBT youth supplement their interventions by adding examples of gay youth to the materials used in evidence-based programs, much as they do when serving other minority populations. Much rarer is the formal adaptation of EBP, none of which has been recognized by the national registries. Four such modified interventions are discussed below.

Motivational interviewing (MI) is an evidence-based approach, which Parsons, Lelutiu-Weinberger, Botsko, and Golub (2014) adapted to address substance use and unprotected anal intercourse (UAI) among young gay and bisexual men. In comparison to standard education sessions about drug use and UAI, the MI intervention was more effective, reducing drug use by 67% compared to 50% in the educational intervention. Although the outcomes of this adaptation are promising, the details of the intervention are not readily available nor are they recognized on the national registries of EBPs.

Cognitive behavioral therapy (CBT) is a commonly used theory in evidence-based approaches that Craig, Austin, and Alessi (2013) have adapted for serving addicted sexual minority youth, including those who identify as gay, lesbian, bisexual and queer. Where traditional CBT has been critiqued for its focus on the individual over the environment, as well as deficits over strengths, this modified approach is designed to empower youth, collaboratively identifying client strengths, and distinguishing between environmental realities (i.e., heterosexism) and cognitive distortions. Although not fully discussed by the researchers, this approach would require extensive cultural training on the contextual realities of gay male youth.

More recently, Reback and Shoptaw (2014) developed a gay-specific CBT approach that was combined with contingency management (CM) for older youth and adults (18 and older). CM, a recognized EBP among heterosexual youth and adults (nrepp.samhsa.gov), involves adjusting a client's environment to maximize the potential for continued abstinence and to reward behaviors that promote abstinence (Stanger, Ryan, Scherer, Norton, & Budney, 2015). The researchers found comparable reductions in substance use when compared to gay-specific CBT alone, but those who received the combined treatment reported significantly fewer sexual partners. From a holistic health perspective, there appears to be advantages to this combination of EBP.

Keepin' it REAL, is an evidence-based prevention program adapted across multiple cultural groups through a National Institutes of Health funded multisite grant. Goldbach and Steiker (2011) modified this approach to LGBT youth using grounded theory methods to solicit client input and determine how to effectively change the program materials to be more culturally relevant. Participants identified the need for gender-non-specific names (e.g., Jessie) and pronouns (e.g., hir) in the intervention materials and the need to include more references to sexual activity and participation in "adult gay situations," such as sneaking into gay bars when describing high risk activities. The youth also rejected claims that the stressors are completely different between "gays" and "straights," but recognized there was an added layer of stress related to being a sexual minority. To date, the outcomes of this modified intervention are yet to be reported. Furthermore, like CBT, *Keepin' it REAL* has not been adopted to meet the specific needs of gay male youth separate from the larger grouping of sexual minorities, and may require additional modifications to do so effectively.

In total, there is little information about the effectiveness of adapted EBPs and the degree to which they may improve treatment outcomes; however, these programs use many gay-affirming practices to make materials relevant and to recognize the larger contextual factors that increase minority stress and impede recovery. Such practices are consistent with best practices in providing gay-affirming treatment.

Gay Affirming Treatment

When using gay-affirming treatment approaches for clients with SUDs, counselors create a safe and supportive space where youth may explore and accept their identities as gay individuals and better understand the interplay between sexual orientation, social marginalization, and SUDs (Chaney & Brubaker, 2014). They also recognize the strengths of gay youth including their resilience in coping with negative environmental stressors (Herrick, Egan, Coulter, Friedman, & Stall, 2014). Upon initial contact with gay youth, counselors assess sexual identity development and determine appropriate individual and family counseling interventions (Chaney & Brubaker, 2014). Attending to the language of gay youth culture is also important, using relevant treatment examples and scenarios (Goldbach & Steiker, 2011). By creating safe and affirming spaces, gay youth may develop needed skills and strategies to overcome minority stress and build positive supports among friends, in their school, and at home (Chaney & Brubaker, 2014).

Chaney and Brubaker (2014) suggested attending to eight topics when offering gay-affirming counseling services, each of which is offered here with applications pertaining to gay youth. This model utilizes a holistic, wellness approach for gay youth (Dew, Myers & Wightman, 2006; Myers & Sweeney, 2004) that aligns with the Association for Lesbian, Gay, Bisexual, and Transgender Issues in Counseling (ALGBTIC) *Competencies for Counseling with Lesbian, Gay, Bisexual, Queer, Questioning, Intersex, and Ally Individuals* (2013). This is not intended as an exhaustive list, but rather an initial list of key counseling considerations. Counselors are encouraged to consult the ALGBTIC (2013) *Competencies* as well as the *2014 American Counseling Association (ACA) Code of Ethics* for additional considerations with gay male youth.

1. **Association and socialization.** As gay male youth engage with peers and older adults who use substances, it is important to explore socialization patterns and affiliations that may promote substance use. The use of phone applications, social media, and the internet should all be assessed, especially as these youth may seek out sex partners and use substances.

2. **Heterosexism and internalized heterosexism.** Given the high rates of bullying, harassment and violence against gay youth, counselors

should assess for these events and any related trauma (Goldbach, Fisher, & Dunlap, 2015) and provide education concerning the relationship between marginalization, internalized heterosexism, and —SUDs. Exploring the meaning of gay male identity is particularly important as these youth may use substances in a compensatory manner to counter negative societal messages.

3. **Social support.** While seeking to reduce their substance use, gay male youth will benefit from positive social supports including affirming parents, teachers, peers, gay-straight alliances, and affirming mutual support groups (Birkett & Espelage , 2009; Heck, Flentje, & Cochran, 2011).

4. **Family issues.** Assessing the degree of family support, whether or not the client has come out to his family, and their reactions are all important when counseling gay male youth (Padilla et al., 2010). If a client has not come out, counselors should explore with their clients how families have reacted to other out gay men and adolescents, be they family members, neighbors, or even public figures in the media. This information may provide an indication of gay-affirming family support clients may or may not receive while in the early stages of recovery.

5. **Same-sex sexual behavior.** Counselors who practice gay-affirming treatment will engage in developmentally appropriate discussions about risky same-sex behavior among gay male youth and the role that substances have played in managing difficult emotions or facilitating sexual experiences (Parsons et al., 2014; Rosario et al., 2014). Examples of such discussions may include safe-sex practices and an exploration of how certain drugs may be used prior or during sexual encounters.

6. **Sexually-transmitting infections (STIs) and other medical issues.** Age appropriate discussions about sexual behavior, needle sharing, and the impact of substance use on one's physical and mental health can empower gay male youth to make informed decisions and engage in harm reduction strategies should they continue to use. Discussions about condoms, needle-exchange programs, and maintaining emergency doses of naloxone (Narcan) may be warranted, depending on the age of the youth and type of drugs being used.

7. **Multiple oppressed identities.** When working with ethnic minority youth, it is important to explore the intersectionality of multiple identities (Wynn & West-Olatunji, 2009). As youth move through this

period of identity development, it is important that counselors understand the fluidity of this process and how young clients may be self-empowered to identify themselves as they deem appropriate. In this conversation, counselors need to be culturally competent, discussing the client's worldview and deconstructing how culture defines gay manhood. The *Multicultural and Social Justice Counseling Competencies* (MSJCC; Ratts, Singh, Nassar-McMillan, Butler, & McCullough, 2015) are an essential resource to this end. Education about minority stress and its connection to substance use behavior is particularly important in these conversations.

8. **Religion and spirituality.** Although there are increasingly affirming supports among religions, there remains much religious abuse that occurs towards young gay men (Wood & Conley, 2014). This abuse may come in many forms including religiously enshrouded verbal assaults from spiritual leaders, bullying in order to conform to the norms of the community, or neglect when seeking support during the coming out process (Wood & Conley, 2014). Gay male youth in early recovery may need guidance in navigating such difficult terrain, especially if they have not come out to their family and/or faith community. Again, conversations about minority stress and social supports may enhance awareness about substance abuse triggers and strategies to build a recovery network.

Together, these topics and strategies serve to address many of the particular needs of gay youth with SUDs. The follow section will present a case to better exemplify these practices.

Case Study

Mikhail is a 19 year old Chaldean American. He referred himself to counseling because he realized that his drug use was compromising his physical health and college grades, but he said, "I can't seem to stop!" An extensive psychosocial assessment of Mikhail revealed the following: Mikhail was born and raised in Iraq, but immigrated to the United States with his parents and four older brothers when he was seven years old. He did not speak English when he arrived to the States, but picked up some English from watching cartoons and watching American music videos.

Due to his limited English speaking skills, he had a difficult time socializing and succeeding academically in elementary school. Though his early academic experiences were a struggle, he excelled in high school and is currently a first year, pre-medicine student at a reputable university in a large Midwest, metropolitan city.

Mikhail reported that he "always knew" he was gay, but had never told anyone especially his family because "they are super strict Roman Catholics." Mikhail started exploring his sexual identity as soon as he left home to attend college, meeting other young, gay males with whom he would socialize. Even though he was underage, he regularly snuck into gay bars and circuit parties. His initiation to drugs began with taking "Molly" (ecstasy) and snorting cocaine, which was introduced to him by his friends to enhance the club experience. "The rush was amazing! From the beginning, I just wanted more." Although he had no sexual experiences prior to attending college, he began engaging in sexual activities with multiple partners while intoxicated. He reported that the ecstasy and cocaine enhanced the sexual experience ("it makes sex totally hot") and helped him not to feel guilty. Upon further questioning, Mikhail revealed that he sometimes smokes crystal meth prior to having sex and finds himself wanting "Tina" (the street name for crystal methamphetamine) even when he is not engaged in sexual activity. Recently, Mikhail was diagnosed with gonorrhea, but has been treated and is no longer infected.

Increasingly, Mikhail has distanced himself from his family and primarily socialized with his gay friends. He stated, "They get me. They accept me for me, and I do not have to hide who I am with them. There is no room in my Chaldean life for me to be gay. My parents would disown me, and the church says I am going to hell!" Although he was not failing his current courses, his grades were rapidly declining and he cut classes to "PNP" (party-n-play) with guys he met on Grindr, a phone application used to meet gay men online. Realizing his life was "falling apart," Mikhail pleaded, "I'm letting my family down. I'm letting myself down. This isn't who I am. I need help."

At the onset of counseling, Mikhail was referred to the campus medical center for a complete medical assessment. Mikhail and his counselor then worked together to craft a treatment plan that integrated cognitive-behavioral strategies and contingency management interventions to help him achieve his treatment goals because this combination has been found to be exceptionally effective for gay males who struggle with stimulant use disorders, particularly methamphetamine (Shoptaw et al., 2005). Mikhail agreed to abstain from all mood-altering substances and attend a minimum of three 12-step meetings per week during a one-month period. Additionally, he agreed to have daily contact with a 12-step sponsor. Once these goals were met, Mikhail and his counselor started to explore in greater depth some of the unique factors that had contributed to his substance use. These factors include his identities as a gay, Chaldean male, internalized shame, fears about coming out to his family, and the relationship between his drug use and sexual behavior.

One facet of a gay-affirming approach to substance abuse treatment involves counselors communicating acceptance of nonheterosexual orientations (Hill, 2009). When Mikhail revealed his sexual identity, rather than pathologizing Mikhail or expressing surprise, his counselor replied, "It took a lot of courage for you to share that. Thank you for trusting me enough to tell me." These types of nonjudgmental, strengths-based responses demonstrate empathy.

Gay-affirming substance abuse treatment also involves exploring how an individual's sexual orientation intersects with other aspects of his/her identities (Chaney & Brubaker, 2014; Hill, 2009). Gathering information about Mikhail's spiritual and religious beliefs and their influence on his sexual orientation was crucial. The Association for Spiritual, Ethical, and Religious Values in Counseling (ASERVIC) *Spiritual Competencies* suggests that clinicians acknowledge and explore clients' spiritual and religious beliefs because they can influence a client's well-being (2009). Over several sessions, Mikhail's counselor explored the following questions: How does your Chaldean heritage view individuals who identify as gay? What does masculinity mean to you and how is it expressed by Chaldeans? What does it mean for you to be a gay, Chaldean male? How would you describe your relationship with the Roman Catholic church and how its teachings have affected your identity? Once these questions had been processed, Mikhail and his counselor objectively examined how these areas may have contributed to his use of substances.

Throughout the counseling process, the counselor worked with Mikhail to help him understand the influences of oppression and shame on the development and maintenance of his substance use. When utilizing a gay-affirmative approach to substance abuse treatment, it is imperative to teach clients about internalized shame associated with heterosexist messages and attitudes and its relationship to substance use (Chaney &

Brubaker, 2014). The MSJCC refer to this process as helping clients to develop critical consciousness, or the ability to deconstruct social myths that are commonly used to marginalize others (Ratts et al., 2015).

Gay-affirming substance use treatment providers should understand that most non-heterosexual clients will have what Johnson (2012) called a coming out narrative. The narrative could be related to coming out to oneself or to others. In the case of Mikhail, his narrative is multi-faceted. During the counseling process, Mikhail came to realize that some of his substance use was a way to regulate anxiety associated with hiding his identity from family and a perceived fear of rejection if he chose to disclose his orientation. In counseling, a decision matrix was utilized to explore the pros and cons of coming out to his family. With the counselor's help, Mikhail decided he would come out to an aunt to whom he felt particularly close. This intervention followed the recommendations of the MSJCC (2015) to assist clients with identifying family or friends who might serve as sources of support. In session, Mikhail and his counselor engaged in coming out role-plays, which provided Mikhail the opportunity to anticipate various reactions to his disclosure. Decisions about coming out should be made with extreme caution. Disclosure may not be the right decision for all clients.

An important component of gay-affirming substance abuse counseling is for counselors to discuss same-sex sexual behavior with clients (Chaney & Brubaker, 2014). Due to Mikhail demonstrating a pattern of high-risk behaviors including combining drugs and sexual activities, having multiple partners, and contracting a sexually transmitted infection, the counselor included sexual health education as part of treatment plan. Further, because substance use and sexual behavior is linked to unprotected sex among gay males (Kashubeck-West & Szymanski, 2008), the counselor collaborated with Mikhail on crafting a risk reduction plan. Action steps that comprised the risk reduction plan included (a) decrease the number of sex partners, (b) make condoms easily accessible at all times, and (c) engage in lower risk sexual behaviors (e.g., masturbation, oral sex rather than anal intercourse, etc.). The counselor also explored the meaning of substance use in relation to sexual activity by asking questions about Mikhail's feelings, thoughts, and attitudes about same-sex sexual behavior. In counseling, Mikhail came to realize that he felt a great deal of sexual shame. The counselor helped Mikhail to understand the origins of his sexual shame by discussing its potential relationships to his cultural and spiritual backgrounds and internalized heterosexism, which allowed Mikhail to externalize some of the shame.

This case study illustrates how substance use can be strongly influenced by one's sexual identity. That is not to say that a gay sexual orientation is the problem, rather the consequences of living in a heterosexist culture can contribute to and maintain SUDs among many gay males. Mikhail's story also underscores characteristics of a gay-affirming approach for treating SUDs among gay male youth.

Conclusion and Future Directions

Given the higher rates of substance use among gay male populations, much of which is rooted in stressors associated with being a sexual minority, there is a great need for counselors to understand and adopt best practices for serving this population. As noted in the prior case discussion, engaging with gay youth requires counselors to understand family and societal biases that often become internalized and may lead to increased substance use. One danger that unprepared counselors may encounter is the temptation to ostracize gay culture, suggesting to their clients that socializing with other gay males might be problematic. By doing so, counselors risk failing to see the deeper social marginalization of the gay community, much of which drives alcohol and drug use. Counselors may be well-equipped to serve this unique population by helping clients deconstruct heteronormative messages, develop affirming social supports, and engage in intrapsychic and interpersonal healing.

More collaborative research is needed to understand how to effectively adapt and create new EBP, using the language and examples of the population, as well as addressing the concerns posed by critics of traditional approaches that fail to address the larger systemic concerns. These practices need to be evaluated, and when shown to be effective, recognized by the national registries of EBP.

For these programs to be effective, it is essential that agencies and clinicians embrace gay–affirming practices that respect gay culture and relationships. Agencies can demonstrate this by offering regular safe-space education and in-service training on how to effectively work with gay youth (Chaney & Brubaker, 2014). Modifying intake forms to include nonheterosexist language, challenging oppressive attitudes and biased assumptions among colleagues, and displaying safe-space stickers may all be ways to increase the climate of treatment programs. Counselors working within agencies are needed to advocate for such changes and track outcomes to evaluate the success of programs in attracting and retaining sexual minority clients. Together, these changes can foster a more therapeutic and socially-just climate for gay male youth.

References

Adam, M., & Guttierrez, V. (2011). Working with gay men and lesbian women with addiction concerns. In G. W. Lawson & A. W. Lawson (Eds.), *Alcoholism and substance abuse in diverse populations* (pp. 2 13—225). Austin, TX: Pro-Ed.

ALGBTIC LGBQQIA Competencies Taskforce, A. L. C., Harper, A., Finnerty, P., Martinez, M., Brace, A., Crethar, H. C., . . . & Kocet, M. (2013). Association for Lesbian, Gay, Bisexual, and Transgender Issues in Counseling Competencies for Counseling with Lesbian, Gay, Bisexual, Queer, Questioning, Intersex, and Ally Individuals: Approved by the ALGBTIC Board on June 22, 2012. *Journal of LGBT Issues in Counseling, 7*(1), 2-43.

Amadio, D. M. (2006). Internalized heterosexism, alcohol use, and alcohol-related problems among lesbians and gay men. *Addictive Behaviors, 31*, 1153-1162. doi: 10.1016/j.addbeh.2005.08.013

American Counseling Association. (2014). *Code of Ethics*. Alexandria, VA: Author.

Association for Spiritual, Ethical, and Religious Values in Counseling. (2009). *Spiritual competencies*. Retrieved fres/

Birkett, M. A., & Espelage, D. L. (2009). LBG and questioning students in schools: The moderating effects of homophobic bullying and school climate on negative outcomes. *Journal of Youth and Adolescence, 38*, 989-1000. doi:10.1007/s10964-008-9389-1

Blashill, A. J., & Safren, S. A. (2014). Sexual orientation and anabolic-androgenic steroids in U.S. adolescent boys. *Pediatrics, 133*, 469-475. doi:10.1542/peds.2013-2768

Bontempo, D. E., & D'Augelli, A. R. (2002). Effects of at-school victimization and sexual orientation on lesbian, gay, or bisexual youths' health risk behavior. *Journal of Adolescent Health, 30*, 364-374.

Brannigan, R., Schackman, B. R., Falco, M., & Millman, R. B. (2004). The quality of highly regarded adolescent substance abuse treatment programs. *Archives of Pediatrics & Adolescent Medicine, 158*, 904-909. doi:10.1001/archpedi.158.9.904

Buchman, D. Z., Skinner, W., & Illes, J. (2010). Negotiating the relationship between addiction, ethics, and brain science. *American Journal of Bioethics Neuroscience, 1*(1), 36-45. doi: 10.1080/21507740903508609

Burns, M. N., Ryan, D. T., Garofalo, R., Newcomb, M. E., & Mustanski, B. (2015). Mental health disorders in young urban sexual minority men. *Journal of Adolescent Health, 56*, 52-58. doi:10.1016/j.jadohealth.2014.07.018

Carrion, V. G., & Lock, J. (1997). The coming out process: Developmental stages for sexual minority youth. *Clinical Child Psychology and Psychiatry, 2*(3), 369-377. doi: 10.1177/1359104597023005

Centers for Disease Control and Prevention. (2015). *HIV among gay and bisexual men*. Retrieved from http://www.cdc.gov/hiv/group/msm/index.html

Chaney, M. P., & Brubaker, M. (2014). The impact of substance abuse and addiction in the lives of gay men, adolescents, and boys. In M. M. Kocet (Ed.), *Counseling gay men, adolescents, and boys: A strengths-based guide for helping professionals and educators* (pp. 109-128). New York: Routledge.

Cochran, B. N., Peavy, K. M., & Robohm, J. S. (2007). Do specialized services exist for LGBT individuals seeking treatment for substance misuse? A study of available treatment programs. *Substance Use & Misuse, 42*, 161—176.

Corliss, H. L., Rosaria, M., Wypij, D., Wylie, S. A., Frazier, A. L., & Austin, S. B. (2010). Sexual orientation and drug use in a longitudinal cohort study of U.S. adolescents. *Addictive Behaviors, 35,* 517-521. doi:10.1016/j.addbeh.2009.12.019

Corliss, H. L., Rosario, M., Birkett, M. A., Newcomb, M. E., Buchting, F. O., & Matthews, A. K. (2014). Sexual orientation disparities in adolescent cigarette smoking: Intersections with race/ethnicity, gender, and age. *American Journal of Public Health, 104,* 1137-1147. doi:10.2105/AJPH.2013.301819

Craig, S. L., Austin, A., & Alessi, E. (2013). Gay affirmative cognitive behavioral therapy for sexual minority youth: A clinical adaptation. *Clinical Social Work Journal, 41,* 258-266. doi:10.1007/s10615-012-0427-9

Dew, B. J., Myers, J. E., & Wightman, L. F. (2006). Wellness in adult gay males. *Journal of LGBT Issues in Counseling, 1,* 23-40. doi:10.1300/J462v01n01_03

DiPlacidio, J. (1998). Minority stress among lesbians, gay men, and bisexuals: A consequence of heterosexism, homophobia, and stigmatization. In G. M. Herek (Ed.), *Stigma and sexual orientation: Understanding prejudice against lesbians, gays, and bisexuals* (pp. 138-159). Thousand Oaks, CA: Sage.

Fergusson, D. M., Horwood, L. J., & Beautrais, A. L. (1999). Is sexual orientation related to mental health programs and suicidality in young people? *Archives of General Psychiatry, 56,* 876-880.

Friedman, M. S., Marshal, M. P., Wright, E. R., & Stall, R. (2007). Early gay-related development, adolescent victimization and adult health outcomes among gay and bisexual males. *AIDS Behavior, 12,* 891-902.

Gay, Lesbian, & Straight Education Network. (2015). *The 2013 National School Climate Survey.* Retrieved from www.glsen.org.

Ghaziani, A., & Cook, T. D. (2005). Reducing HIV infections at circuit parties: From description to explanation and principles of intervention design. *Journal of the International Association of Physicians in AIDS Care, 4*(2), 32-46. doi:10.1177/1545109705277978

Goldbach, J., Fisher, B. W., & Dunlap, S. (2015). Traumatic experiences and drug use by LGB adolescents: A critical review of minority stress. *Journal of Social Work Practice in the Addictions, 15,* 90-113. doi:10.1080/1533256X.2014.996227

Goldbach, J. T., Schrager, S. M., Dunlap, S. L., & Holloway, I. W. (2015). The application of minority stress theory to marijuana use among sexual minority adolescents. *Substance Use & Misuse, 50*(3), 366-375. doi:10.3109/10826084.2014.980958

Goldbach, J. T., & Steiker, L. K. H. (2011). An examination of cultural adaptations performed by LGBT-identified youths to a culturally grounded, evidence-based substance intervention. *Journal of Gay and Lesbian Social Services, 23,* 188-203. doi:10.1080/10538720.2011.560135

Goldbach, J. T., Tanner-Smith, E. E., Bagwell, M., & Dunlap, S. (2014). Minority stress and substance use in sexual minority adolescents: A meta-analysis. *Prevention Science, 15,* 350-363. doi:10.1007/s11121-013-0393-7

Goldstein, M. A. (2011). Adolescent substance abuse. *The Mass General Hospital for Children Adolescent Medicine Handbook, 3,*155-165. doi:10.1007/978-1-4419-6845-6_19

Hatzenbuehler, M. L. (2009). How does sexual minority stigma "get under the skin"? A psychological mediation framework. *Psychological Bulletin, 135,* 707-730. doi:10.1037/a0016441

Hatzenbuehler, M. L., Corbin, W. R., & Fromme, K. (2008). Trajectories and determinants of alcohol use among LGB young adults and their heterosexual peers: Results from a prospective study. *Developmental Psychology, 44*, 81-90.

Heck, N. C., Flentje, A., & Cochran, B. N. (2011). Offsetting risks: High school gay-straight alliances and lesbian, gay, bisexual, and transgender (LGBT) youth. *School Psychology Quarterly, 26*, 161-174. doi:10.1037/a0023226

Hegna, K., & Rossow, I. (2007). What's love got to do with it? Substance use and social integration for young people categorized by same-sex experience and attractions. *Journal of Drug Issues, 37*, 229-255.

Herrick, A. L., Egan, J. E., Coulter, R. W. S., Friedman, M. R., & Stall, R. (2014). Raising sexual minority youths' health levels by incorporating resiliencies into health promotion efforts. *American Journal of Public Health, 104*, 206-210. doi:10.2105/AJPH.2013.301546

Hill, N. L. (2009). Affirmative practice and alternative sexual orientations: Helping clients navigate the coming out process. *Clinical Social Work Journal, 37*, 346-356. doi: 10.1007/s10615-009-0240-2

Jacobus, J., Bava, S., Cohen-Zion, M., Mahmood, O., & Tapert, S. F. (2009). Functional consequences of marijuana use in adolescents. *Pharmacology Biochemistry and Behavior, 92*, 559-565. doi:10.1016/j.pbb.2009.04.001

Johnson, S. D. (2012). Gay affirmative psychotherapy with lesbian, gay, and bisexual individuals: Implications for contemporary psychotherapy research. *American Journal of Orthopsychiatry, 82*(4), 516-522. doi:10.1111/j.1939-0025.2012.01180.x

Jordan, K. M. (2000). Substance abuse among gay, lesbian, bisexual, transgender, and questioning adolescents. *School Psychology Review, 29*(2), 201-206.

Jordan, K. M., & Deluty, R. H. (1998). Coming out for lesbian women: Its relations to anxiety, positive affectivity, self-esteem, and social support. *Journal of Homosexuality, 35*, 41-63.

Kalichman, S. C., & Cain, D. (2004). A prospective study of sensation seeking and alcohol use as predictors of sexual risk behaviors among men and women receiving sexually transmitted infection clinic services. *Psychology of Addictive Behaviors, 18*, 367-373.

Kashubeck-West, S. K., & Szymanski, D. M. (2008). Risky sexual behavior in gay and bisexual men: Internalized heterosexism, sensation seeking, and substance use. *The Counseling Psychologist, 36*(4), 595-614. doi:10.1177/0011000007309633

Kecojevic, A., Wong, C. F., Schrager, S. M., Silva, K., Bloom, J. J., Iverson, E. & Lankenau, S. E. (2012). Initiation in prescription drug misuse: Differences between lesbian, gay, bisexual, transgender (LGBT) and heterosexual high-risk young adults in Los Angeles and New York. *Addictive Behaviors, 37*, 1289-1293. doi:10.1016/j.addbeh.2012.06.006

Lampinen, T. M., McGhee, D., & Martin, I. (2006). Increased risk of "club" drug use among gay and bisexual high school student in British Columbia. *Journal of Adolescent Health, 38*, 458-461. doi:10.10 16/j.jadohealth.2005.04.0 13

Lea, T., Reynolds, R., & de Wit, J. (2013). Alcohol and club drug use among same-sex attracted young people: Associations with frequenting the lesbian and gay scene and other bars and nightclubs. *Substance Use & Misuse, 48*, 129-136. doi:10.3109/10826084.2012.733904

Marshal, M. P., Friedman, M. S., Stall, R., King, K. M., Miles, J., Gold, M. A., & Morse, J. Q. (2008). Sexual orientation and adolescent substance use: A meta-analysis and methodological review. *Addiction, 103*, 546-556.

Marshal, M. P., Friedman, M. S., Stall, R., & Thompson, A. L. (2009). Individual trajectories of substance use in lesbian, gay and bisexual youth and heterosexual youth. *Addiction, 104*, 974-981. doi:10.1111/j.1360-0443.2009.02531.x

Matthews, C. R., Lorah, P., & Fenton, J. (2006). Treatment experiences of gays and lesbians in recovery from addiction: A qualitative inquiry. *Journal of Mental Health Counseling, 28*, 110-132.

Matthews, C. R., & Selvidge, M. M. D. (2005). Lesbian, gay, and bisexual clients' experiences in treatment for addiction. *Journal of Lesbian Studies, 9*, 79-90.

Matthews, C. R., Selvidge, M. M. D., & Fisher, K. (2005). Addictions counselors' attitudes and behaviors toward gay, lesbian, and bisexual clients. *Journal of Counseling & Development, 83*, 57-65.

McCabe, S. E., West, B. T., Hughes, T. L., & Boyd, C. J. (2013). Sexual orientation and substance abuse treatment utilization in the United States: Results from a national survey. *Journal of Substance Abuse Treatment, 44*, 4-12.

Meyer, I. H. (2003). Prejudice, social stress, and mental health in lesbian, gay, and bisexual populations: Conceptual issues and research evidence. *Psychological Beliefs, 129*, 674-697.

Myers, J. E., & Sweeney, T. J. (2004). The indivisible self: An evidence-based model of wellness. *Journal of Individual Psychology, 60*, 234-245.

Newcomb, M. E., Birkett, M., Corliss, H. L. & Mustanski, B. (2014). Sexual orientation, gender, and racial differences in illicit drug use in a sample of high school students. *American Journal of Public Health, 104*, 304-310. doi:10.2105/AJPH.2013.301702

Newcomb, M. E., Clerkin, E. M., & Mustanski, B. (2011). Sensation seeking moderates the effects of alcohol and drug use prior to sex on sexual risk in young men who have sex with men. *AIDS Behavior, 15*, 565-575. doi:10.1007/s10461-010-9832-7

Noell, J. W., & Ochs, L. M. (2001). Relationship of sexual orientation to substance use, suicidal ideation, suicide attempts, and other factors in a population of homeless adolescents. *Journal of Adolescent Health, 29*, 31-36.

Padilla, Y. C., Crisp, C., & Rew, D. L. (2010). Parental acceptance and illegal drug use among gay, lesbian, and bisexual adolescents: Results from a national survey. *Social Work, 55*, 265-275.

Parsons, J. T., Lelutiu-Weinberger, C., Botsko, M., & Golub, S. A. (2014). A randomized control trial utilization motivational interviewing to reduce HIV risk and drug use in young gay and bisexual men. *Journal of Consulting and Clinical Psychology, 82*, 9-18. doi:10.1037/a0035311

Pompili, M., Serafini, G., Innamorati, M., Biondi, M., Siracusano, A., Di Giannantonio, M., . . . Moller-Leimkuhler, A. M. (2012). Substance abuse and suicide risk among adolescents. *European Archives of Psychiatry and Clinical Neuroscience, 262*, 469-485. doi:10.1007/s00406-012-0292-0

Ratts, M. J., Singh, A. A., Nassar-McMillan, S., Butler, S. K., & McCullough, J. R. (2015). *Multicultural and social justice counseling competencies*. Retrieved from http://www.multiculturalcounseling.org/index.php?option=com_content&view=article&id=205:amcd-endorses-multicultural-and-social-justice-counseling-competencies&catid=1:latest&Itemid=123

Reback, C. J., & Shoptaw, S. (2014). Development of an evidence-based, gay-specific cognitive behavioral therapy intervention for methamphetamine-abusing gay and bisexual men. *Addictive Behaviors, 39*, 1286-1291. doi:10.1016/j.addbeh.2011.11.029

Rosario, M., Corliss, H. L., Everett, B. G., Srisner, S. L., Austin, B., Buchting, F. O., & Birkett, M. (2014). Sexual orientation disparities in cancer-related risk behaviors of tobacco, alcohol, sexual behaviors, and diet and physical activity: Pooled youth risk behaviors surveys. *American Journal of Public Health, 104*(2), 245-254.

Rosario, M., Schrimshaw, E., & Hunter, J. (2004). Predictors of substance use overtime among gay, lesbian, and bisexual youths: An examination of three hypotheses. *Addictive Behaviors, 29*(8), 1623-1631.

Rosario, M., Schrimshaw, E., & Hunter, J. (2009). Disclosure of sexual orientation and subsequent substance use and abuse among lesbian, gay, and bisexual youths: Critical role of disclosure reactions. *Psychology of Addictive Behaviors, 23*, 175-184.

Rosario, M., Schrimshaw, E. W., & Hunter, J. (2012). Risk factors for homelessness among lesbian, gay, and bisexual youths: A developmental milestone approach. *Children and Youth Services Review, 34*, 186-193. doi:10.1016/j.childyouth.2011.09.016

Rothman, E. F., Sullivan, M., Keyes, S., & Boehmer, U. (2012). Parents' supportive reactions to sexual orientation disclosure associated with better health: Results from a population-based survey of LGB adults in Massachusetts. *Journal of Homosexuality, 59*, 186-200. doi:10.1080/00918369.2012.648878

Ryan, C., Huebner, D., Diaz, R. M., & Sanchez, J. (2009). Family rejection as a predictor of negative health outcomes in White and Latino lesbian, gay, and bisexual young adults. *Pediatrics, 123*, 346-352.

Shoptaw, S., Reback, C. J., Peck, J. A., Yang, X., Rotheram-Fuller, E., Larkins, S., ... Hucks-Ortiz, C. (2005). Behavioral treatment approaches for methamphetamine dependence and HIV-related sexual risk behaviors among urban gay and bisexual men. *Drug and Alcohol Dependence, 78*, 125-134. doi:10.1016/j.drugalcdep.2004.10.004

Stanger, C., Ryan, S. R., Scherer, E. A., Norton, G. E., & Budney, A. J. (2015). Clinic—and home-based contingency management plus parent training for adolescent cannabis use disorders. *Journal of the American Academy of Child & Adolescent Psychiatry, 54*(6), 445-453. doi:10.1016/j.jaac.2015.02.009

Steiker, L. K. H. (2008). Making drug and alcohol prevention relevant: Adapting evidence-based curricula to unique adolescent cultures. *Family & Community Health, 31*, S52-S60. doi:10.1097/01.FCH.0000304018.13255.f6

Stevens, P., & Smith, R. L. (2013). Etiology of substance abuse: Why people use. In *Substance abuse counseling: Theory and practice* (5th ed., pp. 98-121). Boston, MA: Pearson.

Substance Abuse and Mental Health Services Administration. (2014). *Results from the 2013 national survey on drug use and health: Summary of national findings.* (NSDUH Series H-48, HHS, Publication No. SMA 14-4863). Rockville, MD: Author.

Szymanski, D. M., & Gupta, A. (2009). Examining the relationship between multiple internalized oppressions, African American lesbian, gay, bisexual, and questioning persons' self-esteem and psychological distress. *Journal of Counseling Psychology, 56*(1), 110-118. doi:10.1037/a0011298l

United Nations General Assembly. (2001). *Implementation of the world programme of action for youth to the year 2000 and beyond: Report of the Secretary General* (56th session, A/56/180). Retrieved from http://www.youthpolicy.org/basics/ 2001_WPAY_Implementation_Report.pdf

Weber, G. N. (2008). Using to numb the pain: Substance use and abuse among lesbian, gay, and bisexual individuals. *Journal of Mental Health Counseling, 30*(1), 31-48.

Wood, A. W., & Conley, A. H. (2014). Loss of religious or spiritual identities among the LBGT population. *Counseling and Values, 59*, 95-111. doi:10.1002/j.2161-007X.2014.00044.x

Wright, E. R., & Perry, B. L. (2006). Sexual identity distress, social support, and the health of gay, lesbian, and bisexual youth. *Lesbian, Gay, Bisexual, and Transgender Health, 5*, 81-110. doi:10.1300/J082v51n01_05

Wynn, R., & West-Olatunji, C. W. (2009). Use of culture-centered counseling theory with ethnically diverse LGBT clients. *Journal of LGBT Issues in Counseling, 3*, 198-214.

9

The Importance of Storytelling for Older Women in Alcoholics Anonymous

Lauren S. Ermann, Gerard Lawson, and Penny L. Burge[1]

Aging and Storytelling

As adults age, telling stories about life experiences can be a beneficial process. Butler (1963) first introduced the idea of the life review process, and suggested its importance for older adults. He described it as a, "naturally occurring, universal mental process characterized by the progressive return to consciousness of past experiences" (p. 66). Haber (2006) illustrated that Erikson's (1950) eighth stage of psychosocial development, integrity vs. despair, was positively influenced by conducting life reviews, by minimizing despair and helping to acquire ego integ-

---

1. Lauren S. Ermann, Department of Counselor Education, Radford University; Gerard Lawson and Penny L. Burge, Department of Educational Research and Evaluation, Virginia Tech. The manuscript is based on data from a doctoral dissertation. Data from the dissertation is also used in other original manuscripts but focus and findings are not replicated. Correspondence concerning this article should be addressed to Lauren Ermann, Department of Counselor Education, Radford University, P.O. Box 6994, Radford, VA, 24142. Email: lermann@radford.edu

rity. Gergen and Gergen (1983) identified that when configuring self-narratives, the storyteller must create, "coherent connections among life events" (p. 255). Parker (1995) found that although heavily researched, there had been no successful attempts thus far to solidify the concept of reminiscence into a theory, so she proposed applying Atchley's (1989) Continuity Theory of Normal Aging as a theoretical framework when evaluating reminiscence. According to Atchley, "Continuity Theory thus offers a parsimonious explanation for and description of the ways adults employ concepts of their past to conceive of their future and structure their choices in response to the changes brought about by normal aging" (p. 183). Parker suggested that memory recall through reminiscence is integral for an individual to maintain a sense of continuity. She asserted that, "individuals build these life stories as they age, and these stories incorporate past events into an organized sequence, giving them a personal meaning and a sense of continuity" (p. 521).

Battista and Almond (1973) defined meaning as "positive life regard" (p. 410). While the experience of searching for meaning is an important component of human existence throughout one's life (Frankl, 1959), it can be particularly important in older age due to significant losses in dimensions of family, health and independence. For older adults, "making meaning" of their life experiences can be a positive means to counter the losses associated with aging (Kropf & Tandy, 1998).

Alcoholics Anonymous (AA) and Storytelling

AA was established by Bill Wilson and Dr. Bob Smith circa 1935 as method of achieving alcoholism recovery (Alcoholics Anonymous World Services, 2001). The only requirement of AA members is a desire to cease drinking. With anonymity being paramount, AA strives to achieve complete abstinence following the motto, "one day at a time" (Alcoholics Anonymous, n.d.).

The narrative element (storytelling) is inextricably linked to AA (Cain, 1991; Humphreys, 2000; Jensen, 2000; Pollner & Stein, 1996). Narratives told in AA can be viewed as a model, demonstrating the definition and meaning of alcoholism to other members. An individual then determines if she is an alcoholic by comparing her story with those of other alcoholics in AA. Cain (1991) explains this process,

As the AA member learns the AA story model, and learns to place the events and experiences of his own life into the model, he learns to tell and to understand his own life as an AA life, and himself as an AA alcoholic (p. 215).

Humphreys (2000) further described the AA narrative by presenting five types of AA stories including the "Drunk-a-Log." This type of story, commonly depicted in the *Big Book*, described a member's "personal account of descent into alcoholism and recovery through A.A." (p. 498). As the member grew to better understand the AA process, her drunk-a-log narratives were reconstructed in ways that better articulated the AA philosophy using the model, "experience, strength, and hope" and "what we used to be like, what happened, and what we are like now" (Jensen, 2000, p.11).

Gaps in Research

While some literature exists that addresses women in AA (Alcoholics Anonymous World Services, 2001; Blume, 1991; Beckman, 1993; Katz, 2002; Matheson & McCollum, 2008; Nakken, 2002; The National Center on Addiction and Substance Abuse at Columbia University, 2006; Pagliaro & Pagliaro, 2000; Sanders, 2006; Timko, Moos, Finney & Connell, 2002; Travis, 2009) or older adults in AA (Alcoholics Anonymous World Services, 2001; Mosher-Ashley & Rabon, 2001; Rathbone-McCuan, 1988; Satre, Blow, Chi, & Weisner, 2007; Satre, Mertens, Areán, & Weisner, 2004; Schiff, 1988; Washburn, 1996), there is a dearth of scholarship specific to older women in AA. To address these notable gaps, the author conducted a novel study to better understand the lived experiences of older women in AA through their eyes. Specific themes emerged from this research including the topic of this paper which addresses the importance of storytelling for older women in AA. Here again, there exists a sizeable gap in the literature. While current research articulates the benefits of storytelling in the aging process (Butler, 1963; Gergan & Gergan, 1983; Haber, 2006; Parker, 1995), or explains the model of, and value in, storytelling in AA (Cain, 1991; Humphreys, 2000; Jensen, 2000; Pollner & Stein, 1996), there is no literature that links these two concepts with a focus on women. This research is the first step in exploring the value of narrative experience for older women in AA through the following questions: (1) "Have you ever told your story in AA? How did telling your story to the other members impact you?" and (2) "Do you share in meetings? What's it like revealing parts of yourself in this way? How does sharing impact you?"

Methods
Phenomenology

In an effort to better understand the narrative experience for older women in AA, the interviewer employed a qualitative approach. A qualitative method is appropriate because it is conducted in the participant's natural setting, and is interpretive in that, "it assumes that humans use what they see and hear and feel to make meaning of social phenomena" (Rossman & Rallis, 2012, p. 6). Because context plays an integral role in qualitative inquiry, the researcher sought to understand the influence it has on the participants' actions. This method's "inherent openness and flexibility" allowed the researcher to modify the research design and focus as new areas were explored (Maxwell, 2005, p. 22).

The researcher employed the qualitative tradition of phenomenology with its purposeful and deliberate goal of describing "the depth and meaning of participants' lived experiences" (Hays & Wood, 2011, p. 291). Utilizing a phenomenological approach, the researcher sought to understand the processes involved in constructing narratives in the context of AA meetings. These narratives were viewed through the eyes of women age 50 and older.

As discussed by Moustakas (1994), and Hays & Wood (2011), the researcher ensured that four key steps were adhered to throughout the phenomenological data analysis. First, the author bracketed her experiences. The phenomena of interest organically emerged after research identified holes in the literature, and research questions were conceptualized without preconceived ideas or assumptions about possible outcomes or findings. The researcher refrained from applying her own previous experiences or personal biases about the phenomena of interest (older women or members of AA).

Second, the researcher methodically read through each interview transcript (totaling over 300 pages for all 27 interviews). The transcripts were then re-read using a qualitative data analysis and research software,

Atlas TI, to highlight potential statements relevant to the processes involved in constructing narratives in AA. Next, highlighted statements were read again, being tentatively open-coded for possible subcategories, categories, or themes (Rossman & Rallis, 2012; Saldaña, 2009).

The third step employed a constant comparison method that involved re-reading all coded statements. Some coded statements became over-arching themes, while others became categories and subcategories within these themes. Other coded statements were absorbed by broader codes, while some were renamed to be more inclusive and precise. Finally, a number of codes (i.e., themes, categories, and subcategories) were deemed important, but not necessarily relevant to this paper's particular research question, and will be addressed in future papers. Codes contained analogous and differing experiences related to that particular area in an effort to illustrate the complexity and uniqueness of each woman's responses. Participants' interviews exhibited marked internal consistency, revealing an array of common themes. A second researcher reviewed the transcripts and codes to ensure that no important concepts were missed, and to help identify constructs.

Finally, the researcher assembled the codes into a table in a detailed description of this data analysis process containing themes, categories, and subcategories relevant to the research questions (see Table 1).

As Wertz (2005) explains, "The phenomenological approach emphasizes the importance of returning to psychological subject matter with an open attitude and evoking fresh, detailed descriptions that capture the richness and complexity of psychological life as it is concretely lived" (p. 176). To that end, the author used the codes in the table as the outline, while allowing the participants' own words to illuminate detailed descriptions of the processes involved in constructing narratives in the context of AA meetings. The resulting findings were steeped in the phenomenological ideology that "psychological reality—its meanings and subjective processes—can be faithfully discovered" (Wertz, 2005, p. 175).

Research Team

The research team was comprised of a male and female faculty member and one female doctoral student with varying degrees of knowledge and experience with AA, and varying degrees of work experience with individuals with addictions. Research team members also had unique personal experiences relating to older women. These previous experiences could have potentially influenced the researchers' expectations for findings, and the lens through which they viewed the women in AA. It is possible, too, that research team members might have expected the women to behave in predetermined ways based on their own frames of reference. To safeguard against this, researchers *bracketed* their experiences to avoid personal biases permeating the research (Hays & Wood, 2011; Moustakas, 1994).

Participants

Fourteen participants were recruited through the help of a confederate, a member of the AA community, who used a prewritten script to ask peers in AA who fit the study criteria (active members who regularly attended AA meetings weekly for the previous year, women age 50 and older, English speakers) to participate. Fourteen older women in AA were interviewed, and all but one considered herself an active member of AA. The women ranged from age 52 to 81 and were all of Caucasian decent. Participants' highest levels of education varied: three completed graduate school, three completed some years of graduate school, two completed a Bachelor's degree, one completed an Associate's degree, three completed some college, one graduated from high school, and one obtained a GED. About three-quarters of the women were single, about two-thirds of the women had children, and about one-third of the women had grandchildren. A little over half of the women were employed, and all but one of the remaining were retired. Table 2 illustrates more detailed demographic information about the participants.

Procedure

A total of 27 mostly face-to-face sessions occurred over a one year period. For all but one participant, two interviews were conducted. The second interviews occurred within four weeks of the first. Typically interview sessions lasted one to two hours and were held in private homes, offices, and eating establishments (only when requested by the participants.) In eating establishments, care was taken to procure seating away from other people to ensure that the participants felt comfortable, and to maintain their privacy. Three of the second interviews were held over the telephone due to illness or scheduling conflicts, and the rest were held in person.

There was an established protocol for questions, but broad streams of inquiry were developed as necessary to address the research question. Both interviews were phenomenological in nature with the exception of a brief demographic survey given at the beginning of interview one. In every case, strict measures protected the confidentiality of interviewees. Approval was sought from the IRB before any interviews occurred, and the researcher followed all IRB protocols including ensuring that an Informed Consent Document that was signed by each participant and followed throughout the research. In addition, pseudonyms were used and all identifying information was obscured in order to preserve participant confidentiality.

Data Analysis and Quality/Rigor

The researcher worked towards the goal of developing precise, detailed descriptions of the data. Following each interview, the researcher transcribed the audio recording, adding additional notes with observations about the participants' nonverbal behavior and information about the setting from the researcher's field notes. The researcher conducted member checks: within four weeks of each interview the participant was given a typed transcript to review for accuracy in both words and overall meaning (Creswell & Miller, 2010). Transcripts (totaling over 300 pages for all 27 interviews) were read meticulously, and excerpts that reflected the meaning of the phenomena of interest were highlighted. These excerpts were later open-coded using a constant comparison method to incorporate analogous and differing experiences, and then grouped into categories and subcategories. These categories and subcategories were organized according to themes across the narratives that addressed the research question (Rossman & Rallis, 2012; Saldaña, 2009). Table 1 gives a detailed description of the data analysis process. Participants' interviews exhibited marked internal consistency, revealing an array of common themes in their experiences. A second researcher also reviewed the transcripts and codes to ensure no important concepts were missed, and to help identify constructs.

Findings

In addressing the research question, "How was the narrative aspect of AA experienced by the participants?" the women explained the process of storytelling, and articulated the ways that they were positively affected by their participation. Emerging from this was the theme of the importance of storytelling. This theme was explored from the perspective of both the storyteller and the listener.

The Importance of Storytelling for the Speaker

Twelve out of the 14 women reported that the act of telling their stories in AA positively affected them. One woman suggested that telling her story had no effect on her at all, and one projected a negative attitude toward sharing. Women further articulated subcategories regarding the important aspects of speaking to the AA group: (1) Fulfillment of a desire to give back to the AA program, (2) Acceptance and feeling a part of something, (3) Transcendence beyond early feelings of anxiety or discomfort related to sharing and public sharing, (4) Remembrance of important past events, and (5) A spiritual experience.

A way to give back. Some women noted a desire to give back to the AA program, and cited storytelling as an important way to achieve that goal. One strong motivator was sense of obligation. Of the 14 women interviewed, 11 women, without being prompted, indicated feeling an obligation to give back. Five specifically indicated that sharing their personal stories from alcoholism to sobriety with others is their way to repay that obligation. Some women also indicated a desire to "pay it forward"—they were grateful for having heard more experienced members' stories, and now wanted to tell their stories to inspire others who may not be as far along in their sobriety. Along those lines, storytelling was also mentioned by some as a way to demonstrate service, one of the hallmarks of the AA program. Often, this storytelling was achieved through two common models: (1) "What we used to be like, What happened, and What we are like now," and (2) "Experience, Strength, and Hope" (Jensen, 2000, p. 11).

The researcher met with Susan, 66, at a local diner for dinner. She had just finished a full day at her job and was still dressed in her work clothes. Susan had been sober for 34 years, and was a long-standing member of the AA community. She discussed her harrowing experiences with alcohol, including a promiscuous period where she would leave her children at home and spend evenings with various men. She explained how sharing that story with others, and illustrating how she attained sobriety, fulfilled a sense of obligation, and was a requirement of the program:

> That's what we have to do in order to carry the message to stay sober... You have to give away what you've been given and someone carried the message to me. They were willing to be honest and tell me what happened to them and how they got sober.

Meg, 61, is a pillar in the AA community. Other women in this study mentioned her frequently as a mentor and friend. At our second meeting, Meg received a visitor—a young woman in AA whom Meg sponsors. Meg explained that she preferred her visitor remain present in her home during the interview. Although the young woman stayed in another room, Meg insisted that she had "nothing to hide." It appears that Meg's influence in the AA community is large—she sponsors numbers of women and has an ability to quote directly from *The Big Book* by memory. A retiree with over 14 years of sobriety, she frequently alluded to how hearing others' stories in AA helped her achieve sobriety, and how she hoped to do the same for others through her storytelling:

> It gives me the opportunity to give back... it's basically my way of being able to participate in AA as somebody who's been through the process, and it's the way I say thank you to the people who helped me get out of the hole... AA says, "Batter up!" and I just stand at the plate.

Rose, 64, is a close friend of Meg's with 27 years of sobriety. She was a very recent retiree from a prominent position as a political staffer, who was finding the transition from work to retirement challenging. Rose was stylish, funny, and sensitive, and was easily touched by emotion when discussing her gratitude towards AA. She expressed how the service aspect of AA can be met through sharing stories at meetings:

> And meetings are also important for me now because it's part of my service... because I think that at 27 years it's a service to open your mouth and say what's going on with you so the people with one year can go, "oh, ok."

Hannah, 61, is a practicing doctor with five year's sobriety. She ushered me into her office where, between back-to-back appointments, she made time to speak to me because of her appreciation for the AA program and a desire to help illuminate the benefits of the program to others. Hannah rejected the idea that there was an obligation to use storytelling at meetings but rather emphasized that all elements of AA, including storytelling, were suggestions meant simply to help others:

> You don't have to do anything. You don't have to sit for the whole meeting . . . you don't have to do anything. Nothing is required — ever. There are suggestions and some of those suggestions . . . like it's suggested that you pull a rip cord when you jump out of a plane. You don't have to. Here's the program, here's some suggestions, here's what's worked for us, take it or leave it.

Acceptance and feeling a part of a group. Many of the women expressed that a valuable benefit of storytelling in AA is that it gave them a sense of group acceptance and belonging. Sometimes this occurred because of the actual act of sharing the story with the group. Other times this happened because of the positive feedback received from the group as a result of storytelling. Rose tearfully explained that to her, the importance of storytelling is that it ultimately brought her a sense of community:

> And so for me, sharing is a way to contribute and a way to participate and be a part of. That's probably the most important because I'm sharing what's supposed to be coming through me, like when I'm up talking, not just when I raise my hand.

Meg illustrated how sharing her story was significant for her because of the positive feedback that it incurred. This feedback generated a sense of acknowledgment and validation in the group:

> I've learned stuff about myself that I didn't know until I heard myself say it. But part of it is also being accepted and having people come up afterwards and say, "I'm really glad you shared that" . . . Sometimes it validates me.

Overcoming anxiety about public sharing. Seven women described overcoming early feelings of discomfort or anxiety associated with sharing with the group. Early concerns centered on being judged or just a general sense of fear related to public speaking, but women expressed that they were able to conquer their fears and speak to the group with positive results. (An eighth woman was never able to overcome her anxiety.) Mary, 58, is working in the banking industry. With six years sobriety, the experience of becoming sober was still relatively recent. Like Rose, Mary also considered Meg a strong mentor and friend in the AA community. Mary described having had a strong sense of shame about her alcoholism, and gave a powerful analogy to describe the process of how her nervous feelings the first time she told her story to the AA group gave way to relief at the positive outcome:

> I could liken it to the first time feeling like I was stark naked in front of the group . . . Like, "Go ahead and look." And then me looking back like, "ok, they didn't leave the room, they didn't reject me, I think it's going to be ok."

Like Mary, Susan discussed the initial fear of sharing her story in public. However, she also acknowledged the benefits derived from overcoming these fears:

> And so for me, when I got started it was scary . . . And what we're doing is sharing from the heart, and I've never found that anywhere else. Once I got acclimated to the fact that people weren't going to reject me or run me out of AA, it can be very rewarding.

Similarly, Linda, 52, a professional in the counseling field, articulated the benefits of overcoming her trepidation and sharing her story with the group. Being in the mental health profession, Linda's perspective was particularly poignant because often her comments merged the viewpoint of both a recovering alcoholic and a professional in the counseling field:

> I guess I feel there's that piece of just doing something that's uncomfortable that's stretching that feels like I'm doing the right thing . . . but inevitably it always ends up feeling good, and I always end up feeling like whatever comes out of my mouth was supposed to come out of my mouth sort of like this process (laughs). It always just feels like great afterward . . . I guess one of the things is just being able to get outside myself.

Reminding the speaker of her past struggles. Seven women expressed the benefit of storytelling because it reminded them of their past struggles in alcoholism. This idea of being reminded is positively associated with feelings of gratitude, focus, progress, and humility. For some women, retelling the past was a way to acknowledge previous struggles but also to celebrate the ability to overcome hurdles. Hannah explained why it was particularly necessary for AA members to be reminded of their past experiences related to drinking:

> It's nice to go back and review it. Like I said, we have quick forgetters and sometimes slow learners, but to remember how I felt, what hooked me in, the struggles I had, it's good to go back and review that . . . And it reminds you of who you are and where you came from . . .

Dianne, 69, was a retiree with over 31 years of sobriety. When we met in her home, Dianne told me a bit about her days of alcoholism, and how she constantly feared that she might black out and miss a call to come in to work. She echoed Hannah's sentiments when discussing why remembering and sharing these painful early experiences is so important to the recovery process:

> So in that sense, I think it really now lets me remember. And keeps me focused. And then an extreme amount of gratitude for the way things are now . . . a big piece of it is so you remember, so you remember what the pain was like and how miserable it was.

Spiritual experience. Spirituality is a critical component of the AA storytelling experience. A number of women discussed acknowledging a higher power before telling their stories to the group in the form of praying for help and guidance. Prayer was mentioned in helping women choose what to say to the group or to quell anxiety about public speaking. One woman referred to sharing, and hearing what is shared, as her "spiritual medicine." Susan mentioned spirituality throughout her interview; it was clearly of great importance to her within the context of the AA experience. Unlike the others, however, she expressed that the act of telling her story was in itself a spiritual experience, crediting her word choices to God:

> Well for one thing it is a spiritual experience because I always pray before I talk, I don't try to plan what I talk, I never take notes, and I know it's God's thing . . . I don't know what he wants me to share. He knows who's there and what message they need to hear—I don't . . . So I don't have a canned talk. I'm open to the spirit and that's what my sponsor told me from the very beginning: "Let the spirit direct you."

Importance of Storytelling for the Listener

Six out of 14 women also discussed the positive effects that the narrative process of AA had on the listeners of these stories. Some women perceived the benefit of listening to stories in AA as learning from others in the program. Other women mentioned that listening to stories in AA allowed them to identify with the speaker's story.

Learning from others in the program. Another important component of listening to others' stories, was hearing what other members of AA had gone through in their road to sobriety. Besides offering them a sense of clarity and comfort, the stories also contained useful suggestions for attaining and maintaining sobriety. Meg explained how particularly newer, younger members can learn from the stories of more experienced, older members:

> In storytelling, that is the real benefit of meetings, in storytelling, is that somebody who's 25 can come in and listen to somebody like me who's 60 and I can say, "This is what happened to me," or, "I didn't think it would ever happen to me, but this is where alcohol took me. And if alcohol is taking you to places you don't want to go, you don't have to keep going until you're desperate."

Likewise, Nancy expressed the altruistic desire for members to share stories in order to benefit others in the program, "I think there's a general feeling within AA that you want to share in hopes that you might help someone else." Listening to others tell their stories in AA was important because it allowed women the opportunity to hear the stories and perspectives of other members. In turn, women benefitted by learning from, and emulating others' experiences.

Identifying with the speaker's story. Women understood the importance of identifying with the speakers' stories, and the value of the listener finding commonalities with the speaker. Similar stories of struggle and grief around alcoholism that ultimately culminate in successful abstinence and better overall quality of life, offered listeners a sense of peace and salvation. Mary expressed the relief she felt as a listener in AA, hearing another woman's story that resonated with her:

> I preferred speaker meetings where I was hearing other alcoholics share their story and it gave me hope, a lot of hope. And it made me feel like, "oh my god, I'm not the only one who feels this way, or behaves this way."

As a speaker, Hannah hoped that someone like Mary might relate to her struggles and be roused to make positive changes like she had.

> It is a big important part of giving back, hopefully to get someone to be attracted to the program by your story and your sobriety and to say that, "yes, I felt like you feel and that they have something that I'd like."

Benefit to listeners a welcome "side effect." The women articulated that storytelling is utilized foremost as a tool to help them maintain their own sobriety. Having positive effects on the listeners is a welcome result, but that is viewed as secondary in importance—as a "side effect" of sharing. Susan expressed this perspective in her description of speaking at meetings:

> So that's good for me, and if it helps somebody else, great. But you see it's helping me to stay sober. That's the whole point of telling your story; it helps that person to stay sober.

At age 81, Louise was the oldest participant—she was 12 years older than the next oldest woman in the study. We met at her home, filled with pictures of her three children. She lived alone, and looked and acted years younger than her age might suggest. Louise offered a unique perspective because she spoke, not just as a recovering alcoholic, but as a woman who by virtue of her age, had years of life experience behind her. She discussed her early drinking experiences as a teenager, and several efforts to attain sobriety until the final time, 29 years ago. Like Susan, Louise also explained that the primary reason for telling her stories is to maintain her own abstinence from alcohol:

> And I've done what I can, and if telling my story to you, pretend you were an alcoholic, if that helps you in some way not continue to drink, then I've done a good job . . . And it's about helping me. About helping me get it out and laying it on the table and letting people see dirty laundry, so to speak.

Discussion

With the original research question, "How was the narrative aspect of AA experienced by the participants," the author sought to better understand the ways in which older women conceptualized and utilized the narrative process within AA. The results of this study suggest the storytelling element of AA has significant benefits to older women members, reflective of how Parker (1995) viewed reminiscence through Atchley's (1989) Continuity Theory of Normal Aging. Through this framework, AA narratives can be understood as "lifestories" that are critical in creating continuity for older adults (p. 521). Thus, the women's descriptions of the value of constructing and sharing stories in AA supported Parker's understanding of reminiscence. These AA stories encompass a holistic view, incorporating past experiences into a meaningful present narrative that is important in establishing a sense of continuity. For older women in AA, composing and retelling life stories was also a critical component in helping them to acquire and sustain their sobriety.

AA members utilize two overlapping storytelling models: "what we used to be like (experience), what happened (strength), and what we are like now (hope)" (Jensen, 2000, p. 11). These models merge perceptions about the past and present (negative alcoholic experiences, positive feelings about successful abstention from drinking,) and incorporate conceptualizations of a productive, sober future. Often, the resulting AA stories are actually life stories, since they encompass decades, and in many cases, nearly the entirety, of the participants' lives. Constructing these AA life stories (reminiscence) allows older women to verbally arrange the events of their lives into a streamlined story, achieving a sense of continuity as described by Parker (1995).

Limitations

This was a homogeneous sample racially (Caucasian), socio-economically (middle to upper-middle class), and geographically (living in and around a small urban community in a mid-Atlantic state). And with the exception of one woman (81 years old), the demographic was mostly "young-old" with the rest of the women ranging in age from 52 to 69. This study might have differed had the participants been more culturally diverse, since some cultures emphasize the storytelling tradition over others. In addition, this study mostly addressed "young-old" women. There could be differences in the importance of storytelling for the "young-old" women compared to women who are "old-old." Therefore, it would be advantageous to replicate this study with a group of women in their much later years, women with various cultural backgrounds, and women living in rural environments to determine if these variables affect how older women experience AA. Although the confederate made connecting with AA members easy, it was understood that the researcher was an "outsider" and not a member of AA. Perhaps interviewees may have censored themselves (either purposefully or unconsciously) or may have been protective of the AA program when speaking with the researcher who did not have the same personal connection to the AA community.

Implications for Future Research

This study was just the beginning step in addressing holes in the research related to older women and AA by exploring the storytelling experience. Suggestions for future research involve both the sample and the focus. To more fully understand the narrative experience for older women in AA, it is important to address women with diverse socioeconomic and racial backgrounds, as this research was only conducted with a homogenous group of white women within a relatively small geographic area. A larger geographic area could also be canvassed to include urban and rural areas in other regions of the country. Moreover, with one exception of a woman who was 81, the women in this study ranged from age 52 to 69. Additional research could focus on women in their 70s and 80s which could possibly yield different results.

There are additional focus areas within the greater context of older women in AA that were not addressed by the research. Other areas for investigation may include exploring age and gender as they relate to the AA experience for older women. The researchers hope that this study is only the first step towards exploring and better understanding older women and AA. It is through this continued research that counselors and other mental health practitioners can determine best practices for older women with addictions.

Implications for Addiction Counselors

This study has elucidated important information regarding the value of storytelling for older female clients with addictions issues. The women in this study explain that through the construction of an oral history, they have the ability to piece together disparate events in their lives into a unified whole. In particular, seemingly random or unhappy past situations can be applied to the greater story, imbuing it with an overall sense of meaning. This process can assist older women to accept the challenges of aging by inviting them to recall, and then draw upon, previously used strengths to help solve present issues. Therefore, constructing and then sharing one's story instills a sense of continuity into an older individual's life view (Parker, 1995).

Just as older women in AA derived benefits from the storytelling aspects of the program, counselors may consider that techniques incorporating storytelling may be beneficial to older women with addictions. Several therapeutic modalities highlight this storytelling element: reminiscence, life review, and narrative therapy.

Burnside and Haight (1992) explain that reminiscence is an interactive process that involves recalling distant memories to others, and having others share in response, and may prove effective in achieving a sense of resolution and purpose. Through the interactive story-telling element of distant past experiences, reminiscence can improve quality of life, reduce isolation, and increase self-esteem (Burnside & Haight). Counselors may wish to create "reminiscence groups" for older women with addictions that might provide needed support during their efforts towards sobriety. Traditional therapeutic group counseling may also be beneficial since hearing an applicable story from an individual in a similar situation might serve as an effective strategy towards achieving and maintaining sobriety. In this vein, group counseling practices may also be beneficial as an avenue for both sharing stories and listening to others' stories.

Life review, on the other hand is often a one-on-one experience that involves one person sharing memories of an entire life span with another in a one-way conversation, and contains an evaluative component for the sharer (Burnside & Haight, 1992). Haight and Haight (2007) outlined a structured life review that is beneficial for older adults. This process is conducted in eight, hour-long visits, where a counselor or health practitioner (therapeutic listener) asks an older adult scripted questions addressing events and feelings related to specific stages in life like childhood, adolescence, young adulthood, and older adulthood. This process of structured recall helps older adults to attain greater meaning, acceptance, and a new sense of vigor and enthusiasm (p. 175). Counselors who work with older female clients with addictions could utilize this model by allowing these women the space to conduct their own life review in the safety of the counseling room.

Finally, narrative therapy is another therapeutic modality that highlights storytelling that counselors may find beneficial when working with older women with addictions (White, 1995; White & Epston, 1990). This modality makes use of the personal narrative, and incorporates the storytelling process into the counseling realm. Narrative therapy is a process by which clients are invited to recreate personal narratives (life stories) by deconstructing or challenging the "problem" story, and "re-authoring" narratives into more functional stories. This construction of a new, more positive narrative, is another way that clients can create meaning in their lives (White, 1995; White & Epston, 1990).

As the population of older women grows, it is imperative that counselors and other mental health practitioners be prepared to work with this population and address its unique needs. Results from this study suggest that utilizing a narrative component in counseling can be a useful step towards assisting older women with attaining and maintaining sobriety.

References

Alcoholics Anonymous World Services. (2001). *Alcoholics Anonymous: The story of how many thousands of men and women have recovered from alcoholism* (4th ed.). New York, NY: Author.

Alcoholics Anonymous. Retrieved from http://www.aa.org

Atchley, R. (1989). A continuity theory of normal aging. *The Gerontologist, 29,* 137-144. doi:10.1093/geront/29.2.183

Battista, J., & Almond, R. (1973). The development of meaning in life. *Psychiatry: Interpersonal and Biological Processes, 36*(4), 409-427. doi:10.1521/00332747.1973.11023774

Beckman, L. J. (1993). Alcoholics Anonymous and gender issues. In: B. S. McCrady & W. R. Miller (Eds.), *Research on Alcoholics Anonymous: Opportunities and Alternatives* (pp. 233-248). New Brunswick, NJ: Rutgers Center of Alcohol Studies.

Blume, S. B. (1991). Women, alcohol and drugs. In: N. S. Miller (Ed.), *Comprehensive Handbook of Drug and Alcohol Addictions* (pp. 147-178). New York, NY: Marcel Dekker.

Burnside, I., & Haight, B. K. (1992). Reminiscence and life review: analyzing each concept. *Journal of Advanced Nursing, 17,* 855-862. doi:10.1111/j.1365-2648.1992.tb02008.x

Butler, R. (1963). The life review: An interpretation of reminiscence in the aged. *Psychiatry, 26,* 65-76.

Cain, C. (1991). Personal stories: Identity acquisition and self-understanding in Alcoholics Anonymous. *Ethos, 19*(2), 210-251. doi:10.1525/eth.1991.19.2.02a00040

Creswell, J. W., & Miller, D. L. (2010). Determining validity in qualitative inquiry. *Theory Into Practice, 39* (3), 124-130.

Erikson, E. (1950). *Childhood and society.* New York, NY: W. W. Norton.

Frankl, V. E. (1959). *Man's search for meaning.* Boston, MA: Beacon Press.

Gergen, K., & Gergen, M. (1983). Narratives of the self. In T. Sabin & K. Scheibe (Eds.), *Studies in social identity* (pp. 254-273). New York, NY: Praeger. doi:10.1016/S0065-2601(08)60223-3

Haber, D. (2006). Life review: Implementation, theory, research, and therapy. *International Journal of Aging and Human Development, 63*(2), 153-171. doi:10.2190/DA9G-RHK5-N9JP-T6CC

Haight, B. K., & Haight, B. S. (2007). *The handbook of structured life review.* Baltimore, MD: Health Professions Press.

Hays, D. G., & Wood, C. (2011). Infusing qualitative traditions in counseling research designs. *Journal of Counseling & Development, 89,* 288-295. doi:10.1002/j.1556-6678.2011.tb00091.x

Humphreys, K. (2000). Community narratives and personal stories in Alcoholics Anonymous. *Journal of Community Psychology, 28*(5), 495-506. doi:10.1002/1520-6629(200009)28:5<495::AID-JCOP3>3.0.CO;2-W

Jensen, G. H. (2000). *Storytelling in Alcoholics Anonymous: A Rhetorical Analysis.* Carbondale, IL: Southern Illinois University Press.

Katz, R. S. (2002). Older women and addictions. In S. L. A. Straussner & S. Brown (Eds.), *The Handbook of Addiction Treatment for Women* (pp. 272-297). San Francisco, CA: Jossey-Bass.

Kropf, N. P., & Tandy, C. (1998). Narrative therapy with older clients: The use of a "meaning-making" approach. *Clinical Gerontologist, 18*(4), 3—16. doi:10.1300/j018v18n04_02

Matheson, J. L., & McCollum, E. E. (2008). Using metaphors to explore the experiences of powerlessness among women in 12-step recovery. *Substance Use & Misuse, 43*(8-9), 1027-1044. doi:10.1080/10826080801914287

Maxwell, J. A. (2005). *Qualitative research design: An interactive approach* (2nd ed.). Thousand Oaks, CA: Sage.

Mosher-Ashley, P., & Rabon, C. E. (2001). A comparison of older and younger adults attending Alcoholics Anonymous. *Clinical Gerontologist, 24*(1/2), 27-37. doi:10.1300/j018v24n01_03

Moustakas, C. (1994). *Phenomenological research methods.* Thousand Oaks, CA: Sage.

Nakken, J. M. (2002). Reflections of the past, present and possible future of women's alcoholism treatment. *Alcoholism Treatment Quarterly, 20*(3/4), 147-155. doi:10.1300/J020v20n03_09

Pagliaro, A. M., & Pagliaro, L. A. (2000). *Substance use among women.* Philadelphia, PA: Brunner/Mazel.

Parker, R. G. (1995). Reminiscence: A continuity theory framework. *The Gerontologist, 35*(4), 515-525. doi:10.1093/geront/35.4.515

Pollner, M., & Stein, J. (1996). Narrative mapping of social worlds: The voice of experience in Alcoholics Anonymous. *Symbolic Interaction, 19*(3), 203-223. doi:10.1525/si.1996.19.3.203

Rathbone-McCuan, E. (1988). Group intervention for alcohol-related problems among elderly and their families. In B. W. MacLennan, S. Shura, & M. B. Weiner (Eds.), *Group Psychotherapies for the Elderly* (pp. 139-148). Madison, CT: International Universities Press.

Rossman, G. B., & Rallis, S. F. (2012). *Learning in the field: An introduction to qualitative research* (3rd ed.). Thousand Oaks, CA: Sage.

Saldaña, J. (2009). *The Coding Manual for Qualitative Researchers.* Thousand Oaks, CA: Sage.

Sanders, J. M. (2006). Women and the twelve steps of Alcoholics Anonymous. *Alcoholism Treatment Quarterly, 24*(3), 3-39. doi:10.1300/J020v24n03_02

Satre, D. D., Blow, F. C., Chi, F. W., & Weisner, C. (2007). Gender differences in seven-year alcohol and drug treatment outcomes among older adults. *American Journal on Addictions, 16*, 216-221. doi:10.1080/10550490701375673

Satre, D. D., Mertens, J. R., Areán, P. A., & Weisner, C. (2004). Five-year alcohol and drug treatment outcomes of older adults versus middle-aged and younger adults in a managed care program. *Addiction, 99*(10), 1286-1287. doi:10.1111/j.1360-0443.2004.00831.x

Schiff, S. M. (1988). Treatment approaches for older alcoholics. *Generations: Journal of the American Society on Aging, 12*(4), 41-45.

The National Center on Addiction and Substance Abuse at Columbia University (CASA). (2006). *Women Under the Influence.* Baltimore, MD: The Johns Hopkins University Press.

Timko, C., Moos, R. H., Finney, J. W., & Connell, E. G. (2002). Gender differences in help-utilization and the 8-year course of alcohol abuse. *Addiction, 97*(7), 877-889. doi:10.1046/j.1360-0443.2002.00099.x

Travis, T. (2009). "Handles to hang on to our sobriety": Commonplace books and surrendered masculinity in Alcoholics Anonymous. *Men and Masculinities, 12*(2), 175-200. doi:10.1177/1097184X08318182

Washburn, N. (1996). AA through the eyes of its older members. *Journal of Geriatric Psychiatry, 29*(2), 185-204.

Wertz, F. J. (2005). Phenomenological research methods for counseling psychology. *Journal of Counseling Psychology, 52*(2), 167-177. doi:10.1037/0022-0167.52.2.167

White, M. (1995). *Re-Authoring lives: Interviews and essays*. Adelaide, Australia: Dulwich Centre.

White, M., & Epston, D. (1990). *Narrative means to therapeutic ends*. Adelaide, Australia: Dulwich Centre.

Table 1
Data Analysis Process

Research Question: How was the narrative aspect of AA Experienced?		
Theme: The Importance of Storytelling for Older Women in AA		
Categories	A. Telling story: Effect on storyteller	B. Telling Story: Intended effect on listener
Subcategories and Supporting Codes	Sense of obligation to give back	Learning from others
	Guilt	Clarity from listening
	Gratitude	Comfort from listening
	Obligation	Suggestions
	Pay back	Identifying with speaker
	Pay forward	Identify (relate)
	Acceptance	Hope
	Community	Similarities
	Love	Relief
	Community Belonging	Benefit to listener "side effect"
	Positive Feedback	Story for me
	Caring	Listeners Secondary
	Overcoming anxiety	
	Nervous beginning	
	Fear of speaking	
	Fear of judgment	
	Relief	
	Reminding of past	
	Memories	
	Past sadness	
	Grateful for past	
	Telling stories about past	
	Spiritual experience	
	Pray for guidance	
	Pray for words	
	Speaking is spiritual	

Table 2

Study Participant Demographic Information and AA History

	Age	Schooling (NF=not finished)	Years sober in AA	Years drinking before AA	What prompted AA?
Meg	61	Master's (NF)	15	33	Difficulty staying sober before annual blood work
Nancy	59	Master's (NF)	2	10	Nervous breakdown
Rose	64	Law school	27	21	Having to travel with husband's family sober
Susan	66	Bachelor's	34	18	Joined a group with AA members in it
Beth	58	Bachelor's (NF)	5	19	Didn't want to live the way she was living anymore
Betty	64	Bachelor's (NF)	25	22	Work identified it and she went to treatment
Brenda	56	Master's (NF)	27	15	Friends dying
Dianne	69	Bachelor's (NF)	32	20	Blacked out, forgot to pick up son
Ginny	57	High school	1	11	Car crash with son in car, drinking
Hannah	61	Medical school	5	14	Depressed, mandatory because of DUI
Linda	52	Master's	24	16	Boyfriend's ultimatum
Louise	81	Associate's	29	10	Realization that alcohol was killing her
Mary	58	Bachelor's	6	20	Lost job, mother died, taken to emergency room
Ruth	54	GED	17	27	In psych unit, realized she had same disease as parents

10

The Impact of Addictions Education on Attitudes of Students

AMANUEL HAILE ASFAW, KEVIN VANCE, KYOUNGHO LEE, DAVID MEGGITT, JANE WARREN, JENNIFER WEATHERFORD, AND GRANT SASSE[1]

As far back as 1962, Chafetz et al. studied the lack of follow through for treatment (less than one percent) for persons who were defined as "alcoholics" and who had sought services initially in the emergency room. This lack of follow-through was a concern. Chafetz et al., (1962) adapted the initial emergency room protocol by increasing contact and found 65% of the enhanced contact group sought follow up services compared to 5.4% of the group which received no additional contact following the emergency room event. Contact was defined as the patients being seen and supported by social workers, beyond just the emergency session. Basically "prior to the initiation of this study, virtually no alcoholics came to the alcohol clinic as a consequence of emergency-ward admission" (Chafetz et al., 1962, p. 404). In fact, patients were genuinely helped with

---

1. Amanuel Haile Asfaw, Department of Psychological Science and Counseling, Austin Peay State University; Kevin Vance, Kyoungho Lee, David Meggitt, Jane Warren, and Jennifer Weatherford, Professional Studies Department, Counselor Education Program, University of Wyoming, Laramie, WY 82071; Grant Sasse, Counselor Education Program, University of Alaska, Anchorage, AK 99508-4614. Correspondence concerning this article should be addressed to Amanuel Haile Asfaw, Department of Psychological Science and Counseling, Austin Peay State University, Clarksville, TN 37044. E-mail: asfawa@apsu.edu or haamanuel@gmail.com

follow-up support, once the attitudes of the initial first responders included hope with a positive prognosis approach.

Relatedly, researchers have consistently found that a nonjudgmental and therapeutic bond with clients is associated with positive treatment outcomes (Horvath, Del Re, Flückiger, & Symonds, 2011; Miller, 2000; Norcross & Lambert, 2011; Norcross & Wampold, 2011; Rogers, 1975); this therapeutic bond is enhanced when the counselor believes a client can change (Dollarhide & Oliver, 2014), and the client has hope for change (Koehn & Cutcliffe, 2012). Lambert and Barley (2001) posited that factors related to successful counseling outcomes include "therapist credibility, skill, empathic understanding, and affirmation of the patient, along with the ability to engage the patient . . . " (p. 358).

Researchers need to assess how educators are preparing counselors for practice and, in particular, addressing student attitudes that might impact treatment. We need to bridge our classroom experiences to clinical effectiveness, with goals of enhancing the counseling profession and establishing evidence-based teaching practices that impact students' work with clients (Minton, Morris, & Yaites, 2014). Evidence-based practices are interventions found to be successful in helping a person achieve his or her goals, have been empirically validated, and have credibility due to repeated successes. Specifically, more attention is needed to evidence-based teaching strategies that impact effectiveness in addictions treatment and beliefs about the stigma of addictions.

Impact of Stigma in Addictions Treatment

Stigmas are a form of negative attitudes and were originally used to define a lower moral status of a person or group of persons (Lay & McGuire, 2008). "*Stigma* is another term for prejudice or negative stereotyping" (Corrigan & Penn, 1999, p. 766). Research shows that people with substance abuse and addiction problems experience stigma; they are considered responsible for their plight, provoking more social rejection, and are at greater risk for social discrimination (Schomerus et al., 2011b). From a stratified random sample of people in the United States, Corrigan, Kuwabara, and O'Shaughnessy (2009) found that people who were labeled as drug addicts were less likely to be given help compared to those individuals with mental illness or in a wheelchair. There are studies which demonstrate the existence of negative attitudes and stigmas toward persons with addictions (Adams & Madson, 2007; Gerace, Hughes, & Spunt, 1995; Nellis, Greene, & Mauer, 2008; Spaid & Squires, 2005). Kelly, Saitz, and Wakeman (2016) and Saitz (2015) clearly supported how the use of stigmatizing language toward addictions can worsen clinical care. "There is great opportunity to improve the care for people with or at risk for alcohol and other drug use disorders, to address endemic and related epidemic conditions that have long been ignored or poorly addressed" (Saitz, 2015, p. 430).

The Center for Substance Abuse Treatment (CSAT, 2006) suggested that attitudes in helping professionals "need to be considered within the framework of stigma and its consequences for the counselor, the client, and the field" (p. 164). A counselor's capacity to empathize with clients experiencing addictions problems can be impacted by stigmas, biases, and assumptions (Ballon & Skinner, 2008). Research suggests that helping professionals risk delivering incompetent, biased, and ineffective services to clients when they do not recognize the negative biases, stereotypes, and beliefs they possess (Blagen, 2007; Boysen, 2010; Koch, 2008; Koch, Sneed, Davis, & Benshoff, 2007; Lay & McGuire, 2008; McLellan, Lewis, O'Brien, & Kleber, 2000; Stadler, Suh, Cobia, Middleton, & Carney, 2006; Stein, 2003; Steinfeldt & Steinfeldt, 2012).

Although acknowledgment of attitudes occurs through self-awareness, automatic reactions happen without knowledge or conscious effort; consequently, the perceiver may not even recognize their own prejudices and biases (Bessenoff & Sherman, 2000). Although Livingston, Milnes, Fang, and Amari (2012) reported that substance use disorders were more stigmatized than other health conditions they found evidence that stigma and automatic unrecognized stereotyping were reduced through education, positive stories, and contact with stigmatized individuals.

Professional counselors have a high number of clients with primary addictions problems; consequently, addictions education is necessary for all counseling students (Lee, 2014). Counselors-in-training (CIT) and professional helpers bring biases, experiences, and beliefs regarding substance use, substance abuse, and addictions into their training and interventions (Broadus, Hartje, Roget, Cahoon, & Clinkinbeard, 2010; Chappel, Veach, & Krug, 1985; Crabb & Linton, 2007; McKim et al., 2014). These biases may hinder the therapeutic alliance; however they can be addressed through education.

Reducing Negative Attitudes and Stigma Through Education

It is not easy to develop new attitudes and empathetic capacity for persons struggling with substance use and abuse problems (Vadlamudi, Adams, Hogan, Wu, & Wahid, 2008). However, recognizing one's own preexisting attitudes and stigma may enhance any helper's ability to more accurately understand substance abuse clients (Martinez & Murphy-Parker, 2003). One way to become aware of one's negative attitudes is through education. It is important to investigate the best methods for enhancing positive attitudes in addictions education (Lee, 2014; Osborn & Lewis, 2005).

There is considerable research identifying ways in education to address stigma. Corrigan and Penn (1999) identified three strategies to reduce stigma and negative attitudes: protest, education, and contact. They also noted that education efforts are augmented by face-to-face contact with persons who are stigmatized. Carroll (2000) reported that students in internships who completed a minimum of three semester hours of addictions counseling were able to more adequately identify a substance abuse problem and appropriately treat or refer clients with substance abuse problems, compared to those who received less substance abuse training. Sias, Lambie, and Foster (2006) reported that substance abuse education was positively correlated with conceptual development and moral reasoning in substance abuse counselors.

Although research suggests that didactic and experiential education *can* address negative attitudes and stigma (Corrigan & Penn, 1999; Lloyd, 2010; Vadlamudi et al., 2008), *how* education is delivered is important (Nagda, Gurin, & Lopez, 2003). To effectively address substance abuse problems, education needs to be relevant, and experiential to adequately prepare students for many complexities in addictions-related work (Dawes-Diaz, 2007; Hardwood, Kowalski, & Ameen, 2004; Lee, 2014; Quinn, 2010; Salyers, Ritchie, Cochrane, & Roseman, 2006; Sheehan, Walker, & Reiter, 2008; Whittinghill, Carroll, & Morgan, 2004).

Experiential Education

Experiential education is one effective way to address attitudes and beliefs. Kolb (1984) combined experientially based education with reflective learning to promote self—and attitude awareness; he found students became cognizant of negative attitudes. In general, deep change requires life experiences to be engaging cognitively, emotionally, and interpersonally (Manners & Durkin, 2000). Research results suggest that experiential education may influence students' potentially negative biases (Giannetti, Sieppert, & Holosko, 2002). Osborn and Lewis (2005) supported experiential educational strategies suggesting they could not only enhance awareness of biases, but also promote treatment integrity. Ballon and Skinner (2008) found that reflective journaling altered psychiatric providers' ability to address beliefs and stereotypes of addictive disorders and was related to their providing more effective services. Vadlamudi et al. (2008) showed that education had a positive effect on the attitudes and beliefs about substance using clients in primary care nurses; however, the education approach included both didactic and experiential (role play) methods.

In addition, research suggests that direct experience with recovering persons changes attitudes. Mogar, Helm, Snedeker, Snedeker, and Wilson (1969) found treatment optimism was higher in staff who worked with individuals suffering with alcoholism compared to those who had no contact with alcoholism treatment. In their study on attitude changes in nurses, Martinez and Murphy-Parker (2003) reported that education assisted nurses in having more accurate beliefs; however to have direct work with the person wanting sobriety was the most effective teaching strategy. Crabb and Linton (2007) showed how belief systems of substance abuse counselors were altered due to "activating events" (p. 16) such as a conversation, reading research, or clinical experience. Challenging their students' personal stereotypes about people with addictions, Sias and Goodwin (2007) requested that students attend 12-step meetings, which was found to alter their former negative beliefs about substance abusers. Moran and Milsom (2015) showed how experiential and interactive learning such as hearing guest speakers and class discussions facilitated knowledge acquisition.

Measuring Changes in Attitudes through Education

There have been numerous studies assessing addictions attitude changes in medical students and nurses. For example in 1987, Chappel and Veach studied 212 medical students who finished a substance abuse education program. They used the Substance Abuse Attitudes Survey (SAAS) to measure changes in five attitudes toward alcohol and drug use; results indicated that students' mean scores for all measures changed significantly in a positive direction during the first three years of the study. Hagemaster, Handley, Plumlee, Sullivan, and Stanley (1993) found attitudinal changes in practicing nurses who completed an alcohol and drug educational program. Specifically, their results, using the SAAS, revealed decreased permissiveness and increased treatment intervention beliefs. In nurses who completed substance abuse education, Gerace et al. (1995), who also used the SAAS, found increases in treatment optimism scores.

There has been a limited number of studies evaluating addictions attitudes changes in helping professionals such as social workers or counselors. Stein (2003) investigated attitude changes toward substance abuse in social work students who completed a 4-hour substance abuse course. From this study there were higher treatment intervention and optimism scores in students who had known someone with a drug problem. Also using the SAAS, Richmond and Foster (2003) studied 103 mental health professionals. They found practitioners who possessed postgraduate level education showed less moralistic and increased treatment optimism toward persons with addictions, compared to those who have not received postgraduate level education. From their findings, they suggested that postgraduate courses could contribute to a decrease in moralistic attitudes and an increase in treatment optimism. They suggested further research was needed to ascertain how and if postgraduate addictions education might impact attitudes toward substance abuse.

To the best knowledge of the present researchers, a study examining addiction attitudes in first year counselors-in-training is lacking. This gap is addressed by this current study, given the participants were all in their first year of training and their attitudes were assessed using the SAAS to measure five attitudes: non-stereotyping, permissiveness, nonmoralism, treatment optimism, and treatment intervention. We intended to examine whether there were statistically significant differences between pretest and post-test scores of participants on the five attitudes measured by the SAAS.

Method

Participants

This study included data collection from students in two separate addictions courses utilizing the same curricula. Participants were first year master's-level counseling students ($N = 36$) enrolled in a Council for the Accreditation of Counseling and Related Educational Programs (CACREP, 2009) accredited training program within the Rocky Mountain region. In the first year of the study, there were 18 participants; in the second year there were 18 participants.

Specific demographic identifiers in the first year (2013) were: 6 males (33%) and 12 females (67%). A majority of these students self-identified as Caucasian ($n = 13$, 72%); with a small percentage being other self-identified races: Asian ($n = 1$, 6 %), Mexican-American or Chicano ($n = 2$, 11%), and other ($n = 2$, 11%). These participants ranged in age with ten 20-25 year olds (55%) and eight 26-30 year olds (44%). For the second year (2014), there were 5 males (27%) and 13 females (73%). A majority of these students self-identified as Caucasian ($n = 17$, 94%), with a small percentage self-identifying as other ($n = 1$, 6%). Second year participants ranged in age from 20-35 years old (age 20-25, $n = 7$, 39%; age 26-30, $n = 9$, 50%; age 31-35, $n = 2$, 11%). None of the participants had been working at substance treatment sites at the time of the research, but a few of them had conducted substance abuse assessments during their first year practicum training at the university counseling training clinic.

Intervention (Addictions and Counseling Course)

The 15-week addictions and counseling course included both experiential and didactic activities and focused on treatment simulation, promotion of understanding, contact with recovering persons, and addictions-related content from the course textbooks and class presentations. The course was based on the curriculum described in the five experiential activities in addictions education (Warren, Hof, McGriff, & Morris, 2012). However, it is important to note, the instructors of the activities followed important ethical considerations such as privacy, allowing students to process and choose not to participate in the activities in order to protect their well-being (Morrissette & Gadbois, 2006).

Treatment Simulation

The Change-Behavior. Each student was invited to commit to a potentially beneficial behavior change for the duration of the semester. The intention of requiring a change behavior was to provide students with an experience similar to that of a client in treatment, who is asked to change their behavior. The activities they chose were diverse such as abstinence from sugar, video games, and chocolate; increases in walking or daily exercise; completion of all homework before Sunday; using a shopping list at the grocery store, and attending church more often.

Weekly Journaling. Journal writing can promote self-awareness and enhance professional and personal growth (Ballon & Skinner, 2008; Griffith & Frieden, 2000; La Torre, 2005). The weekly journaling experience was intended to provide a way to process and reflect upon experiences, and to identify emotions (Gladding, 2007; Hagedorn, 2011).

Piggy Bank. A piggy bank was given to each student at mid-semester to replicate Contingency Management (CM) which is a strategy often employed in actual treatment settings. Contingency Management is based upon the idea that rewarded behavior will continue. Research suggests that incentives such as restaurant gift certificates, clothing, movie theater tickets, and money, support drug abstinence (Higgins & Petry, 1999). The piggy bank was referred to as Prefer Immediate Gratification (PIG) and was intended to serve as a reminder of the difficulties in deferring gratification. Students were asked to place pennies into the piggy bank every time they were successful with their change-behavior, thereby reinforcing their change-behavior.

Recovery Plan. Regarding their change-behavior, during the final class, students shared what they had learned over the semester and disclosed how their post class recovery plans addressed readiness for change, withdrawal, treatment acceptance, relapse potential, and recovery support. These plans were modeled after the American Society of Addiction Medicine (ASAM, 2007) placement criteria. The ASAM is a widely used aftercare planning and placement guideline used with clients with substance abuse and dependency problems. In addition, success in recovery has been correlated with having a recovery plan (Lee et al., 2010).

Coin. Clients in treatment receive coins to recognize success in sobriety (Hazelden, 2009). At the end of the class, after sharing their recovery plans, each student received a coin intended to mirror how a client may celebrate sobriety. Each coin was engraved with an inspirational quote to honor the completion of the class.

Promotion of Understanding

Watching a Movie. Research offers considerable evidence of how movies can promote learning in diverse areas such as group dynamics (Armstrong & Berg, 2005; Moe, Autry, Olson, & Johnson, 2014), family theories (Shepard & Brew, 2005), multicultural awareness (Villalba & Redmond, 2008), and diagnosis (Pearson, 2006). Films can help students "walk in the shoes of others," bring issues into the classroom, simulate real counseling experiences, and enhance "student learning" (Armstrong & Berg, 2005, p. 136).

Hearing Stories of Recovery. Research suggests stigmas are reduced through contact with the individuals who are stigmatized (Corrigan & Penn, 1999). Livingston et al. (2012) showed evidence that social stigma can be reduced through hearing positive stories of people who have substance use disorders; contact-based educational programs were effective in reducing stigmas with counselors, medical students and police officers. In this class, diverse speakers shared their stories of their addictions and their recoveries. These speakers were men and women who came from differing settings (Alcoholics Anonymous [AA], prison, etc.); and experienced various addictions (alcohol, marijuana, methamphetamine, etc.).

Didactic. The class incorporated assigned readings, videos, and article discussions in the classes to augment learning. The course topics covered etiology, diagnosis, withdrawal, readiness for change, triggers, relapse, social support, medications, spirituality, interventions, and prevention. There was one primary text, *Substance Abuse Counseling: Theory and Practice* (Stevens & Smith, 2009). More specific class information can be obtained from the primary author.

Procedure

The Institutional Review Board of the university approved the research for both years of this study; the procedures were the same in each year. To protect the rights and confidentially of participants, participation was voluntary. The SAAS was administered on the first day of class and at the conclusion of the 15-week (three-credit hour) addictions counseling course. The researchers briefly explained the study, provided the informed consent, and then invited students to complete the pre-class SAAS survey. Upon completion, students placed the survey into an envelope along with the blank post-class SAAS survey form for later use. Each student wrote his or her name on the envelope, which were then collected by the researchers, and subsequently stored in a locked cabinet until the last day of the course. During the final class, the envelopes were redistributed to each student to complete the post-class SAAS survey form. When finished, students placed all forms into a box. Students kept the envelopes with their names; thereby the surveys contained no identifying information. Each pre and post-class survey was sequentially coded to allow matching of the pre-post responses. If a student chose not to participate in the study, he or she left the survey instruments blank and the researchers were unable to identify him or her (data were kept anonymous to the researchers). Students were informed that participation in the study would not have any impact on their grades.

Instrument

The SAAS is a 50-item instrument designed to measure attitudes toward substance abuse. Each item is scored on a five point Likert-scale with responses ranging from 1 (*strongly disagree*) to 5 (*strongly agree*). The five attitude measures include the following scales: (a) *Permissiveness*: a tolerant and accepting attitude toward substance use; (b) *Non-stereotyping*: non-reliance on popular societal stereotypes of substance use and substance users; (c) *Treatment Intervention*: orientation towards perceiving substance use/misuse in the context of treatment and intervention; (d) *Treatment Optimism*: an optimistic perception of early intervention and treatment, relapse, and outcome; and (e) *Non-moralism*: absence/avoidance of moralistic perspective when considering substance use and substance users addressing such issues as law, will power, religion, and punitive approaches.

When scoring the 50-item SAAS, the raw-score is obtained for each of the five attitude measures and then transformed into independent T-scores using a conversion table provided by the questionnaire designers (Veach & Chappel, 1999). In a factor analysis of the SAAS, the alpha reliability coefficient of the four attitude measures ranged from .63 to .819, (Treatment Intervention, .63; Treatment Optimism, .67; Non-moralism, .67; Permissiveness, .77; Non-stereotypes, 0.81) (Chappel, Veach, & Krug, 1985). The research on the SAAS indicates the five factors are stable (Chappel et al., 1985; Stein, 2003). The SAAS scale is considered to have adequate reliability and validity (Chappel et al., 1985; Chappel & Veach, 1987; Gerace el al., 1995; Hagemaster et al., 1993; Richmond & Foster, 2003). Together the scores on the SAAS are considered to offer "a relatively comprehensive evaluation of factors that are believed to influence responses of health care providers to patients having problems with substance misuse or addiction" (Gerace et al., 1995, p. 290). The optimum attitude for constructive work with substance misusers is considered to be a mean score of 50 or above for each score (Richmond & Foster, 2003).

Analysis

The researchers employed a pretest-post-test design for this analysis. The course was required for all enrolled counseling students; therefore, there was no control group. Analysis was computed using the IBM Statistical Program for Social Sciences (SPSS) version 22.0. Modified Bonferroni alpha levels were employed to determine significance, thus reducing the possibility of family-wise error (Olejnik, Li, Supattathum, & Huberty, 1997). Results were considered significant at the $p = .0125$ level; the result of dividing an alpha-level of .05 by four, one for each attitude measure analyzed. Paired t-tests were tabulated to calculate pretest and posttest differences.

Results

Paired sample *t*-tests were computed for the five attitude measures to evaluate change over the semester for all students. The analyses revealed that treatment optimism scores significantly increased from $M = 20.89$ to $M = 49.75$, $t(35) = 17.186$, $p < .01$ (see Table 1).

The effect size was very large (Cohen's $d = 3.74$). The permissiveness, non-stereotyping, treatment intervention, and non-moralism scores showed no statistically significant changes.

Discussion

This study measured how students' attitudes toward addictions might change following completion of an addictions education class. The class included experiential and didactic educational strategies. The results revealed significant changes in one attitude measure: treatment optimism: from pre-class ($M = 20.32$) to post-class ($M = 48.41$). In general, a positive change in treatment optimism responses means that the research participants see drug and alcohol addictions as treatable disorder and clients can be helped even if they relapse. This change parallels the findings from similar studies where treatment optimism increased following substance abuse education (Gerace et al., 1995; Richmond & Foster, 2003).

Optimism supports a humanistic view which is promoted by the counseling profession. Essentially, humanistic beliefs are positive; they emphasize the dignity and responsibility of each person highlighting the wellness orientation. The humanistic approach is one of support, healing, and hope with the client as the expert and the counselor as the coach and fellow constructor of new stories (Dollarhide & Oliver, 2014).

Moreover, these findings are similar to studies finding optimism is higher in providers who had contact with individuals in recovery (Chappel et al., 1985; Mogar et al., 1969; Stein, 2003). Our speculation is the stories of recovering persons served in a role of providing contact, similar to that promoted by Corrigan and Penn (1999), Livingston et al. (2012), and Martinez and Murphy-Parker (2003). Students were able to hear recovering people's previous struggles and current successes, which challenged their previous beliefs and assumptions regarding addictions interventions. Additionally, Sias and Goodwin (2007) found counseling students' treatment attitudes more positive subsequent to attendance at 12-step meetings. Although the attendance of meetings may be a more natural form of contact, the six speakers from the AA member panel may have served as a form of contact to expose students to recovery.

Moran and Milsom (2015) also found that listening to guest speakers facilitated learning. Real person contact is a powerful way to impact negative beliefs (Corrigan & Penn, 1999). Hearing about the devastating impacts of substance use may have enabled students to more effectively understand the impact of substance use and abuse and hear the client's perspective and struggles; research suggests that stories of recovery can reduce stigma (Livingston et al., 2012). In addition, these real life experiences, like engaging in their own change behavior, keeping a journal of progress, and receiving a coin at the end of their program, were personally meaningful; emotional engagement is essential to transformation and change from education (Ballon & Skinner, 2008; Kolb, 1984; Manners & Durkin, 2000; Nagda et al., 2003; Osborn & Lewis, 2005).

There were no significant changes in the other four scores (permissiveness; non-stereotyping, treatment intervention and non-moralism), therefore, we can only offer speculation about the lack of statistical significance in changes. The SAAS scores of 50 or above are considered optimal for constructive work with individuals who have substance abuse problems (Richmond & Foster, 2003) and the students in this study scored a SAAS score of above 50 on 3 of the 4 scales where nonsignificant pre and post-test results were found.

Our results showed high scores $(M > 50)$ (see Table 1) in three pre-class measures: non-stereotyping ($M = 52.92$), non-moralism ($M = 50.44$), and permissiveness ($M = 50.83$). Our speculation is that these first year students may have already had open-minded attitudes. For example, non-stereotyping, which refers to not relying on popular societal stereotypes of both substance abuse and persons using substances (Chappel et al., 1985; Richmond & Foster, 2003), suggests that students' already had non-stereotyped assumptions. Stereotypic attitudes include beliefs such as no one can ever recover from heroin use, people who use marijuana do not respect authority, and people who wear hippie clothing use psychedelic drugs. Media promote attitudes and lifestyles which show substance use connected to sexual attractiveness or social competencies. A non-stereotyping approach may allow a professional helper to offer a not-knowing mindset and be fully present with clients, laying aside personal views and values, and entering "another's world without prejudice" (Rogers, 1975, p. 4). This nonjudgmental approach can lay a foundation for an effective therapeutic relationship (Miller, 2000; Norcross & Lambert, 2011).

High non-moralism scores ($M = 50.44$) reflect nonjudgmental attitudes as opposed to stereotypical ones. The scores of non-moralism showed practically no change between the pre—and the post-class assessments ($M = 50.44$ to 50.50). High moralism reflects factors such as "alcoholism implies weak will power," "clergyman should not use," and "chronic alcoholics should be legally committed." We can only speculate that the high non-moralism may indicate that the students did not hold core moral belief systems which lower their view of substance users. In our review of the literature, non-moralism score changes were infrequently reported; consequently, this is an area that needs further investigation.

High permissiveness scores historically reflect tolerant and accepting attitudes toward substance use. The pre—and post-class measures of permissiveness ($M = 50.83$ to 50.58) did not show significant change, other than a very slight reduction. Permissiveness reflects factors such as the importance of parents teaching children rules about substance use and not tolerating smoking in teens. One interpretation of more permissiveness is more tolerance. We speculate that students hearing the stories of the devastating experiences of substance use and abuse on the lives of the speakers could have reinforced negative outcomes of substance abuse, thus not increasing their permissiveness. The results from our study are similar to those found in other studies. Hagemaster et al. (1993) found decreased permissiveness in practicing nurses who completed an alcohol and drug educational program and Veach and Chappel (1990) found lower permissiveness scores in recovering addictions physicians compared to non-recovering peers.

Treatment intervention measures refer to the importance of group, family, paraprofessionals, and long-term therapy related to the effectiveness of substance abuse treatment. Equating substance abuse with treatment suggests a positive expectation. Treatment intervention scores were quite low at pre-class ($M = 41.97$) and did not show significant changes post-class ($M = 43.81$) in this study. Perhaps because the first year students did not have the actual experience of doing counseling yet, having positive treatment intervention expectations was not a part of their thinking. In a number of studies where treatment intervention scores increased, such as Chappel et al. (1985), the findings were ones in which the participants (physicians) had provided treatment showed significant changes in treatment intervention scores.

Implications for Addictions Education

In general, research has shown that education can play a pivotal role in addressing attitudes toward substance abuse in helping professionals (Carroll, 2000; Osborn & Lewis, 2005; Sias & Goodwin, 2007). There are many ways the experiential teaching can be designed, and there is no one right way.

Different programs will have unique regional and local issues. Finding speakers who themselves are in recovery can be done in numerous ways such as contacting a local AA group, the local drug courts, and the state department of treatment for substance abuse disorders. Each of these contacts will have ideas and often themselves will have speakers to talk to any class about the process of recovery, and what has worked and what has not worked. A recent example of a "local" issue is the opioid use crisis which may look different in New Hampshire compared to Colorado.

The journaling experience can be open-ended such as write about your experience each week with your change. Or it can include prompts that may be more related to the topic of the week. For example, if the class is focused on Motivational Interviewing (MI), that week the prompt could be, "Write about what helped you and what hindered you in your change behavior and relate that to empathy, rolling with resistance, and ambivalence in MI." Or, if the focus is on family and recovery, the journal prompt could be, "Identify how your role in your family is related to the change behavior you have chosen."

In this class a piggy bank was given to each student at mid-semester to replicate CM which is a strategy often employed in actual treatment settings. Although there is debate in the literature whether or not CM is the most effective intervention and if it based on internal or external incentives (Drug and Alcohol Findings, 2016), the hope in this class is that the students can experience a sense of self-reward when they are successful and "walk in the shoes" of a client in the process of change. Clients in treatment may receive rewards such as time with their families, attendance to a movie, or even a coin.

Measuring the impact of education on attitudes toward persons who work with substance abuse is imperative not only because negative attitudes may hinder effective treatment (Blagen, 2007; Lay & McGuire, 2008), but also because our counseling profession can be enhanced through rigor in our evaluation of pedagogical work (Minton et al., 2014; Moran & Milsom, 2015). There are additional ways attitudes could be measured such as use of other attitude measures such as the Alcohol Knowledge Scale [AKS] (Giannetti et al., 2002), the Marcus Alcoholism Questionnaire [(MAQ] (Martinez & Murphy-Parker, 2003); the Substance Abuse Knowledge Survey [SAKS] (Gerace et al., 1995); the Substance Abuse Experience Survey [SAES] (Gerace et al.,1995); and the Self Stigma in Alcohol Dependence Scale [SSAD] (Schomerus et al, 2011a). All of these instruments could add depth to the findings.

Overall, counselors' attitudes and stigma may impact their connections with clients and the level of empathy they show towards them. There is considerable research showing the relationship between the client and the counselor is the most predictive variable to the outcome being positive for the client (Lambert & Barley, 2001; Norcross & Lambert, 2011; Norcross & Wampold, 2011; Rogers, 1975); and experiential education enhances empathy in a relationship (Corrigan & Penn, 1999).

Limitations of the Study

Results from this study need to be interpreted relative to some limitations. Because there was not a control group, it can be hard to assure that changes occurred solely due to the class experience. Additionally, we cannot assume that the changes in treatment optimism, as measured by the SAAS, will necessarily translate into effective empathetic counseling. A convenience sample was used including only students in a Rocky Mountain based training program where there is limited diversity, thus generalizability is limited. And finally, the analysis used the single-group pretest post-test measures and this can have internal validity threats such as history and maturation. Even with the limitations to this study, it remains important to measure attitudes towards all aspects of addictions.

Future Research Directions

Researchers may want to replicate this study in diverse settings and training programs to further enhance confidence in any changes of the SAAS measures. In depth narrative feedback from students might provide insight into what attitude changes mean individually. Research could evaluate more in-detail the demographic variables such as age, gender, personal experiences with addictions, and phase in counselor training to determine if there are differential changes based on personal factors. Conducting a similar study on students two and four years later, once they have some clinical experience, would add depth to understanding attitude change. Another focus could be identifying changes in use of terminology from pre-class to post-class such as using Wordle (McNaught & Lam, 2010), as language can be both a creator of and a reflection of attitudes (Kelly et al., 2016; Saitz, 2015). Additionally, it might be interesting to explore whether brief educational interventions have similar effects compared to a semester long class.

Conclusion

Research shows that training programs can address negative attitudes, stereotypes, and stigma (Blagen, 2007; Steinfeldt & Steinfeldt, 2012). Educators can enhance awareness through providing activities that challenge students to think critically, thus they can identify such factors as internal narratives, myths, and misunderstandings about addictions (Ballon & Skinner, 2008; Lay & McGuire, 2008). Empathy is foundational to effective counseling (Horvath et al., 2011; Miller, 2000; Rogers, 1975); however, without an open mind, treatment can lack genuine caring and connection (Mogar et al., 1969; Richmond & Foster, 2003). "Humanistic beliefs about the healing process include an emphasis on empathy and the core conditions in the counseling relationship; fostering individual, relational, and group agency; the freedom, right, responsibility, and ability of the client to choose goals . . ." (Dollarhide & Oliver, 2014, p. 203). Educators can help students to recognize their biases that can impair the therapeutic alliance (Blagen, 2007; Boysen, 2010; Spaid & Squires, 2005). An important goal of addictions education is to enable an unconditional, nonjudgmental, and empathetic relationship with persons in all aspects of substance abuse work.

References

Adams, J. B., & Madson, M. B. (2007). Reflection and outlook for the future of addictionstreatment and training: An interview with William R. Miller. *Journal of Teaching in the Addictions, 5,* 95-109. doi:10.1300/J188v05n01_07

American Society of Addiction Medicine. (2007). *American Society of Addiction Medicine (ASAM) publishes Second Edition-Revised of Patient Placement Criteria* (ASAM PPC-2R). Chevy Chase, MD: Author. Retrieved from http://www.asam.org/PatientPlacementCriteria.html

Armstrong, S. A., & Berg, R. C. (2005). Demonstrating group process using *12 Angry Men*. *Journal of Specialists in Group Work, 30,* 135-144. doi:10.1080/01933920590925986

Ballon, B. C., & Skinner, W. (2008). "Attitude is a little thing that makes a big difference": Reflection techniques for addiction psychiatry training. *Academic Psychiatry, 32,* 218-224. doi:10.1176/appi.ap.32.3.218

Bessenoff, G. R., & Sherman, J. W. (2000). Automatic and controlled components of prejudice toward fat people: Evaluation versus stereotype activation. *Social Cognition, 18,* 329-353. doi:10.1521/soco.2000.18.4.329

Blagen, M. T. (2007). A research-based, experiential model for teaching a required addictive behaviors course to clinical counseling students. *Vistas 2007 Online*. Retrieved from http://counselingoutfitters.com/vistas/vistas07/Blagen.htm

Boysen, G. A. (2010). Integrating implicit bias into counselor education. *Counselor Education and Supervision, 49,* 210-227. doi:10.1002/j.1556-6978.2010.tb00099.x

Broadus, A. D., Hartje, J. A, Roget, N. A., Cahoon, K. L., & Clinkinbeard, S. S. (2010). Attitudes about addiction: A national study of addiction educators. *Journal of Drug Education, 40,* 281-298. doi:10.2190/DE.40.3.e

Carroll J. J. (2000). Counseling students' conceptions of substance-dependence and related initial interventions. *Journal of Addictions & Offender Counseling, 20,* 84-93. doi: 10.1002/j.2161-1874.2000.tb00145.x

Center for Substance Abuse Treatment. (2006). *Addiction Counseling Competencies: The Knowledge, Skills, and Attitudes of Professional Practice*. Retrieved from http://store.samhsa.gov/product/TAP-21-Addiction-Counseling-Competencies/SMA08-4171

Chafetz, M. E., Blane, H. T., Abram, H. S., Goler, J., McCourt, W. F., Clarke, E., & Meyers, W. (1962). Establishing treatment relations with alcoholics. *Journal of Nervous and Mental Diseases, 134,* 395-409. doi:10.1097/00005053-196205000-00001

Chappel, J. N., & Veach, T. L. (1987). Effect of a course on students' attitudes toward substance abuse and its treatment. *Journal of Medical Education, 62,* 394-400.

Chappel, J. N., Veach, T. L., & Krug, R. (1985). The substance abuse attitude survey. *Journal of Studies on Alcohol, 46,* 48-52. doi:10.15288/jsa.1985.46.48

Corrigan, P. W., & Penn, D. L. (1999). Lessons from social psychology on discrediting psychiatric stigma. *American Psychologist, 54,* 765-776. doi:10.1037/0003-066X.54.9.765

Corrigan, P. W., Kuwabara S. A, & O'Shaughnessy, J. (2009). The public stigma of mental illness and drug addiction: Findings form a stratified random sample. *Journal of Social Work, 9,* 139-147. doi:10.1177/1468017308101818

Council for the Accreditation of Counseling and Related Educational Programs. (2009). Proposed *CACREP accreditation manual*—effective date July 1, 2009. Alexandria, VA: Author. Retrieved from http://www.cacrep.org/2009standards.html

Crabb A. C., & Linton, J. M. (2007). A qualitative study of recovering and nonrecovering substance abuse counselors' belief systems. *Journal of Addictions & Offender Counseling, 28,* 4-20. doi:10.1002/j.2161-1874.2007.tb00028.x

Dawes-Diaz, M. L. (2007). *Education and training in substance abuse: Counselor perceptions and recommendations.* (Doctoral dissertation). Available from ProQuest Dissertations and Theses database. (ATT 3293150).

Dollarhide, C. T., & Oliver, K. (2014). Humanistic professional identity: The transtheoretical tie that binds. *The Journal of Humanistic Counseling, 53,* 203-217. doi:10.1002/j.2161-1939.2014.00057.x

Drug and Alcohol Findings. (2016). "Should we offer prizes for not using drugs?" Retrieved from http://findings.org.uk/PHP/dl.php?file=hot_CM.hot

Gerace, L. M., Hughes, T. L., & Spunt, J. (1995). Improving nurses' responses toward substance-misusing patients: A clinical evaluation project. *Archives of Psychiatric Nursing, 9,* 286-294. doi:10.1016/S0883-9417(95)80048-4

Giannetti, V. J., Sieppert, J. D., & Holosko, M. J. (2002). Attitudes and knowledge concerning alcohol abuse: Curriculum implications. *Journal of Health and Social Policy, 15,* 45-58. doi:10.1300/J045v15n01_03

Gladding, S. T. (2007). Tapping into the wellspring of wellness. *Journal of Humanistic Counseling, Education and Development, 46,* 114-119. doi:10.1002/j.2161-1939.2007.tb00029.x

Griffith, B. A., & Frieden, G. (2000). Facilitating reflective thinking in counselor education. *Counselor Education and Supervision, 40,* 82-93. doi:10.1002/j.1556-6978.2000.tb01240.x

Hagedorn, W. B. (2011). Using letters to navigate resistance and ambivalence: Experiential implications for group counseling. *Journal of Addictions & Offender Counseling, 31,* 108-126. doi:10.1002/j.2161-1874.2011.tb00071.x

Hagemaster, J., Handley, S., Plumlee, A., Sullivan, E., & Stanley, S. (1993). Developing educational programmes for nurses that meet today's addiction challenges. *Nurse Education Today, 13,* 421-425. doi:10.1016/0260-6917(93)90117-K

Hardwood, H. J., Kowalski, J., & Ameen, A. (2004). The need for substance abuse training among mental health professionals. *Administration and Policy in Mental Health, 32,* 189-205. doi:10.1023/B:APIH.0000042746.79349.64

Hazelden. (2009). *Recovery medallions and tokens to inspire and celebrate.* Retrieved from http://www.hazelden.org/web/public/custommedallions.page

Higgins, S. T., & Petry, N. M. (1999). Contingency management: Incentives for sobriety. *Alcohol Research and Health, 23,* 122-127.

Horvath, A. O., Del Re, A. C., Flückiger, C., & Symonds, D. (2011). Alliance in individual psychotherapy. *Psychotherapy, 48,* 9-16. doi:10.1037/a0022186

Kelly, J. F., Saitz, R., & Wakeman, S. (2016). Language, substance abuse disorders, and policy: The need to reach consensus on an "Addiction-ary." *Alcoholism Treatment Quarterly, 34,* 116-134. doi:10.1080/07347324.2016.1113103

Koch, D. S. (2008). Finally parity? The impact of reductionistic anachronisms on substance abuse counselor education and practice. *Journal of Teaching in the Addictions, 7,* 1-3. doi:10.1080/15332700802077158

Koch, D. S., Sneed, Z., Davis, S. J., & Benshoff, J. J. (2007). A pilot study of the relationship between counselor trainees' characteristics and attitudes toward substance abuse. *Journal of Teaching in the Addictions, 5,* 97-100. doi:10.1300/J188v05n02_07

Koehn, C., & Cutcliffe, J. R. (2012). The inspiration of hope in substance abuse counseling. *Journal of Humanistic Counseling, 51,* 78-98. doi:10.1002/j.2161-1939.2012.00007.x

Kolb, D. A. (1984). *Experiential learning: Experience as the source of learning and development.* New York, NY: Prentice Hall.

Lambert, M. J., & Barley, D. E. (2001). Research summary on the therapeutic relationship and psychotherapy outcome. *Psychotherapy, Theory, Research, Practice, Training, 38,* 357-361. doi:10.1037/0033-3204.38.4.357

La Torre, M. A. (2005). Self-reflection: An important process for the therapist. *Perspectives in Psychiatric Care, 41,* 85-87. doi:10.1111/j.1744-6163.2005.00019.x

Lay, K., & McGuire, L. (2008). Teaching students to deconstruct life experience with addictions: A structured reflection exercise. *Journal of Teaching and Addictions, 7,* 145-163. doi:10.1080/15332700802269227

Lee, C. S., Baird, J., Longabaugh, R., Nirenberg, T. D., Mellow, J. M., & Woolard, R. N. (2010). Change plan as an active ingredient of brief motivational interventions for reducing negative consequences of drinking in hazardous drinking emergency-department patients. *Journal of Studies on Alcohol and Drugs, 71,* 726-733. doi:10.15288/jsad.2010.71.726

Lee, T. K. (2014). Addiction education and training for counselors: A qualitative study of five experts. *Journal of Addictions & Offender Counseling, 35,* 67-80. doi:10.1002/j.2161-1874.2014.00027.x

Livingston, J. D., Milnes, T., Fang, M. L., & Amari, E. (2012). The effectiveness of interventions for reducing stigma related to substance use disorders: A systematic review. *Addiction, 107,* 39-50. doi:10.1111/j.1360-0443.2011.03601.x

Lloyd, C. (2010). *Sinning and sinned against: The stigmatization of problem drug users.* The UK Drug Policy Commission (UKDPC). Retrieved from http//www.ukdpc.org.uk/reports.shtmlT

Manners, J., & Durkin, K. (2000). Processes involved in adult ego development: A conceptual framework. *Developmental Review, 20,* 475-523. doi:10.1006/drev.2000.0508

Martinez, R., & Murphy-Parker, D. (2003). Examining the relationship of addiction education and beliefs of nursing students toward persons with alcohol problems. *Archives of Psychiatric Nursing, 27,* 156-164. doi:10.1016/S0883-9417(03)00086-4

McKim, C., Warren, J., Asfaw A. H., Balich, R., Nolte, M., Perkins, D., Sasse, G., & Zakaria, N. S. (2014). An integrative model of recovery: A qualitative study of perceptions six counseling doctoral students. *Research in Psychology and Behavioral Sciences, 2,* 17-23. doi:10:12691/rpbs-2-1-4.

McLellan, A. T., Lewis, D. C., O'Brien, C. P., & Kleber, H. D. (2000). Drug dependence, a chronic medical illness: Implications for treatment, insurance, and outcome evaluation. *Journal of the American Medical Association, 284,* 1689-1695. doi:10.1001/jama.284.13.1689

McNaught, C. & Lam, P. (2010). Using Wordle as a supplementary research tool. *The Qualitative Report, 15,* 630-643.

Miller, W. R. (2000). Rediscovering fire: Small interventions, large effects. *Psychology of Addictive Behaviors, 14,* 6-18. doi:10.1037//0893-164X.14.I.6

Minton, C. A. B., Morris, C. A. W., & Yaites, L. D. (2014). Pedagogy in counselor education: A 10-year content analysis of journals. *Counselor Education and Supervision, 53,* 162-177. doi:10.1002/j.1556-6978.2014.00055.x

Moe, J., Autry, L., Olson, J. S., & Johnson, K. F. (2014). Teaching group work with *The Great Debaters*. *Counselor Education and Supervision, 53*, 204-218. doi:0.1002/j.1556-6978.2014.00058.x

Mogar, R. E., Helm, S. T., Snedeker, M. R., Snedeker, M. H., & Wilson, W. M. (1969). Staff attitudes toward the alcoholic patient. *Archives of General Psychiatry, 21*, 449-454. doi:10.1001/archpsyc.1969.01740220065007

Moran, K., & Milsom, A. (2015). The flipped classroom in counselor education. *Counselor Education and Supervision, 54*, 32-43. doi:10.1002/j.1556-6978.2015.00068.x

Morrissette, P. J., & Gadbois, S. (2006). Ethical considerations of counselor education teaching strategies, *Counseling and Values, 50*, 131-141. doi:10.1002/j.2161-007X.2006.tb00049.x

Nagda, B. R., Gurin, P., & Lopez, G. E. (2003). Transformative pedagogy for democracy and social justice. *Race, Ethnicity and Education, 6*, 165-191. doi:10.1080/13613320308199

Nellis, A., Greene, J., & Mauer, M. (2008). Reducing racial disparity in the criminal justice system: A manual for practitioners and policymakers. *The Sentencing Project*. Retrieved from http://www.sentencingproject.org

National Institute on Drug Abuse (NIDA). (2012). Evidence-based practices. Retrieved from www.drugabuse.gov/category/drug-topics/evidence-based-practices

Norcross, J. C., & Lambert, M. (2011). Psychotherapy relationships that work II. *Psychotherapy, 48*, 4-8. doi:10.1037/a0022180

Norcross, J. C., & Wampold, B. E. (2011). Evidence-based therapy relationships: Research conclusions and clinical practices. *Psychotherapy, 48*, 98-102. doi:10.1037/a0022161

Olejnik, S., Li, J., Supattathum, S., & Huberty, C. (1997). Multiple testing and statistical power with modified Bonferroni procedures. *Journal of Educational and Behavioral Statistics 22*, 389-406. doi:10.2307/1165229

Osborn, C. J., & Lewis, T. F. (2005). Experiential training in substance abuse counseling: Curricular design and instructional practices. *Journal of Teaching in the Addictions, 3*, 41-56. doi:10.1300/J188v03n02_04j

Pearson, Q. (2006). Using the film *The Hours* to teach diagnosis. *Journal of Humanistic Counseling, Education, & Development, 45*, 70-78. doi:10.1002/j.2161-1939.2006.tb00006.x

Quinn, G. (2010). Institutional denial or minimization: Substance abuse training in social work education. *Substance Abuse, 31*, 8-11. doi:10.1080/08897070903442475

Richmond, I., & Foster, J. (2003). Negative attitudes towards people with co-morbid mental health and substance misuse problems: An investigation of mental health professionals. *Journal of Mental Health, 12*, 393-403. doi:10.1080/0963823031000153439

Rogers, C. R. (1975). Empathetic: An unappreciated way of being. *The Counseling Psychologist, 5*, 2-10. doi:10.1177/001100007500500202

Saitz, R. (2015). Things that work, things that don't work, and things that matter-Including words. *Journal of Addiction Medicine, 9*, 429-430. doi:10.1097/ADM.0000000000000170

Salyers, K. M., Ritchie, M. H., Cochrane, W. S., & Roseman, C. P. (2006). Inclusion of substance abuse training in CACREP-Accredited programs. *Journal of Addictions & Offender Counseling, 27*, 47-58. doi: 10.1002/j.2161-1874.2006.tb00018.x

Schomerus, G., Corrigan, P. W., Klauer, T., Kuwert, P., Freyberger, H. J., & Lucht, M. (2011a). Self-stigma in alcohol dependence: Consequences for drinking-refusal self-efficacy. *Drug and Alcohol Dependence, 114*, 12-17. doi:10.1016/j.drugalcdep.2010.08.013

Schomerus, G., Lucht, M., Holzinger, A., Matschinger, H., Carta, M., & Angermeyer, M. (2011b). The stigma of alcohol dependence compared with other mental disorders: A review of population studies. *Alcohol and Alcoholism, 46*,105-112. doi:10.1093/alcalc/agq089

Sheehan, T. J., Walker, C., & Reiter, D. (2008). Teaching addiction counseling: A comparison of social interdependence methods and traditional lecture-based instruction. *Journal of Teaching and Addictions, 6,* 49-58. doi:10.1080/15332700802126344

Shepard, D, S., & Brew. L. (2005). Teaching theories of couples counseling: the use of popular movies. *The Family Journal, 13,* 406-415. doi:10.1177/1066480705278470e

Sias, S. M., & Goodwin, L. R. (2007). Students' reactions to attending 12-step meetings: Implications for counselor education. *Journal of Addictions & Offender Counseling, 27,* 113-126. doi:10.1002/j.2161-1874.2007.tb00025.x

Sias, S. M., Lambie, G. W., & Foster, V. A. (2006). Conceptual and moral development of substance abuse counselors: Implications for training. *Journal of Addictions & Offender Counseling, 26,* 99-110. doi:10.1002/j.2161-1874.2006.tb00011.x

Spaid, W. A., & Squires, S. P. (2005). Changing social work students' attitudes toward substance abusers through the use of an abstinence assignment: A pilot study. *Journal of Teaching in the Addictions, 4,* 45-62. doi:10.1300/J188v04n02_03

Stadler, H. A., Suh, S., Cobia, D. C., Middleton, R. A., & Carney, J. S. (2006). Reimagining counselor education with diversity as a core value. *Counselor Education and Supervision, 45,* 193-206. doi:10.1002/j.1556-6978.2006.tb00142.x

Stein, J. B. (2003). Attitudes of social work students about substance abuse: Can a brief educational experience make a difference? *Journal of Social Work Practice in the Addictions, 3,* 77-99. doi:10.1300/J160v03n01_06

Steinfeldt, J. A., & Steinfeldt, M. C. (2012). Multicultural training intervention to address American Indian stereotypes. *Counselor Education and Supervision, 51,* 17-32. doi:10.1002/j.1556-6978.2012.00002.x

Stevens, P., & Smith, R. L. (2009). *Substance abuse counseling: Theory and practice* (4th ed.). Upper Saddle River, NJ: Merrill Prentice-Hall.

Vadlamudi, R. S., Adams, S., Hogan, B., Wu, T., & Wahid, Z. (2008). Nurses' attitudes, beliefs, and confidence levels regarding care for those who abuse alcohol: Impact of educational intervention. *Nurse Education in Practice, 8,* 290-298. doi:10.1016/j.nepr.2007.10.003

Veach, T. L., & Chappel, J. N. (1990). Physician attitudes in chemical dependency: The effects of personal experience and recovery. *Substance Abuse, 11,* 97-101.

Veach, T. L., & Chappel, J. (1999). *Self Scoring Substance Abuse Attitude* (SAAS). Office of Medical Education, Reno, Nevada.

Villalba, J. A., & Redmond, R. E. (2008). *Crash:* Using a popular film as an experiential learning activity in a multicultural counseling course. *Counselor Education and Supervision, 47,* 264-276. doi:10.1002/j.1556-6978.2008.tb00056.x

Warren, J., Hof, K., McGriff, D., & Morris, L. B. (2012). Five experiential learning activities in addictions education. *Journal of Creativity in Mental Health, 7,* 2-17. doi:10.1080/15401383.2012.710172

Whittinghill, D., Carroll, J. J., & Morgan, O. (2004). Curriculum standards for the education of professional substance abuse counselors. *Journal of Teaching in the Addictions, 3,* 63-76. doi:10.1300/J188v03n02_06

Table 1

Substance Abuse Attitudes Survey (SAAS) Subscale Scores (Paired-sample t-test)

Subscale	Pretest t Score Mean (SD)	Post-test t Score Mean (SD)	t-statistic (35 df)	Cohen's d	Significance
Permissiveness	50.83 (10.28)	50.58 (9.04)	.214	-	.832
Nonstereotyping	52.92 (8.22)	52.73 (6.88)	.561	-	.578
Treatment Intervention	41.97 (7.11)	43.81 (10.30)	1.454	-	.155
Treatment Optimism	20.89 (2.42)	49.75 (10.63)	17.186	3.74	.000
Nonmoralism	50.44 (8.78)	50.50 (8.24)	.046	-	.964

11

Wearing their Shoes

Creating Counselors' Understanding of Addiction through Empathy

Christina Rosen and Geoffrey G. Yager[1]

Counselors in general recognize the value of empathy in (a) helping to establish a solid therapeutic relationship through communicating understanding of the client's emotions and feelings and (b) encouraging a client's full exploration of all existing concerns. The skill of communicating empathy is perhaps even more important with addictions counselors because their work often confronts them with feelings of "being stuck" or "actively resisted," or "directly challenged." For example, it is commonplace for an addictions counselor to experience (a) a client's frustration in not feeling understood, (b) a client's direct expression of resistance to being involved in mandated counseling, (c) a client's somewhat indirect signal that understanding is crucial when often asked, "Are you (the

---

1. Christina Rosen, Human Development and Psychological Counseling, Reich College of Education, Appalachian State University; Geoffrey Yager, Counseling Program, School of Human Services, College of Education, Criminal Justice, and Human Services, University of Cincinnati. Correspondence concerning this article should be addressed to Christina Rosen, Human Development and Psychological Counseling, Reich College of Education, Room 336D Appalachian State University, Boone, NC 28608. Email: rosencm@appstate.edu

counselor) in recovery yourself?" or (d) a client's attack on the counselor for either minimizing the impact of addiction (or, on the other hand, for seeing much larger impact of the addiction than the client is ready to admit). For experienced addictions counselors, all of these possibilities will occur from time to time, and as those who work in the field of addictions also know, individuals with addiction concerns are all too often judged harshly from a moralistic viewpoint. To overcome the negative expectations generated by such a perspective, substance abusing clients desperately need to encounter counselors who are both non-judgmental and empathic.

This article is addressed to counselor educators and supervisors who work in the field of addictions. It explains one method to increase the addictions counselors' understanding of clients' world through empathy and, using this information, to enhance the therapeutic connection with those who have come for help.

The method proposed to encourage more effective use of empathy is the Cognitive Self-Instructional Training Model of Empathy Training. For purposes of this article, we have chosen to use the acronym CSIME to abbreviate the model (i.e., Cognitive Self-Instructional Modeling for Empathy—to be pronounced as "Sesame," similar to the "magic words" employed to open a cave of hidden treasure in "Ali Baba and the Forty Thieves"). This approach to empathy training was first proposed by Ochiltree, Yager, and Brekke's (1975). Essentially, this model describes a plan for increasing students' and professional counselors' ability to "wear their client's shoes." In a very concrete manner, Ochiltree et al. outline an approach to building the skills of empathy and cultural awareness in trainees and supervisees. Developing these skills directly enhances the therapeutic alliance (Garza, Falls, & Bruhn, 2009; Grace, Kivlighan, & Kunce, 1995; Neukrug, Bayne, Dean-Nganga, & Pusateri, 2013; Norcross, & Wampold, 2011; Pickover, 2013). In the specific case of addictions counseling, these same skills are especially essential for counselors who worry they are unable to understand the client because they themselves are not in recovery from substance abuse (Angus & Kagan, 2007; Conner, Rosen, Wexler, & Brown, 2010; Fiorentine, & Hillhouse, 1999; Miller, 1985; & Nguyen, Clark, & Belgrave, 2011).

Therapeutic alliances

One very well established approach for the addictions field asserts that the purpose of counseling someone with an SUD (substance use disorder) is to engage the client and increasing the motivation and ability to change (Feldstein, & Forchimes, 2007; Miller, 1985; Miller, Benefiew, & Tonigan 1993; Norcross & Wampold, 2011). Seeing counseling in this way tends to create a different understanding the counselor and client interaction (Norcross, & Wampold, 2011). One apparent impact of this newer view of therapeutic interactions has been that some addiction counselors have moved to focus exclusively on the use of techniques to motivate the client to change. Unfortunately, such an exclusive focus tends to result in the counselor's losing attention to the development of the counseling relationship *between* client and counselor. In mastering the techniques of change, these counselors seem to have lost the necessary and crucial concentration required to develop effective and quality empathy. Although the achievements of the motivational interviewing approach are clearly valuable, a counselor may miss the important step of connecting with the client by moving too quickly to motivational efforts (Gaume, Bertholet, Faouzi, Gmel, & Daeppen, 2010; Gaume, Gmel, Faouzi, & Daeppen, 2009). It is initially crucial that counselors use empathy to communicate a clear effort to understand their clients while building an effective therapeutic relationship (Campbell et al., 2013; Marlow et al., 2012, Rogers 1951; Shaffer, & Hasegawa, 1984). As supervisors, our role is to assist counselors in recognizing they have not mastered either the technique or intention of motivational interviewing unless and until a therapeutic relationship has been solidly initiated.

CSIME can effectively promote a counselor's empathic abilities. The cognitive self-instructional model is not generally known within the counseling discipline or the substance abuse field. This approach is based on the empathy training model inspired by Rogers (1951) and developed by Carkhuff (1969). In the early 1970s, Meichenbaum and his colleagues (Meichenbaum, 1971, 1973; Meichenbaum & Goodman, 1971; Meichenbaum & Cameron, 1973) created the self-instructional modeling approach to developing skills. Ochiltree et al. (1975) described how the self-instructional approach would apply to developing empathy. Over the past six decades, the skills that Rogers (1951) described in his writings have been delineated as "micro-skills," "basic skills," and, even, "motivational interviewing skills." Attention to developing skills has resulted in the expansion of Rogers' initial understandings to other professional disciplines. For example, physicians have been trained to use micro listening skills through brief interventions and motivational interviewing to assess and reduce substance use in patients while enhancing appropriate referrals (Brown et al., 2010; Kaner, Dickinson et al., 2009; Kaner, Bland et al., 2013). The awareness of relationship-building skills has provided the field of addictions with a surge in energy, encouraging respectful treatment of clients diagnosed with a substance use disorder (SUD) rather than the harsh confrontation that had previously been prevalent. For far too long, many in our society have taken a moral view of substance abuse: "If substances are a problem, pull yourself up by your own bootstraps and STOP using them! If you don't, clearly you are not morally competent to handle your own life!" A counselor's direct communication of understanding through empathy can serve to counteract these negative communications.

Research serves to support the importance of the relationship in effective counseling (Angus & Kagan, 2007; Campbell, et al., 2013; Norcross & Wampold, 2011). One of the key elements is the client's perception of feeling heard by the counselor (Garza et al., 2009; Gerdes, Segal, Jackson, & Mullins, 2011; Grace, Kivlighan, & Kunce, 1995; Marlow et al., 2012; Neukrug et al., 2013). This connection between the counselor and client is the most important element in creating client change (Horvath & Bedi, 2002; Miller, 1985). As such, it is important for the counselor to slow down and provide clear and effective communication describing what has been heard. Despite its importance, there are very few specific, concrete models providing a road map to assist students and professional counselors in building and delivering empathy statements.

Counselors much act to concentrate on direct listening skills *with no agenda attached* (i.e., counselors need to go beyond a simple, focused agenda on "motivating" the client.). To accomplish this "direct listening" skill, substance abuse counselor educators and site supervisors must focus trainees (i.e., students or professional colleagues) on developing effective empathy *without an exclusive* concern on motivating a client toward change. Furthermore, field supervisors need to monitor substance abuse counselors to identify any needed remediation related the now often-overlooked skill of empathy. Even with a clinician who had previously developed solid empathy skills, feelings of burnout and being overwhelmed with paperwork can quickly produce a lack of focus on the core skill of understanding.

Foundation

For over 30 years, the authors of this article have implemented a method for training counselors to develop empathy. In this time, there has been an opportunity to explore fully the role of a student counselor's self-talk on developing empathy skills. This model of teaching empathy has also been used both directly and indirectly in supervision (in course work and with professional counselor supervisors). The method assists counselors in taking a verbal step back, slowing down the process, and pausing in order to listen to and integrate more completely the client's point of view. Such slowing down is in direct contrast to a typical student's tendency (a) to think of a response before the client has finished talking and (b) to deliver that next response before the client has truly processed what has been stated already. Often, a client is simply not yet ready to move the next step toward an overall counseling goal. Pausing to reestablish the client-counselor connection (alliance) via CSIME has empowered professional counselors to examine their perceptions of the client and to recognize the impact that perceptions have on the counselor-client relationship (Ochiltree, et al., 1975).

Model

Cognitive self-instructional modeling training provides just such a road map through six simple questions dedicated to training student counselors and professionals in developing empathy statements. In essence, taking the time to think through these questions and answer each one virtually guarantees that the counselor's next response will convey the counselor's sincere effort to communicate understanding of the client and his/her issues. These are the questions:

1. How can I pat myself on the back for something I've actually said or for something I may have learned about the client? [Essentially, this "odd" initial question is designed to push the counselor out of the very ingrained and unhelpful habit of focusing immediately and almost exclusively on "what I've done wrong." Redirecting attention to the positive aspects of the counseling session serves to free up a counselor's openness and creativity.]

2. What has the client expressed verbally about his/her emotions?

3. What has the client indicated nonverbally about his/her emotions?

4. How do I feel right now? [This question is also unusual and almost appears irrelevant. But . . . we so often "know things" that we don't immediately have words to express. Awareness of our own feelings as counselors may later lead to valuable insights about the client.]

5. How would I feel if I had experienced the same situation that the client has described to me? [If I were this client, with the same background and life experiences, how might I feel in the situation that has just been discussed? —Not 'How would I feel?' but 'How would I feel if I were really this person?'].

6. How can I combine the emotions that I have identified in the above question with the content that I heard as I listened to the client, in order to make a response that clarifies what I understood? I will say the response once to myself before I speak it aloud. "You feel [emotional word] because [content]."

Most counseling programs teach Client Centered therapy in their techniques course. Typically students are taught paraphrasing, summary statements and empathy statements such as "you feel ___," "I heard you say _____." Often, the counselor in training, knowing that feelings are important, reverts to "How are you feeling?" when an emotional word isn't immediately identified. Essentially, many students are left to try and figure out what the feeling "should be" with minimal or no instruction on the steps toward developing an effective empathy statement. Employing CSIME gives a developing counselor concrete, slowly-paced steps to generate emotional words and communicate understanding.

To address the specifics of this approach, the process will be described step by step. In most cases, CSIME is introduced within a pre-practicum, techniques, or practicum class as students work to practice in groups. The six questions are explained to everyone in the class with a direct effort to generate answers for each question. These practices may involve creating responses as a group to role-played or video representations of client statements. As a second step, role-plays with students smaller groups are initiated (three to four with a student supervisor) with the small group generating answers to the questions. As the skill of each student counselor increases, students begin to abbreviate the questions and need less help to generate likely client emotions. The next step in the learning occurs with student counselors in role-play situations generating responses aloud individually. These practice role-plays are recorded so that the supervisor can review the trainee's clarity in answering the questions. The final stage is that the student counselor thinks the questions silently, practicing the empathy responses in role-plays that are recorded and reviewed by the supervisor.

Purpose

This sections articulates the purpose of CISME's and the various ways CISME has been used. CISME has been primarily used to teach students how to understand a client and to develop their responses to the client. For student counselors, this model takes the guessing or "magic" away from the response by breaking the process into six questions. For professional substance abuse counselors, the thinking process gives the supervisor a chance to refresh and enhance his/her supervisees' skills. The supervisor uses the questions as a means to slow the counselor's response time, thereby avoiding the quick responses to any client statement, particularly if this takes the form of extreme emotions or an attack. Such a contemplative response is particularly helpful for substance abuse counselors who are dealing with a client's feeling of hostility, fear, or impending disaster. This method can assist substance abuse counselors to detach from their personal reaction to the emotions of the client while staying focused on listening and understanding the client's feelings and worldview.

Example

Client: "I am so angry that you have misinterpreted my life so negatively! Just because I've lost a job doesn't mean that alcohol had anything to do with it. I was ready to quit just before that time that I was hung over and late. They let me go because they knew I was moving on."
Counselor: [After having thought carefully through the six questions of self-instructional modeling] "You are feeling angry and judged because in my mind, I'm making a connection between your being late to work after drinking and the fact they let you go."

This response, of course, appears to be a fine client centered reflection, and that is exactly what it is. The use of CSIME, therefore, does not necessarily engender responses different from good Rogerian empathy, but it tends to accomplish the creation of such responses with reduced tension and anxiety.

Supervision

Of course, these same questions can be used effectively in supervision to assist a substance abuse counselor's treatment choices when stuck with a client. Bernard and Goodyear (2008) and Culter et al. (2009) recognized that even seasoned counselors need supervision to work through feeling of being stuck, burned out, fatigued, and forgetful (e.g., about the importance of empathy). It is possible for any counselor, regardless of experience, to struggle with understanding a client or to avoid interpreting something a client has said as a personal attack. CSIME has been used as a tool to assist counselors to slow down, pause, and think about the process while developing a statement. This effort moves the counselor away from a place of being completely reactive to a place of careful contemplation and intentionality.

Instructions for teaching/supervising

How can the supervisor help the beginning counselor to get to a place of contemplation and intentionality? The use of the six questions is a great place to start because it is relatively clear when a student counselor has actually taken the time to ask the questions silently. If the student is making on-going reactive responses (i.e., responses without pausing and asking the questions), the supervisor can directly share this observation with the counselor and initiate an exploratory discussion. In most cases, the telltale sign of a student's neglecting the questions is the absence of a pause and a lowered quality (i.e., either the emotion is not quite correct or the content has not been addressed clearly) in his/her empathy statements.

A secondary use, of the Cognitive Self-instructional Training, for clinical supervisors, came directly from work in the mental health field specializing in substance abuse and mental health treatment (e.g., dual diagnosis). In reflecting on comments from clients and students, the authors became aware that cognitive self-instructional modeling had been incorporated as a way of being with clients, peers, and supervisees. For example, abbreviated versions of these questions, with associated pauses before responding, had become an integral part of these counselors' approach to their work. Clients often felt deeply heard, as did peers and supervisees. When resistance and conflict inevitably came up in counseling or in consultation with peers, these same empathy skills tended to eliminate the unwanted responses of argument or debate. Counselors' reactivity to anger and stress had been greatly reduced by being able to slow down the process and develop understanding of the listener's point of view.

As clinical supervisors, these questions can be adapted for supervision with substance abuse counselors and mental health counselors, helping supervisees feel empowered, unstuck, and understood. Too often in the past, these supervisees had not been listening completely or understanding their counselor supervisees. Instead, they were thinking of responses before the supervisee had finished talking, leaving these individuals with a sense of not being heard. After supervision and the new awareness, supervisees began reporting an improvement in the relationship with the client as well as movement in working on treatment goals. In addition, supervisees felt more accepted, connected, and understood by the supervisor.

Counselor educators

Addiction Courses and Clinical Experiences

Having briefly discussed the role of the supervisor, how does CSIME impact counselor educators? Counselor educators can readily adapt these same questions in teaching internships or substance abuse related courses. The purpose of using this technique is in instructing students on understanding the client from the client's situation and perspective concerning substance use, recovery, and relapse. Sometimes this instruction may involve all six questions directly to build empathy, and sometimes it can be illustrated through the teacher modeling responses to questions by students or in class activities around recovery, or in demonstrations of counseling skills. As university supervisors teaching internship courses, the questions can be introduced (or re-introduced), as needed, to assist students as a means to slow down response time (i.e., developing a pause) and to increase the quality of listening to the client. Therefore, depending on the purpose of revisiting CSIME will determine if all six questions are used to increase quality of listening or sometimes the questions are addressed as a means to guide an increased student understanding of the client's perspective.

Students' response

Counseling students in addictions classes taught by one of the authors often ask if the implementation of these six questions serve as an aspect of motivational interviewing. The answer, of course, is "No." The six questions are a one way to teach each skill; empathy, paraphrasing and challenging statements. The self-instructional modeling approach is merely a way to teach students to understand the client's world by "walking in their shoes." Moreover, when a counselor/supervisor demonstrates this technique without saying the questions aloud or telling the students what the instructors is doing, students are likely through role-play to feel deeply understood and unable to hide their feeling. Students thereby have a personal experience of the impact of a careful, slow, intentional process of developing an empathy response, which effectively reinforces the importance of practicing such an approach. In the processing of such demonstrations with an experienced instructor, students can begin to clarify the unproductive and less helpful ways to address answering the six questions. Often there is a need to work with new learners to address how each of the following sample questions might keep them from making an effective empathy statement:

> "Maybe I shouldn't say anything about feelings because I'm not certain how the client is feeling?"
> "Do I want to risk 'putting words in the mouth' of my client?"
> "Why don't I just simply suggest what my client needs to do to avoid this uncomfortable situation?"

Counselor self-awareness

Grace et al. (1995) identified a positive correlation between the therapeutic working alliance and the counselor's own insightfulness. Clients rated having a closer relationship with counselors who communicate more self-awareness in session. A by-product of self-instructional modeling training is increasing counselors' self-awareness of internal processes, including thinking dialogues and personal emotions. Livingston et al. (2012) discussed the need for counselors to understand and challenge their own biases and stereotyping in order that they can reduce harm to the therapeutic alliance. For counselors to stay effective and reduce harm to their clients, it is imperative that they understand themselves (i.e., prejudice, myths, and stereotypes). Without this self-knowledge, counselors place themselves at risk of being culturally insensitive.

Counselors will not necessarily share their internal dialogue directly with a supervisor, especially if they are feeling inadequate or culturally incompetent (Rosen-Galvin, 2005). The self-instructional modeling training allows the students to start their reflections with looking at what they did well (Question 1); this moves the focus off what they did not like about themselves or about the client (e.g., "I really was bumbling in my last response." "I hate the way I say "um-hmm" so often." "The client's response was so disrespectful, and I have no idea how to address that.") and onto more positive thoughts. Another way that self-awareness is increased for the counselor is through reflecting on his/her current feelings and thoughts (Question 4), which are separated from the client's feelings, thoughts, and non-verbal behaviors (Questions 2 and 3). Such a change in focus can help to avoid projections, reactions, or confusion around the feelings and thoughts of the client. It gives space to the counselors to check their own emotions before speaking. In addition, counselors rehearse (in Question 6) what they will say before speaking aloud to the client. This process assists counselors to hear themselves prior to speaking, a process directly helpful in building self-awareness and insight. Perls (1969) believed it was important for counselors to know themselves and to be aware (mindful) of their own process and defenses in order to be as effective as possible. Furthermore, Block-Lerner, Adair, Plum, Rhatigan, and Orsillo (2007) reported the need for counselors to know their own emotions before they can be empathic toward a client.

Reactiveness responses

Pausing and reflecting are essential self-awareness builders and valuable tools for any substance abuse counselor. These tools give the counselor time to think and detach before being reactive, especially during times of feeling defensive. For example, novice counselors often believe they cannot counsel someone who has a substance abuse disorder unless they themselves are in recovery from substance abuse. Of course, some professional substance abuse counselors have the same view (Conner et al., 2010). And many times a client will ask if the counselor is in recovery. Clients typically ask these questions in a way that takes counselors by surprise or in a tone that can sound (or may *actually be*) judgmental. Therefore, counselors often feel attacked or judged, leading to feelings of threat or defensiveness. In asking such questions, clients are likely to be merely expressing emotions and thoughts. Clients' motives could vary from being manipulative to wanting to ensure that they are receiving "good treatment." In response to feeling attacked, a novice counselor is likely to feel compelled to be defensive and obligated to answer this question. A professional counselor can often feel annoyed with such questions. Moreover, if counselors respond defensively or with an aggressive tone, clients readily perceive such a reaction as a confirmation that the counselor is not completely trustworthy. Substance abuse clients have indicated that they want a counselor who understands their struggles (Miville, Carlozzi, Gushue, Schara, & Ueda, 2006). Clients prefer counselors who are in recovery because they believe the recovering counselors will likely better understand their experience and, therefore, be more helpful in promoting treatment success (Batson et al. 2003).

Intentional response

The substance abuse counselor using the self-instructional model slows down his/her response and provides an understanding reply instead of a reactive one. By slowing down the reaction/response time, the counselor will cause clients to see the attempts to understand. Counselors accomplish this by reflecting on the six questions before giving the client a response. The questions 1 through 4 help counselors to explore the client's thoughts and feelings as well as their own thoughts and feelings. The fifth question helps the counselor in trying to wear the client's shoes by looking at the client's world (i.e., feelings, thoughts, situation, and experiences). With such introspection, the subsequent response is more accurate for the specific client. The sixth question is the counselor practicing the response before saying the response aloud. By practicing one or more responses, the counselor can hear his/her response before saying it and thereby decide which response best fits. This gives clients a sense of being understood, which builds unconditional positive regard—the therapeutic relationship (Rogers, 1951).

Technique Instructions

The Self-Instruction model's six questions build on each other and must be practiced repeatedly before a counselor can relax and feel comfortable with the questions. Once the counselor masters these questions, the "understanding responses" create for the counselor the ability to provide an empathy statement from the client's perspective.

Case example

Let us suppose that a 45 year old male client has talking with a substance abuse counselor for twenty minutes. During that time, he has been very cognitive in describing his life situation. Emotions have not come up, even though it is clear that he's recently had a very difficult time in his life. He has attempted alcohol treatment unsuccessfully on three occasions. Recently, his wife separated from him with his two children. Having accumulated four DUI arrests, there is a definite possibility that he will be returning to jail. Although it may be on shaky ground, the client still holds his job in the construction field. After having explained all of this to his counselor, he turns to her and states: "I really wonder if this fourth attempt at treatment could possibly be any more helpful than the others. You look like you are only a few years older than my teenage son: how can you really help me?"

What follows are the thoughts a substance abuse counselor might address (in silence) in response to each of the self-instructional questions before answering the client. (a) How can I pat myself on the back for something I've actually said or for something I may have learned about the client? Counselor thought: "I was able to keep quiet and stay calm, and I am answering these questions." (b) What has the client expressed verbally about his/her emotions? Counselor thought: "Hum, no direct feelings were stated by the client." (c) What has the client indicated nonverbally about his/her emotions? Counselor thoughts: "The client's facial expression looks curious; the voice tone sounds a bit abrupt and a bit tense. The client could be feeling nervous, worried, angry, uncertain, cautious, annoyed, or manipulative." (d) How do I feel right now? Counselor thoughts: "Worried, scared, inadequate, uncertain, annoyed, and doubtful—I'm wondering if I can understand and help the client." (e) How would I feel if I had experienced the same situation that the client has described to me? Counselor thoughts: "If I were 45 years old, a white male (this client), on my fourth attempt at treatment, having at least three relapses . . . Being on probation, separated from my spouse and kids, with the threat of going back to jail if I don't stop . . . And, I am trying to hold on to my career. Yet, I have to go to treatment with a counselor that just looks to be barely 25 year old. Who is telling me I have to quit drinking and smoking pot for the rest of my life? -—I think I would feeling angry, worried, scared and stressed (maybe overwhelmed?) with a lot of doubt and little hope." (f) How can I combine the emotions that I have identified in the above question with the content that I heard? Counselor thoughts: "You feel really uncomfortable because, as young as I am, you just aren't sure that I'm going to be able to understand what you've been through." or "You are worried because you think I might not be able to understand your situation and help you."

Having carefully addressed each question, the counselor replies to the client with: "You are worried because you think I might not be able to help you with your recovery."

Discussion

This approach may assist student counselors in reducing the stress and anxiety about being "good" counselors by giving them an avenue to develop empathy. Furthermore, the approach assists supervisors in the field by providing a way to guide supervisees in becoming "unstuck." By asking the supervisees to listen to their own internal process (e.g., feelings and thoughts) and explore misunderstandings with the client, both counselors and clients are allowed to be human, with neither having to be right or wrong. The questions can be infused directly in supervisory sessions with the supervisees (either students or licensed professionals) as recordings or verbatim transcripts are reviewed. Supervisees can appropriately be asked to practice these same questions while at home in front of the television. Of course, to avoid potential embarrassment, they should avoid doing this thinking aloud while in the company of others! Every time the authors have implemented this approach with supervisees, counselors have found the process energizing and valuable.

This structure supports *Motivational Interviewing* and the stages of change (Feldstein & Forchimes, 2007) and it will feel familiar to the experienced counselor. The difference between *Motivational Interviewing* and CSIME model lies in the intentionality on "understanding the client" where that client happens to be *without* any expectation about motivating that client to change. Interestingly, it is likely that change will occur as the client develops trust that the counselor is actively listening without any other agenda. The client is not another number or just another person on the counselor's schedule. Instead, the client feels deeply understood and supported. Therefore, the client is likely to be willing to be more open and honest, and to move toward completing a treatment goal. Finally, this structure gives supervisors and counselor educators a way to provide future counselors with a tool they can carry with them throughout their careers.

References

Angus, L., & Kagan, F. (2007). Empathic relational bonds and personal agency in psychotherapy: Implications for psychotherapy supervision, practice, and research. *Psychotherapy: Theory, Research, Practice, Training,* 44(4), 371-377. doi: 10.1037/0033-3204.44.4.371

Batson, C. D., Lishner, D. A., Carpenter, A., Dulin, L., Harjusola-Webb, S., Stocks, E. L., Gale, S., Omar Hassan, O., & Sampat, B. (2003). "... As you would have them do unto you": Does imagining yourself in the other's place stimulate moral action? *Personality and Social Psychology Bulletin,* 29(9), 1190-1201. doi:10.1177/0146167203254600

Bernard, J. M., & Goodyear, R. K., (2008). *Fundamentals of clinical supervision.* 4th Boston: Allyn & Bacon, Inc.

Block-Lerner, J., Adair, C., Plum, J.C., Rhatigan, D. L., & Orsillo, S. M. (2007). The case for mindfulness-based approaches in the cultivation of empathy: Does non-judgmental, present-moment awareness increase capacity for perspective taking and empathic concern? *Journal of Marital and Family Therapy,* 33, 501-515. doi:10.1111/j.1752-0606.2007.00034.x

Brown, T., Williams, B., Boyle M., Molloy, A., McKenna, L., Molloy, L., & Lewis, B. (2010). Levels of empathy in undergraduate occupational therapy students. *Occupational Therapy International,* 17(3), 135–141. doi:10.1002/oti.297

Campbell, B. K., Manuel, J. K., Manser S. T., Peavy, K. M., Stelmokas, J., MacCarty, D., & Guydish, J. R. (2013). Assessing fidelity of treatment delivery in group and individual 12-step facilitation. *Journal of Substance Abuse Treatment,* 44(2), 169–176. doi: 10.1016/j.jsat.2012.07.003

Carkhuff, R. R. (1969). *Helping and human relations: A primer for lay and professional helpers: Volume I. Selection and training.* Carlsbad, CA: Holt, Rinehart and Winston.

Conner, K. O., Rosen, D., Wexler, S., & Brown, C. (2010). 'It's like night and day. He's White. I'm Black': Shared stigmas between counselors and older adult methadone clients. *Best Practices in Mental Health: An International Journal,* 6(1), 17-32.

Cutler, J. L., Harding, K. J., Mozian, S. A., Wright, L. L., Pica, A. G., Masters, S. R., et al. (2009). Discrediting the notion "working with 'crazies' will make you 'crazy'": Addressing stigma and enhancing empathy in medical student education. *Advances in Health Sciences Education,* 14(4), 487-502.

Feldstein, S. W., & Forchimes, A. A. (2007). Motivational interviewing with underage college drinkers: A preliminary look at the role of empathy and alliance. *American Journal of Drug and Alcohol Abuse,* 33(5), 737-746. doi:10.1080/00952990701522690

Fiorentine, R., & Hillhouse, M. P. (1999). Drug treatment effectiveness and client-counselor empathy: Exploring the effects of gender and ethnic congruency. *Journal of Drug Issues,* 29(1), 59–74.

Garza, Y., Falls, L., & Bruhn, R. A. (2009). Measuring deeper meaning responses: A discrimination scale for play therapists in training. *International Journal of Play Therapy,* 18(3), 147-161. doi:10.1037/a0015548

Gaume, J., Bertholet, N., Faouzi, M., Gmel, G., & Daeppen, J.B. (2010). Counselor motivational interviewing skills and young adult change talk articulation during brief motivational interventions. *Journal of Substance Abuse Treatment,* 39, (3), 272–281. doi:10.1016/j.jsat.2010.06.010

Gaume, J., Gmel, G., Faouzi, M., & Daeppen, J.B., (2009). Counselor skill influences outcomes of brief motivational interventions. *Journal of Substance Abuse Treatment, 37*, (2), 151–159. doi:10.1016/j.jsat.2008.12.001

Gerdes, K. E., Segal, E. A., Jackson, K. F., & Mullins, J. L. (2011). Teaching empathy: A framework rooted in social cognitive neuroscience and social justice. *Journal of Social Work Education, 47*(1), 109-131. doi:10.5175/JSWE.2011.200900085

Grace, M., Kivlighan, D. M., & Kunce, J. (1995). The effect of nonverbal skills training on counselor trainee nonverbal sensitivity and responsiveness and on session impact and working alliance ratings. *Journal of Counseling & Development, 73*(5), 547-552. doi:10.1002/j.1556-6676.1995.tb01792.x

Hector, M. A., Elson, S. E., & Yager, G. G. (1977). Teaching counseling skills through self-management procedures. *Counselor Education and Supervision, 17*, 12-22. doi:10.1002/j.1556-6978.1977.tb01039.x

Horvath, A. O. & Bedi, R. P. (2002). The alliance. In J. C. Norcross (Ed.) *Psychotherapy relationships that work: Therapist contributions and responsiveness to patients* (pp. 37-69), New York, NY: Oxford University Press.

Kaner, E. F., Dickinson, H. O., Beyer, F., Pienaar, E., Schlesinger, C., Campbell, F., Saunders. J.B., Burnand. B., & Heather, N. (2009). The effectiveness of brief alcohol interventions in primary care settings: a systematic review. *Drug and alcohol review, 28*(3), 301-323. doi:10.1111/j.1465-3362.2009.00071.x

Kaner, E., Bland, M., Cassidy, P., Coulton, S., Dale, V., Deluca, P., Gilvarry. E., Godfrey, C., Heather, N., Myles, J., Newbury-Birch, D., Oyefeso, A., Parrott, S., Perryman, K., Phillips, T., Shepherd, J., & Drummond, C. (2013). Effectiveness of screening and brief alcohol intervention in primary care (SIPS trial): pragmatic cluster randomised controlled trial. *BMJ: British Medical Journal, 346*. doi:10.1136/bmj.e8501

Livingston, J. D., Milne, T., Fang, M. L., & Amari, E. (2012). The effectiveness of interventions for reducing stigma related to substance use disorders: A systematic review. *Addiction, 107*(1), 39-50. doi:10.1111/j.1360-0443.2011.03601.x.

Marlow, E., Nyamathi, A., Grajeda, W. T., Bailey, N., Weber, A., & Younger, J. (2012). Nonviolent communication training and empathy in male parolees. *Journal of Correctional Health Care, 18*(1), 8–19. doi:10.1177/1078345811420979.

Meichenbaum, D. H. (1971). Examination of model characteristics in reducing avoidance behaviors. *Journal of Personality and Social Psychology, 17*(3), 298-307. doi: org/10.1037/h0030593

Meichenbaum, D.H. (1973). *Cognitive factors in behavior modification: Modifying what clients say to themselves.* In C.H. Franks & G.T. Wilson (Eds.). Annual Review of Behavior Therapy. NY: Brunner/Mazel. 416-432.

Meichenbaum, D. (1977). *Cognitive behavior modification.* New York: Plenum Press.

Meichenbaum, D.H. & Cameron, E. (1973). Training schizophrenics to talk to themselves: A means of developing attentional controls. *Behavior Therapy, 4*(4), 515-534. doi:10.1016/S0005-7894(73)80003-6

Meichenbaum, D.H. & Goodman, J. (1971). Training impulsive children to talk to themselves: A means of developing self-control. *Journal of Abnormal Psychology, 77*(2), 115-126. doi: 10.1037/h0030773

Miller, W. R. (1985). Motivation for treatment: A review with special emphasis on alcoholism. *Psychological Bulletin, 98*(1), 84. doi:10.1037/

Miller, W.R., Benefield, R. G., & Tonigan, J.S. (1993). Enhancing motivation for change in problem drinking: a controlled comparison of two therapist styles. *Journal of Consulting and Clinical Psychology, 61,* 455–461. doi:10.1037/0022-006X.61.3.455

Miville, M. L., Carlozzi, A. F., Gushue, G. V., Schara, S. L., & Ueda, M. (2006). Mental health counselor qualities for a diverse clientele: Linking empathy, universal-diverse orientation, and emotional intelligence. *Journal of Mental Health Counseling, 28*(2), 151-165.

Neukrug, E., Bayne, H., Dean-Nganga, L., & Pusateri, C. (2013). Creative and novel approaches to empathy: A neo-Rogerian perspective. *Journal of Mental Health Counseling, 35*(1), 29-42.

Norcross, J. C., & Wampold, B. E. (2011). Evidence-based therapy relationships: research conclusions and clinical practices. *Psychotherapy, 48*(1), 98. doi:10.1037/a0022161.

Nguyen, A. B., Clark, T. T., & Belgrave, F. Z. (2011). Empathy and drug use behaviors among African-American adolescents. *Journal of Drug Education, 41*(3), 289–308. doi: 10.2190/DE.41.3.d

Ochiltree, J. Yager, G., & Brekke, D. (1975, April). A cognitive self-instructional modeling approach vs. The Carkhuff Model for training empathy. Paper presented at the American Educational Research Association Annual Meeting, Washington, D.C. (ERIC Document Reproduction Service No. 106 706)

Perls, F. (1969). *In and out of the garbage pail.* Lafayette, CA: Real People Press.

Pickover, S. (2010). Emotional Skills-Building Curriculum. *Journal of Addictions & Offender Counseling, 31*(1), 52-58. doi:10.1002/j.2161-1874.2010.tb00066.x

Rogers, Carl. (1951). *Client-centered therapy: Its current practice, implications, and theory.* London: Constable.

Rosen-Galvin, C. M. (2005). Values, religion and spirituality topics discussed in counseling supervision. (Doctoral dissertation, University of Cincinnati, 2004) *Dissertation Abstract International, 65,* 3323.

Shaffer, W. F., & Hasegawa, C. S. (1984). Use of an empathy algorithm with a role-played client. *Journal of Clinical Psychology, 40* (1), 57–64. doi:10.1002/1097-4679(198401)40:1

12

The New Leaf Experience

College Student Substance Use Treatment and Addiction Counselor Training Clinic

Amy E. Williams, Eleni M. Honderich, and Charles F. Gressard[1]

College student alcohol use remains an ongoing concern for students, faculty, staff, and communities (Wechsler & Nelson, 2008). Alcohol use among college students presents unique precipitating factors, use patterns, and consequences that are embedded within the college experience (Dimeff, Baer, Kivlahan, & Marlatt, 1999; Ham, Zamboanga, Bridges, Casner, & Bacon, 2012; LaBrie, Ehret, Hummer, & Prenovost, 2012; Wechsler & Nelson, 2008). By offering a range of services grounded in motivational interviewing (MI), the New Leaf clinic provides evidence-based support that also has proven effectiveness with college students. This manuscript describes the history, development, and current practices of the New Leaf clinic. Considerations for developing similar clinical programs at universities and colleges are included.

---

1. Amy E. Williams, Department of Counseling, Special Education, and School Psychology, Youngstown State University; Eleni M. Honderich and Charles F. Gressard, School Psychology and Counselor Education, The College of William and Mary. Correspondence concerning this article should be addressed to Amy E. Williams, PO Box 6396, Williamsburg, VA 23188. E-mail: aewilliams@email.wm.edu.

College Student Alcohol Use

College student alcohol expectancies—student beliefs about the positive or negative impact alcohol may have—impact alcohol consumption patterns among college students, with positive expectancies associated with increased alcohol consumption (Ham et al., 2012). These expectancies may influence consumption patterns and put students at risk of negative consequences of alcohol consumption, despite the individual's expectation that excessive alcohol use will result in a positive experience. In addition, the transition to college represents a milestone in a student's life, and this transition and subsequent adjustment to the college setting may influence and be influenced by alcohol use patterns. Of particular note, poor adjustment to the college environment for both males and females has been associated with greater levels of negative alcohol-related consequences (LaBrie et al., 2012). Given the ongoing process of adjustment present throughout an individual's college experience, some students may encounter multiple episodes of alcohol-related consequences stemming from adjustment-related concerns.

Other Drug Use Among College Students

Recent reports of college student drug use indicate that approximately 36% of college students report past year drug use (Dennhardt & Murphy, 2013). Among college-age adults, 5.9% reported daily marijuana use (National Institutes of Health, 2015). Nonmedical use of prescription medications represents a growing concern among college students, with approximately 11% of students reporting nonmedical use of pharmaceutical stimulants. In the same study, 5.4% of students reported use of pharmaceutical opiates for nonmedical reasons, and 3.4% of students reporting nonmedical use of pharmaceutical sedatives and tranquilizers (Preventing Prescription Abuse in the Workplace [PPAW], n.d.). Growing concern related to misuse of prescription medications among college students exists as access to these medications for nonmedical purposes among college students has increased over the past decade (PPAW, n.d.).

Substance Use Interventions and College Students

Strong empirical support exists for the use of behavioral interventions that include personalized feedback, support for harm reduction and moderation efforts, challenging alcohol expectancies, and goal setting for intervening upon high-risk undergraduate student alcohol use (Scott-Sheldon, Carey, Elliot, Garey, & Carey, 2014). Similarly, brief motivational interventions have been found to support college students engaging in high risk drug use (Dennhardt & Murphy, 2013). MI is an evidence-based intervention for helping individuals resolve ambivalence through the process of evoking personal reasons for change and represents an approach congruent with empirically-supported interventions for both alcohol and drug use among college students (Dennhardt & Murphy, 2013; Glasner-Edwards & Rawson, 2010; McGovern, Fox, Xie, & Drake, 2004; Miller & Rollnick, 2013; Scott-Sheldon et al., 2014). MI involves the use of techniques, including open-ended questions, affirmations, reflections, and summaries (the OARS) to help an individual develop discrepancies and articulate reasons for change. These techniques, coupled with the spirit of MI—a way of being that is grounded in the belief that the individual is capable of making changes and that the counselor is a guidepost along the client's journey—provide the client with an experience that is sensitive to individual needs, affirming of the client's strengths, and respectful of client autonomy throughout the process of counseling (Miller & Rose, 2009).

The use of MI has been supported in both individual and group formats with many types of clients and presenting concerns. An MI framework can increase client engagement and motivation to change problematic substance use patterns (Miller & Rollnick, 2013). Multiple studies emphasized efficacy of MI for reducing high-risk alcohol use with college student populations (LaBrie, Feres, Kenney, & Lac, 2009; LaBrie, Thompson, Hutching, Lac, & Buckley, 2007; Lincourt, Kuettel, & Bombardier, 2002; Miller & Rollnick, 2013).

Campus Substance Use Prevalence and Consequences

The following statistics provide an overview of the current state of substance use on the main campus of the university where the New Leaf clinic operates. According to the university's 2015 Annual Campus Security and

Fire Safety Report, a total of 71 liquor law arrests were made across the university's main campus in 2012. During the same year, 276 liquor law violation referrals were referred to university officials stemming from incidents on campus. In 2013, a total of 65 liquor law arrests and 454 liquor law violation referrals occurred stemming from on-campus incidents. In 2014, a total of 44 liquor law arrests were made and 234 liquor law violations were referred to university officials. These rates do not include incidents involving drunk in public or open container violations (2015 Annual Campus Security and Fire Safety Report, 2015). Overall, data obtained from 2012 through 2014 demonstrate a decrease in alcohol-related reporting of incidents over this time period. Interestingly, these decreases parallel increases in the New Leaf clinic's alcohol-related program offerings and annual census, although direct relationships between these two factors cannot be assumed due to the many elements that influence college student alcohol use.

In 2012, there were also a total of 11 drug law arrests and 15 drug law violations reported stemming from events that occurred on campus. In 2013, 14 drug law arrests were reported, along with 28 drug law violation referrals. In 2014, 21 drug law arrests were made, along with 20 referrals to university officials stemming from drug law violations (2015 Annual Campus Security and Fire Safety Report, 2015).

The American College Health Association's National College Health Assessment II (NCHA II) provides descriptive data related to current substance use practices and consequences experienced by undergraduate students on the main campus of the university. The most recent NCHA indicates that among undergraduate students, 75% of students reported using alcohol in the past 30 days, with 14.4% reporting use between 10 and 30 days of the previous month. Among respondents who endorsed any alcohol use, 65.4% reported most recent use resulting in an estimated blood alcohol content (BAC) greater than .10. Among these same students, 46.2% reported consuming 5 or more alcoholic drinks in their most recent drinking session. Among all students participating in the survey, 26.9% reported consuming five or more alcoholic drinks in a sitting one to two times in the past two weeks, and 15% reported consuming five or more drinks three or more times in the past two weeks. Among students who endorsed alcohol use, 57.6% reported they had experienced at least one negative consequence in the previous 12 months due to alcohol use; 43.9% of respondents reported they did something they regretted,

37.6% reported they forgot where they were or what they did, 13.9% reported they had unprotected sex, 13.2% reported they physically injured themselves, 3.1% reported they seriously considered suicide, and 2.2% reported they got in trouble with the police (American College Health Association, 2015).

The NCHA II data also include information on other drug use for the undergraduate students on the university's main campus. The most recent report indicates that 15.6% of participants reported any use of marijuana in the past 30 days, and 7.6% of students reported use of drugs other than marijuana in the past 30 days. In addition, 9.8% of respondents reported past 30 day use of prescription drugs not prescribed to them (American College Health Association, 2015).

The New Leaf Clinic: Early Beginnings and Rapid Growth

The following section describes the establishment of the New Lead clinic, providing justification for its development, along with potential guidelines and expectations (e.g., collaboration among stakeholders) for those interested in developing similar agencies. The New Leaf clinic, located in the College of William and Mary's School of Education, was founded in 2009 following a conversation between Sara Scott, a student enrolled in an addictions counseling course, and Dr. Rick Gressard, the Program Director for the Clinical Mental Health and Addictions Counseling program at William and Mary (R. Gressard, personal communication, September 5, 2013). Traditionally, when a college student at the university received an alcohol-related sanction or was in need of alcohol-related treatment services, students were either referred to agencies in the community or they completed alcohol education training. Student feedback related to this experience spoke to a mismatch between services rendered and student needs; the outpatient treatment groups and the alcohol education courses ranged from being too intensive to not intensive enough depending upon the student's presenting issues. In addition, counselor interns at the university completed 100% of their field experience internship off-campus with little opportunity to learn or practice MI within these settings. As a result of ongoing conversations related to these concerns, Dr. Gressard and Sara Scott identified the potential need for an on-campus clinic that would benefit the university's student population, and provide training opportunities for counselor interns. This project became known as the New Leaf clinic.

Next, consultation with potential stakeholders at the university occurred, including the Dean of Student Conduct and the College Counseling Center. Following these preliminary planning meetings, additional input was sought from across the campus and local community. The college's School of Education, within which the clinic would be housed, became part of the planning process as the Dean of the school became involved. The New Horizons Family Counseling Center, who also provided clinical counseling services through the School of Education, became an additional collaborator as plans for maximizing the use of clinic space for both programs was explored. Additional collaborative relationships were developed with the local substance abuse coalition, campus health services, local mental health service providers, and the county court services unit to inform planning and implementation of the clinic. The needs and benefits of developing the New Leaf clinic were identified, and potential challenges were explored, opening up conversations that included multi-disciplinary engagement between the university and community that supported student growth, development, and well-being.

Brief interventions integrating MI have demonstrated efficacy with college students with a variety of precipitating events leading to referral for substance use intervention (LaBrie, Feres, Kenney, & Lac, 2009; LaBrie et al., 2002; Miller & Rollnick, 2013). This empirical support for MI with college students justified the selection of this technique as the framework for use at the New Leaf Clinic from its inception. The client-centered elements of MI align well with the developmental tasks and psychosocial challenges inherent in the transition to college, which may include tasks such as developing friendships and social networks, managing time and honing study skills, coping with life away from family and hometown friends, and experimenting with mood-altering substances. As a result, the New Leaf clinic's use of MI as a framework for intervention is concordant with research-supported interventions for the college student population that reflects best practices and innovative solutions to problematic substance use on the campus where the New Leaf clinic is located.

In its first three years of existence, the New Leaf clinic provided one type of service to William and Mary students who were referred due to negative alcohol-related consequences: six sessions of MI-based brief-intervention counseling (SSP). In response to an increasing demand for services that differentiate between moderate and high risk behaviors, the New Leaf clinic added the two-session Brief Alcohol Screening and Intervention for College Students (BASICS) program to its offerings in the fall of 2011. In the fall of 2012, an additional one-session, group-based Alcohol Skills Training Program (ASTP) was added to program offerings to address a range of problematic alcohol use among college students at William and Mary. The expansion of services individualized the intervention process for students through the development of a tiered system of care.

As the New Leaf clinic's programs expanded, so, too did self-referrals from students who were interested in exploring change related to their substance use patterns. Voluntary students typically were referred to the Six Session Program (SSP), to maximize the opportunities for these students to explore and make changes to substance use. In addition, student referrals from off-campus entities including attorneys, the court services unit, and mental health service providers allowed students with a variety of substance-related consequences to receive support in making changes through one or more of the New Leaf clinic's tiered program of services.

Although the New Leaf clinic's primary purpose is to provide alcohol/drug brief intervention services to students among the William and Mary community, the clinic also serves additional roles, including addictions counseling training, clinical supervision, and scholarly research opportunities. The clinic operates on a zero-net dollar budget and students are not charged directly for services through the New Leaf Clinic. Student directors are reimbursed as graduate assistants, with one doctoral clinic director position repurposed from a personal graduate assistant to a clinic graduate assistant by the faculty director and the other student director position funded through the dean of students office via fines for students who have been sanctioned for violating substance-related student conduct policies. Master's students in the Clinical Mental Health and Addictions Counseling program are invited to become involved in working with clients in the clinic while receiving training and gaining competency in providing MI-based services on a volunteer basis. Doctoral students provide needed clinical supervision to these master's students and manage the overall day-to-day functioning of the New Leaf clinic. In addition to these two parallel arms, the New Leaf clinic also serves as a site for research that has included: (a) assessing the impact of brief interventions on college student motivation to change and (b) exploring the relationships between developmental levels and risk of alcohol-related consequences.

Clinical, Training, Research, and Sustainability Considerations

The New Leaf clinic serves as a model for supporting the campus community while also advancing the goals of the graduate counseling programs at William and Mary. The following section further expounds on clinical services, training programs, and research opportunities provided by the New Leaf clinic. Clinical developmental considerations are discussed to help set a framework for college/university campuses interested in providing addiction related services on campus. Figure 1 provides a logic model that describes the New Leaf clinic program elements and goals.

Clinical Services

Across the three programs offered through the New Leaf clinic over 300 students were seen during the 2013-14 academic year and included undergraduate and graduate students from a wide cross-section of the William and Mary student community. Part of the clinic's success (e.g., continued growth, popularity with student-clients) can be attributed to the MI foundation in which all services are grounded. The New Leaf clinic uses an MI framework within all tiers of clinical service (i.e., ASTP, BASICS, SSP). The three treatment tiers vary in intensity and a student is referred to a specific clinical program based on individual alcohol/drug consequences (e.g., severity, frequency) by matching services to the student's needs. Because the spectrum of services is provided within the New Leaf clinic, transitioning a student from one program to another to best meet student needs is possible and can be done efficiently.

ASTP program. Of the three New Leaf clinic programs, the ASTP program is considered the least intensive. Developed for high-risk alcohol use among college students, ASTP is a group-based brief intervention that integrates MI within educational and awareness-raising components (Fromme, Marlatt, Baer, & Kivlahan, 1994). Although ASTP was initially developed to span six to eight sessions, the format was modified to address first-time and low-risk student referrals while retaining the program elements that have been most effective in working with students with low-level alcohol-related consequences (S. Menefee, personal communication, August 25, 2014). The ASTP groups combine MI principles and techniques with educational information intended to help students consider ways they may choose to reduce their risk of alcohol-related consequences. This one and a half hour group session focuses on balancing discussion and exploration of options with provision of information and resources that students may choose to use if they are so inclined. The groups typically begin by inviting students to introduce themselves and begin setting group norms related to participation and expectations. Although activities may vary in sequence, all groups provide students with the opportunity to consider the pros and cons of alcohol use, develop discrepancies by identifying campus norms related to alcohol use, and explore expectancies related to alcohol use. In addition, alcohol education related to optimal blood alcohol level for reducing the risk of alcohol-related consequences, discussion of specific impacts on health of high blood alcohol levels, and identification of ways to reduce risks related with high levels of alcohol consumption are presented. Students are supported through MI processes to consider the benefits and consequences of their substance use, and students are empowered to make decisions for themselves without convincing, arguing, or blaming from the facilitator.

Students referred to ASTP typically received a minor alcohol-related infraction that did not involve underage intoxication. In some cases, students are referred through their resident advisor, a coach, or another individual concerned about the student's welfare; most referrals come directly from the Dean of Students office. As ASTP targets students who have a first-time substance-related offense or consequence, students with a second related offense are typically placed in the next tier of treatment: the BASICS program.

BASICS program. The BASICS program is a two-session brief intervention specifically devised for college students with high-risk alcohol use patterns (Dimeff, et al., 1999). BASICS is also included among the Substance Abuse and Mental Health Services Administration's National Registry of Evidence-Based Programs and Practices (SAMHSA, 2015). Compared to the ASTP program, BASICS offers more intensive and individualized services to students.

The BASICS program, like the ASTP program, balances conversations about problematic substance use with the provision of information that the student may choose to avail him or herself of if it seems useful to the student. BASICS is differentiated from ASTP in several ways. First, BASICS is facilitated in a one-on-one setting over two one-hour sessions scheduled approximately a week apart. In addition, during the first session, the client completes online assessments of current alcohol use patterns and related information, which serves as the basis for the conversations that occur in the second session. This allows the facilitator to provide individualized feedback based specifically upon the student's experiences, and also affords the students seen in BASICS opportunities to describe, discuss, and develop discrepancies between current alcohol use patterns and values and goals. As with ASTP, MI is used to support conversations surrounding reducing alcohol-related consequences, exploring the pros and cons of alcohol use, identifying expectancies, and challenging norms. Through the individualized feedback sheets based upon student survey data, the BASICS facilitator can provide individualized support and develop discrepancies related to student alcohol use and to support exploration of change in a relevant and effective way to meet the individual needs of each student.

Overall, students referred to BASICS are typically either involved in an alcohol-related incident where underage consumption/intoxication is present or referred as a result of an incident requiring medical intervention that is subsequently reported to the university. In some cases, students may be referred to BASICS as a result of a city or county law violation such as a public intoxication charge or as a result of a second infraction after successfully completing ASTP. As with ASTP, most referrals come from the Dean of Students office, although other referral sources, such as attorneys or probation officers, may also refer individuals to BASICS.

Six-Session program. Among the three services provided at the New Leaf clinic, SSP is the most intensive; as the name indicates, students participate in a minimum of six individual one-hour long sessions. SSP focuses on developing discrepancies related to client alcohol or other drug use, supporting client self-efficacy, increasing client motivation to change, and delineating and refining plans for change when clients are invested in making changes. These processes all align clearly with the MI spirit, skills, and techniques (Miller & Rollnick, 2013).

The SSP is New Leaf's hallmark program. The sessions are client-centered and focused on issues relevant to the student as it relates to his or her substance use. As with the other programs offered by the clinic, MI is used as framework for conceptualizing student strengths and needs and for facilitating conversations about change. However, within SSP, the sessions are more flexible and responsive to the needs of students who experience social, academic, familial, or emotional stressors that relate to problematic substance use. The intentional reduction of structure in SSP is congruent with an MI philosophy that promotes client-generated motivation for change based upon the client's individual experiences, needs, and goals related to substance use (Miller & Rollnick, 2013).

Students with any kind of illegal drug-related incident are referred directly to SSP. In addition, students with severe alcohol-related consequences, a history of ongoing escalating consequences, or previous attendance in ASTP and BASICS are typically referred to SSP. Attorneys and probation officers regularly refer students to the program as well. Students who seek services on a voluntary basis (i.e., self-referral) are typically placed in SSP as well

Other client services. The New Leaf clinic also provides doctoral students who express interest in providing additional services with a venue for piloting new programs that align with the clinic's goals and mission. Doctoral students have successfully created and facilitated a women's group that used MI to support members in making changes to substance use and groups related to changing alcohol-use culture for athletic teams. In addition, one doctoral student had opportunities to work with family members impacted by a loved one's substance use in conjunction with the family-counseling clinic in the School of Education.

Training Programs

Services are provided by student interns who are currently enrolled in a graduate level counseling program at the college. The master's and doctoral interns who are engaged in practice through the New Leaf clinic receive unparalleled training, practice, and supervision in using MI through providing brief interventions and engaging in evidence-based practice related to substance use counseling in a college-campus setting. Added benefits for the doctoral students include the opportunity to provide ongoing training, mentoring, and support to students who are developing their professional identities as addictions counselors and receiving ample opportunities to hone supervision skills and processes.

Within the counseling program, graduate-level students who enter the Clinical Mental Health and Addictions Counseling program are invited to begin working with the ASTP and BASICS programs before they begin their first semester of coursework. Training in MI and the specific processes involved in ASTP and BASICS occurs over several days prior to the commencement of classes. This allows the new interns to begin working with clients from their first semester in the program. It also allows the new interns an opportunity to practice skills being learned in their basic counseling techniques course with actual clients while also integrating MI processes and skills. Because ASTP and BASICS are relatively structured in format, it is also an appropriate developmental match to support the counseling self-efficacy in these students while also preparing them for their eventual placement with SSP.

Second-year master's students continue to build MI skills in the more flexible and adaptive SSP. These interns have successfully completed practicum and are in the process of completing an off-campus internship, so the flexibility and autonomy they have, coupled with the increased complexity of client concerns, supports ongoing developmental and professional growth. In addition, interns are able to graduate with two full years of clinical experience if they participate in providing services across the three New Leaf clinic programs. This sets the graduates of the master's program in Clinical Mental Health and Addictions Counseling apart from other students in the program, and from other students who graduate from other programs who do not have the benefit of these experiences.

Doctoral students who are involved with the New Leaf clinic have opportunities to provide individual and group supervision to the master's level students working in the clinic. Supervision models align with the developmental framework for counseling supervision, which emphasizes a balance of support, challenge, and reflection while engaging in authentic role-taking experiences to promote both cognitive and professional skill development (Sprinthall, 1994), and also generally involve processes that model MI throughout the supervision process. The weekly supervision also supports consistent skill development, feedback on MI practice, and review of MI-based techniques, principles, and practices congruent with increased competence in effectively using MI in clinical settings (Yahne, Miller, Moyers, & Pirritano, n.d.). As a result, the doctoral supervisors have a high degree of autonomy and can support the needs of individual supervisees in responsive ways. In addition, the supervisors are able to gain valuable supervision experience specifically in the field of addictions counseling, which is not an experience that the doctoral students may have access to in other settings.

Research Opportunities

Interns who are involved with the New Leaf clinic have opportunities for research both through the clinic's ongoing data collection processes and through opportunities for conducting independent research projects. The New Leaf clinic collects periodic assessment data related to frequency and quantity of alcohol use, consequences experienced due to alcohol and other drug use, and motivation to change alcohol and other drug use in order to provide services to clients. These data are also shared within aggregate reports to the university regarding client demographics and have been used as archival data to explore use-related trends, relationships, and responses to intervention for programmatic purposes. In addition, data exist to conduct outcome evaluations for clients seen through the clinic and assess training effectiveness for master's students should students opt to pursue these research areas in the future.

The New Leaf clinic collects and maintains a database with data for clients seen in any of the clinic's three programs. Demographic data and assessment results are all maintained for each client both in the client file and in a secure encrypted database. For SSP, data gathered include assessments that measure frequency and quantity of alcohol use, readiness to change, and consequences experienced as a result of substance use at various service points. For BASICS, the student-completed survey is stored on a separate server as de-identified data. Gathered data provide information that may be useful in exploring changes over time in response to participation in SSP. Because both BASICS and ASTP are brief interventions, no comparable data exist to measure intermediate or long-term outcomes, although this topic has been raised in conversations about future data collection practices.

In addition to the program-based data that are collected and maintained, student researchers are currently in various stages of data collection for individual research projects. Each of the groups proposed by doctoral students—the women's group and the college student athletes group—received IRB approval and involved data collection. In addition, several dissertations have focused upon data collected through the clinic. Another current research project includes a longitudinal qualitative study focusing on the experiences of the master's level interns from the first day of their participation in New Leaf clinic services through their graduation and entry into the profession.

Implications for future research. Additional ideas for research continue to be generated and are typically executable due to the New Leaf clinic's ongoing position as a research clinic. As noted, clinic interns, supervisors, and faculty propose research ideas. Institutions that have similar clinics and or are those that are interested in establishing such clinics might wish to take into consideration this pertinent research facet, remembering that it can be tailored to the cultural population of clients served, along with intern's/faculty's unique interests.

Clinic Development Considerations

The history of the New Leaf clinic was previously discussed, speaking to the development of such clinics being a process. For institutions interested in developing similar program-based substance use services, it is recommended that step-by-step processes be taken into recommendation and each institution assess the specific needs of their community. The New Leaf clinic can be implemented in full (i.e., three-tier service levels) or in part (e.g., BASICS) contingent on individualized needs. The following list of guidelines summarizes the relevant elements that supported the success of the New Leaf clinic that institutions may wish to consider prior to the establishment of similar clinics at their university/college.

- Develop positive relationships with stakeholders from the beginning
- Build on mutual respect, expertise, and shared vision of all stakeholders
- Consider the elements of time, space, and resources before and during the planning and implementation process
- Start small, establish a strong reputation, then expand
- Underscore the benefits for the college, including the administration, and remain flexible to administrative needs, goals, and concerns
- Consider ethical obligations, policies, and regulations from the start for clients, trainees, and doctoral supervisors

For counseling departments without doctoral programs, the challenge of staffing the clinic with supervisors trained to provide supervision to the master's students is an important consideration. The use of the required master's level supervision course as group supervision for students involved in a similar clinic coupled with individual or triadic supervision provided by a faculty member or community partner with MI knowledge and skills may represent an alternative option for these programs. These options are contingent upon program-level faculty motivation, MI expertise, and resource availability; as a result, creative solutions coupled with the active involvement of multiple stakeholders may work particularly well in instances where doctoral students are not available to support the infrastructure of the clinic.

Summary

The New Leaf clinic provides a needed and valuable service to the college community for students who have experienced negative consequences related to substance use. Through collaborating with stakeholders across the campus and larger community, the New Leaf clinic was established as a one-of-a-kind clinic for substance use counseling training, supervision, and research while also supporting college students in examining problematic substance use patterns through the use of MI. The clinic has grown to provide a range of services to clients and a series of clinical opportunities to students in all levels of the masters and doctoral counseling programs.

References

Annual Campus Security and Fire Safety Report. (2015). *William & Mary 2015 annual campus security and fire safety report*. Retrieved from http://www.wm.edu/offices/compliance/_documents/campus_safety_report_2015.pdf

American College Health Association. (2015). *The College of William & Mary undergraduate executive summary: The American College Health Association National College Health Assessment II*. Published digitally: Author.

Dennhardt, A. A., & Murphy, J. G. (2013). Prevention and treatment of college student drug use: A review of the literature. *Addictive Behaviors, 38*, 2607-2618. doi: 10.1016/j.addbeh.2013.06.006

Dimeff, L. A., Baer, J. S., Kivlahan, D. R., & Marlatt, G. A. (1999). *Brief alcohol screening and intervention for college students (BASICS): A harm reduction approach*. New York, NY: Guilford Press.

Fromme, K., Marlatt, G. A., Baer, J. S., & Kivlahan, D. R. (1994). The alcohol skills training program: A group intervention for young adult drinkers. *Journal of Substance Abuse Treatment, 11*(2), 143-154.

Glasner-Edwards, S., & Rawson, R. (2010). Evidence-based practices in addiction treatment: review and recommendations for public policy. *Health Policy, 97*(2-3), 93-104. doi: 10.1016/j.healthpol.2010.05.013

Ham, L. S., Zamboanga, B. L., Bridges, A. J., Casner, H. G., & Bacon, A. K. (2012). Alcohol expectancies and alcohol use frequency: Does drinking context matter? *Cognitive Therapy Research, 37*, 620-632. doi:10.1007/s10608-012-9493-0

LaBrie, J. W., Ehret, P. J., Hummer, J. F., & Prenovost, K. (2012). Adjustment to college life mediates the relationship between drinking motives and alcohol consequences: A look at college adjustment, drinking motives, and drinking outcomes. *Addictive Behaviors, 37*, 379-386. doi:10.1016/j.addbeh.2011.11.018

LaBrie, J. W., Feres, N., Kenney, S. R., & Lac, A. (2009). Family history of alcohol abuse moderates effectiveness of a group motivational enhancement intervention in college women. *Addictive Behaviors, 34*, 415-420. doi:10.1016/j.addbeh.2008.12.006

LaBrie, J. W., Thompson, A. D., Hutching, K., Lac, A., & Buckley, K. (2007). A group motivational interviewing intervention reduces drinking and alcohol-related negative consequences in adjudicated college women. *Addictive Behaviors, 32*, 2549-2562. doi: 10.1016/j.addbeh.2007.05.014

Lincourt, P., Kuettel, T. J., & Bombardier, C. H. (2002). Motivational interviewing in a group setting with mandated clients: A pilot study. *Addictive Behaviors, 27*, 381-391. doi: 10.1016/S0306-4603(01)00179-4

McGovern, M. P., Fox, T. S., Xie, H., & Drake, R. E. (2004). A survey of clinical practices and readiness to adopt evidence-based practices: Dissemination research in an addiction treatment system. *Journal of Substance Abuse Treatment, 26*, 305-312. doi: 10.1016/j.jsat.2004.03.003

Miller, W. R., & Rollnick. S. (2013). *Motivational interviewing: Helping people change* (3rd ed.). New York, NY: Guilford Press.

Miller, W. R. & Rose, G. S. (2009). Toward a theory of motivational interviewing. *American Psychologist, 64*(6), 527-537. doi:10.1037/a0016830

National Institutes of Health. (2015, Dec.). *National Institutes on Drug Abuse: Drug and alcohol use in college-age adults in 2014*. Retrieved from https://www.drugabuse.

gov/related-topics/trends-statistics/infographics/drug-alcohol-use-in-college-age-adults-in-2014

Preventing Prescription Abuse in the Workplace. (n.d.). *Prescription drug misuse among college students*. Retrieved from http://publichealth.hsc.wvu.edu/media/4239/college_students_no-samhsa-logo.pdf

Scott-Sheldon, L. A., Carey, K. B., Elliott, J. C., Garey, L., & Carey, M. P. (2014). Efficacy of alcohol interventions for first-year college students: A meta-analytic review of randomized controlled trials. *Journal of Consulting and Clinical Psychology, 82*, 177-188. doi:10.1037/a0035192

Sprinthall, N. A. (1994). Counseling and social role taking: Promoting moral and ego development. In J. R. Rest & D. Narvaez (Eds.), *Moral development in the professions: Psychology and applied ethics* (pp. 85-100). Hilldale, NJ: Lawrence Erlbaum Associates, Inc.

Substance Abuse and Mental Health Services Administration. (2015, Apr.). *Brief alcohol screening and intervention for college students (BASICS)*. Retrieved from http://www.nrepp.samhsa.gov/ViewIntervention.aspx?id=124

Wechsler, H., & Nelson, T. F. (2008). What we have learned from the Harvard School of Public Health college alcohol study: Focusing attention on college student alcohol consumption and the environmental conditions that promote it. *Journal of Studies on Alcohol and Drugs, 69*, 481-490. doi:10.15288/jsad.2008.69.481

Yahne, C. E., Miller, W. R., Moyers, T. B., & Pirritano, M. (n.d.). *Teaching motivational interviewing to clinicians: A randomized trial of training methods* [PDF document]. Retrieved from http://www.motivationalinterviewing.org/sites/default/files/Teaching%20MI%20to%20Clinicians.pdf

Figure 1. New Leaf Clinic Program Elements Logic Model. Note. 1 = Motivational Interviewing; 2 = Alcohol Skills Training Program; 3 = Brief Alcohol Screening and Intervention for College Students

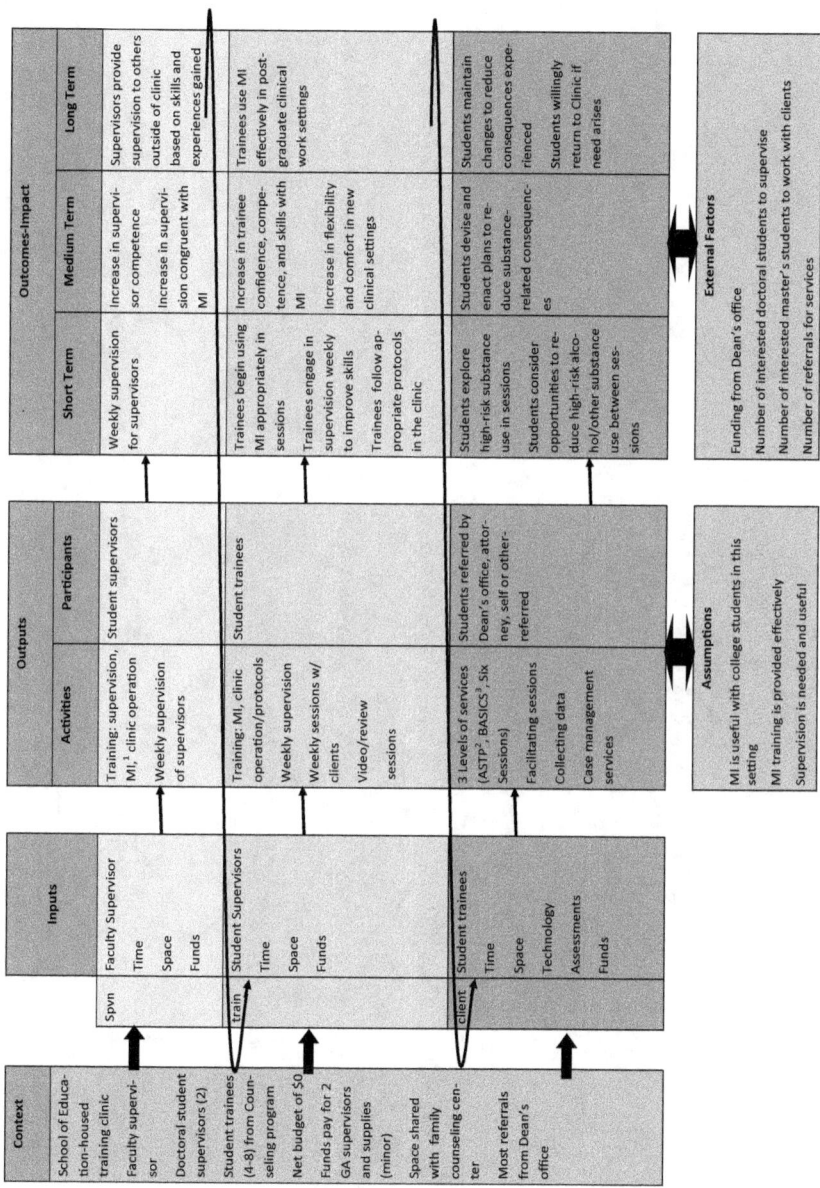

The *Annual Review of Addictions and Offender Counseling, Volume III: Best Practices* is the third volume in a series of peer-reviewed edited books sponsored by the International Association of Addiction and Offender Counselors (IAAOC), a division of the American Counseling Association (ACA). Continuing the mission of the first two volumes, this volume provides a forum for publications addressing a broad array of topics in the field of addictions and offender counseling. Experts in the profession present innovative strategies and recommendations for best practices in drug education, intervention strategies, multicultural considerations, and counselor education.

DR. PAMELA S. LASSITER is an Associate Professor of Counseling in the Department of Counseling at the University of North Carolina at Charlotte. She has over 30 years of work experience in substance abuse treatment and community mental health. Dr. Lassiter holds credentials as a Licensed Professional Counselor, a Licensed Marriage & Family Therapist, and as a Licensed Clinical Addiction Specialist. She serves as Director of the Addictions Program at UNC Charlotte and teaches graduate courses in addiction and mental health counseling. She is also a Past-President of IAAOC and currently the Associate Editor of the *Journal of Addiction and Offender Counseling*.

DR. TREVOR BUSER is an Associate Professor at Rider University, where he teaches coursework in both the clinical mental health counseling and school counseling tracks. His research centers on cognitive predictors of nonsuicidal self-injury. He also brings a dedicated focus on addictions counseling and is editor of the *Journal of Addictions and Offender Counseling*. Dr. Buser is a licensed professional counselor, certified school counselor, and approved clinical supervisor. He has professional experience as a college counselor and private practice counselor. He also served as President of IAAOC.

IAAOC
International
Association
of
Addictions
&
Offender
Counselors

The International Association of Addictions and Offender Counselors (IAAOC) is an organization of professional substance abuse/addictions counselors, corrections counselors, students, and counselor educators who are concerned with improving the lives of individuals exhibiting addictive and/or criminal behaviors. Our mission is to provide leadership in and advancement of the professions of addiction and offender counseling. IAAOC is a division of the American Counseling Association.